A Day-Care Guide
for Administrators,
Teachers, and Parents

The MIT Press
Cambridge, Massachusetts,
and London, England

Contents

**A Day-Care Guide
for Administrators,
Teachers, and Parents**

Richard Ruopp
Brigid O'Farrell
David Warner
Mary Rowe
Ruth Freedman

Copyright © 1973 by
The Massachusetts Institute of Technology

This book was set in IBM Press Roman
by Williams Graphic Service
printed on Decision Offset
and bound in Columbia Millbank Vellum
by Halliday Lithograph Corp.
in the United States of America.

Library of Congress Cataloging in Publication Data
Main entry under title:

A Day-care guide for administrators, teachers, and
    parents.

    Based on A study in child care, 1970-71, prepared
for the Office of Economic Opportunity, by Abt Associates.
    1. Child welfare—United States—Case studies.
2. Day nurseries—United States—Case studies.
3. Evaluation research (Social action programs)—
United States. I. Ruopp, Richard. II. Abt Associates. A study in child care, 1970-71.
HV741.D38   362.7'1   73-3447
ISBN 0-262-18063-4

Preface

The need for day care in the United States is enormous and increasing rapidly. Census figures released in 1967 placed the youth population of the country (under age twenty-five) at 93 million: twice the number we had in 1950. About a quarter of these are poor as defined by the Social Security Index. The number of school-age youth is estimated at about 12.5 million. Of these, 4.5 million are in female-based households, and this number is increasing. Between 4 and 4.5 million preschoolers (under six) have mothers who work, and only about 2 percent of these children are in child-care centers.

Statistics alone can't tell the whole story; they can only help us begin to estimate potential demand for day-care facilities in an economic sense. Many other changes in our society have contributed to current demand and will shape the demand of the future: families are becoming highly mobile; we're seeing rising employment of women, and particularly mothers (an eightfold increase since World War II); and the traditional role of women in America is being seriously challenged by women themselves. Furthermore, the past decade has brought an increased interest in helping the children of the poor to break out of the dependency cycle and improve the quality of their lives. And finally, there has been growing national concern over child-rearing priorities: the public is more aware than ever of the importance of intellectual, social, emotional, and physical growth for balanced, healthy development of the individual.

Demand for day care cuts across social and economic lines. For the middle class, day care may be a means of improving the quality of life or raising the economic status of the family. College- and high-school-educated married women increasingly want the freedom to work, to be involved in community organizations, to continue their education, or to pursue their own interests. For the poor, restricted by inadequate welfare payments, child care can mean financial solvency through freedom to work. Day care can also mean significant benefits to the child in the form of supplemental diet, adequate medical attention, exposure to other children, and many other kinds of life experiences that the poor child would not get at home. Various antipoverty programs, such as Community Action agencies, Head Start, Concentrated Employment programs,

Model Cities, Neighborhood Youth Corps, Work Incentive programs, and others, have become more aware over the past ten years of the importance of day care to the people they represent and to the goals they seek to achieve.

The question of whether or not to provide child care is no longer the issue. What we must decide is what kind and what quality of care should be provided and at what cost to whom. The federal government appears to be moving toward a major role as provider, both directly and indirectly, of day-care programs. Current supply is wholly inadequate in terms of both quantity and quality, and there is reason to believe that neither the government nor the people want to support more of the same. If there were only limited demand and homogeneous need for child care, perhaps the problem could be solved piecemeal, but this isn't the case. The demand is awesome and needs are heterogeneous.

This book seeks to determine from a study of diverse quality programs just what the government may wish to support in the area of good child care. It attempts to develop some guidelines about what good child care is, how much it costs, and how it can be duplicated. We hope this book will be useful to people who are operating, or considering operating, day-care programs, teachers, and parents, if only by pointing out what other people in the field are doing. Please use it, not as a rigid text, but as a guide to considerations you may have overlooked in your planning, or choosing, of a day-care program. Our intent is not to propound hard and fast rules but merely to point out what's working for others and might prove helpful to you.

Richard R. Ruopp
Brigid O'Farrell
David Warner
Mary Rowe
Ruth Freedman

Abt Associates Inc.

Acknowledgments

The study reported herein was performed pursuant to a contract with the Office of Economic Opportunity, Executive Office of the President, Washington, D.C. 20506. The opinions expressed herein are those of the authors and should not be construed as representing the opinions or policy of any agency of the United States Government.

The publishing rights for this book, based on *A Study in Child Care, 1970-71,* have been secured from the Office of Economic Opportunity and from the day-care centers involved. November 1970 data has been updated where possible through continued work with the centers and systems as well as additional child-care work done by Abt Associates Inc.

Many people have contributed their efforts to the development of this book. The staff members of Abt Associates Inc. who were responsible for the original *A Study in Child Care, 1970-71* include: Dr. Richard Anderson, Patricia Bergstein, Patricia Cook, Virginia Demos, Linda Elbow, Dr. Stephen Fitzsimmons, Dr. Evelyn Glenn, Paul Grigorieff, Christine Jerome, John Jerome, Brigid O'Farrell, Kristine Rosenthal, Dr. Mary Rowe, Richard Ruopp, Lynn Thompson, Dr. Jeffrey Travers, Jane Ward, David Warner, Erline Willis, and Sally Zeckhauser. Administrative and clerical support were provided by Patti Burns, Carol Sue Duncan, Frances Pretty Paint, Nancy Sievert, and Rosemary Wilson. Overall contributions were made to the study through the Office of Economic Opportunity by Dr. Walter Stellwagen and Dr. Morris Shepard.

Colleagues whose continued work has been reviewed and used to update our information where possible include: Minnie Berson, Virginia Burke, William Chase, Joseph Curran, E. Belle Evans, Robert Fein, John Jordan, Joseph Lane, Martin Deutsch, Glenn Nimnicht, Richard Rowe, Beth Shub, Marlene Weinstein, and the staffs of the Contracting Corporation of America, Inner City Fund, the Massachusetts Early Education Project, Urban Research Corporation, and the Women's Bureau of the U.S. Department of Labor.

Additional contributions, particularly in the area of costs, have been made by the staff of Abt Associates Inc., including Keith McClellan, Dr. Mary Rowe, and David Warner. Much of this work was done under contract to the U.S. Department of Labor, Welfare Reform Planning Staff (November 19, 1971) under the direction of Nancy Snyder, Task Leader of the WRPS.

Ruth Freedman was responsible for the major reorganizing of the study into book form, with direction and assistance from Brigid O'Farrell and Richard Ruopp. Writing and editing assistance was provided by Christine Jerome throughout the study and the preparation of the book.

We extend a special thanks to the directors, staffs, and children of the day-care centers involved, who provided critical and heartwarming assistance and support.

Introduction

This book is based on *A Study in Child Care, 1970-71,* prepared for the Office of Economic Opportunity. From an original list of 188 centers, the study selected 20 programs, representing the wide diversity of groups interested in providing child care. These included centers and systems located all around the country—on Indian reservations, in the inner city, in mobile trailers, in Appalachia, and in the suburbs. Sponsors, too, were diverse, including employers, unions, private corporations, federal, state, and local agencies, as well as parents. A list of the 20 programs follows.

Single centers

Amalgamated Day Care Center, Chicago, Illinois

American Child Centers, Inc. (Woodmont Center, Nashville, Tennessee)

Avco Day Care Center, Boston, Massachusetts

Casper Day Care Center, Casper, Wyoming

Central City Head Start Day Care Center, Salt Lake City, Utah

5th City Pre-School, Chicago, Illinois

Georgetown University Hospital Day Care Center, Washington, D.C.

Greeley Parent Child Center, Greeley, Colorado

Haight-Ashbury Children's Center, San Francisco, California

Holland Day Care Center, Holland, Michigan

Syracuse University Children's Center, Syracuse, New York

Ute Indian Tribe Day Care Center, Fort Duchesne, Utah

West 80th Street Day Care Center, New York, New York

Systems

Berkeley Unified School District Children's Centers, Berkeley, California

Family Day Care Career Program, New York, New York

Rural Child Care Project, Kentucky Child Welfare Research Foundation, Inc., Kentucky

Mecklenburg County Department of Social Services Day Care Centers, Charlotte, North Carolina

Neighborhood Centers Day Care Association, Houston, Texas

Northwest Rural Opportunities Child Development Centers, Pasco, Washington

Springfield Day Nursery (Brightwood Center), Springfield, Massachusetts

The study interviewed directors, teachers, support staff, children, community people, and parents. Children and teachers were observed in their daily center routines. Much of the observation and interviewing was done by day-care staff who agreed to travel with us, far from their own centers. Budgets were carefully recorded with attention to both dollar and in-kind revenues and expenditures. A panel of child-care experts acted as advisors for the study, and all final case studies were reviewed by the centers involved.

Each of the 20 centers is providing what we consider to be good child care. This does not mean that all aspects of each center operation are outstanding or that elaborate programs are provided. In general, these centers are clean and safe environments, and the children who use them are receiving adequate nutrition and supervision. In addition, at least one aspect of each program or center is notable. Some are truly excellent by virtue of the happiness of the children, the warmth and dedication of the staff members, and the enthusiasm of the parents. We believe that as a group these centers are among the best organizations of their kind in the country.

Parents from different cultures, different social and economic groups, have differing ideas about what kind of care they want for their children. Quality for one group may not mean much for another. For instance, children who've been isolated in the hollows of Kentucky may need, above all, to learn how to talk. Urban, middle-class kids may need to learn how to listen. Black parents may want to see that their children develop pride in their identities as black people; Chicano and Indian parents may want similar emphasis for their children. Special nutrition and health services may be essential for kids whose diets are substandard, while such extras would be unnecessary for others.

Quality from the parent point of view means meeting both child *and* parent needs. In addition to considering the growth and well-being of their children, parents must evaluate child-care programs in terms of cost, location, transportation, and hours of operation. Parents also want programs that respect their rights as parents and consider their concerns. Providing real opportunities for parent involvement gives parents a chance to understand what you're trying to do and why, and it may mean crucial carryover of your goals into the home. It's also a way for teachers to learn more about the children they're working with and for children to gain confidence and pride in themselves.

For day-care directors and staff, there are other concerns. Very few programs can afford whatever they want in terms of staff size and quality, materials, special services, and so on. Most must carefully weigh each expenditure, and the decisions made can have a substantial effect on the quality of care. Understanding and responsive staff members who work closely with the children can provide an environment far superior to one in which kids are parked in front of a television set for eight hours. One of the most impressive characteristics of good centers is the amount of sheer human energy expended in the course of a routine week. However, unless they have phenomenal energy, teachers with too many children to care for will soon be run ragged and will be unable to respond well to all the demands being made on them. Directors and staff members have to budget not only financial but also human resources if they're to be effective. Finally, the child as a total person must not be lost in the shuffle when parent, staff, and community needs are being considered.

The 20 day-care programs we studied reflect the complexity of these concerns. Briefly, here are some of our general findings:

1. Good and excellent child care come in many forms, varying with respect to parents' and providers' values and the resources available. We found that there is no one kind of "quality child care": there are many different kinds.

2. Good and excellent child care are now being offered by a wide variety of sponsors: welfare departments, inner-city community organizations, private industry, religious groups, research foundations. Within school departments, on Indian reservations, in

private homes, in the ghetto, in migrant camps, and in the suburbs, good child care is to be found in heartening profusion.

3. Good and excellent child care are very hard to guarantee. The wide diversity described here has one common base: enormous human effort lies behind every center we visited. The most important aspect of quality child care is the human effort and devotion behind it. A child-care center *is* its director and staff.

4. Good and excellent child care are expensive. People accustomed to costs in lower-quality public schools, people who are familiar with only part-time or volunteer child care, are likely to be taken aback by the real cash costs of full-time care for young children. Costs of child care in our survey range from $1,200 to $4,100 per child per year. (No centers handled infants exclusively, and they are, as a group, even more expensive to care for.) About four-fifths of the real costs of child care are personnel costs; if you know the staff/child ratio at a given center and where that center is located, you can predict within narrow limits how much a child-care arrangement will cost. The staff of a center is its definitive aspect with respect to both quality and cost.

Part I of this book describes the people involved in child care and what they do: the kids, the staff, directors and boards, and parents. Part II delineates basic program components—education, nutrition, health, and supplemental services—and uses examples from the centers we felt were handling these aspects in creative or particularly appropriate ways. While the book as a whole focuses on programs serving children between the ages of three and five, a separate chapter in this section (Chapter 8) describes special programs for infants and school-age children. Part III examines operating costs for day care, outlines start-up activities and their costs, and describes a model center serving 50 children. Part IV consists of detailed case studies of four of the programs we studied: a small urban center, a large urban home-care program, a small program for migrant children, and a large rural child-care system. The appendix contains four summary charts of all 20 centers studied.

Part I   The People

We witnessed [one] scene we wished we could have filmed. During the morning's large-group activity with the five-year-olds, a teacher and his Spanish-speaking assistant were organizing the children for some learning games when one little girl called out, "Mr. Etukudo, when I grow up will you marry me?" At this point, all the girls started chanting that *they* wanted to marry Mr. Etukudo, and every child was out of his seat, reaching up to the teacher to give him a kiss. The process of giving each child a kiss and a hug was certainly a departure from the schedule. The spontaneity, humor, and good-naturedness of this teacher have produced a group of children who relate beautifully with each other and the staff.

Brightwood Day Care Center
Springfield (Mass.) Day Nursery

Kids. They're what day care is all about, and yet it's easier to talk about efficient planning, special grouping, timetables, budgets, boards of directors, health, transportation, nutrition programs, and curricula. The mechanics of day care will take up a good portion of this book, but people, not processes, make good day care happen—people like Mr. Etukudo, whose contracts say nothing about kissing and hugging, about extra hours, extra attention, about really caring.

The 20 day-care centers and systems we studied served thousands of children, some of whom had very special needs. Some children, who lived in isolated areas, needed to learn how to talk and how to deal with other people. Some children were handicapped. Some children were undernourished. Others were underclothed. Still others were obviously not loved. Some needed dental work, some needed glasses. Many, from different cultures, spoke little or no English and faced the prospect of public school with almost no way to communicate. These are special needs, and some of them occur in almost every day-care class. Creative ways to meet many of these needs are discussed in the chapters about nutrition and health, education, and supplemental services.

But there were also at least four basic needs our quality centers were trying to meet in their day-to-day operations, regardless of the environments, cultures, or the special approaches they embodied. Our centers were endeavoring to meet physical needs, meet emotional needs, promote readiness for future learning, and simply let kids be kids.

Meeting Physical Needs

To be physically healthy, children need to be fed adequately. You may be serving families whose kids have never eaten regular meals, or whose experience has been limited to two or three staple items. Such children may be anemic, undernourished, and susceptible to disease. In this case, and particularly if your program is a full-day operation, you may have to provide compensatory nutrition— more than the normal lunch and snack programs associated with what is called maintenance nutrition for children whose diets are adequate. Chapter 6 deals with both kinds of nutrition programs and describes some outstanding approaches to this aspect of day care.

Care should be taken to prevent the spread of communicable diseases through adequate toilet and washing facilities, cooking facilities, and sanitary procedures. In most areas, day-care centers must meet local, state, and/or federal guidelines in these respects before they can begin operation. The majority of centers studied provided either child-size toilets and washstands or adapted adult-size facilities so children could be comfortable with them. Toileting times and routines varied widely, but all children were taught and encouraged to wash their hands after toileting and before meals. Many centers see that teachers who greet the children in the morning also perform a quick health inspection to make sure children are feeling and looking well enough to join in the day's activities. Chapter 6 describes basic and special health needs and some of the creative health programs our quality centers have instituted.

Kids should also be protected from discomfort or danger due to safety hazards and inclement weather. This calls for an adequate physical environment and adult supervision. Again, local, state, and/or federal regulations have been developed to ensure that fire and building safety codes are met before day-care programs can start operation. Conscientious maintenance is also essential for safety, on the playground as well as indoors. In addition, the toys and equipment should be safe: a number of toys have proven to be dangerous in the hands of children. Common sense and adult watchfulness will go a long way toward making your center a safe place for children.

And finally, children need to be able to exercise and to rest. Because a child's muscular development improves rapidly in the preschool years, you must provide activities that will allow kids to strengthen those muscles and practice muscle coordination and control. Most centers have outdoor areas or access to playgrounds with swings, slides, jungle gyms, wagons, tricycles, large blocks and balls, and a variety of other play equipment. Typically, about an hour is set aside daily for outdoor play. When the weather precludes outdoor activity, large-muscle games and exercises are conducted indoors. Exercise is important for another reason, aside from physical development. When children spend between six and eight hours daily in a center, they need a chance simply to let off steam, to run around, to yell, to work off energy. Large-muscle activities provide that outlet.

Small-muscle coordination usually develops naturally through indoor activities such as painting, coloring, pasting, and playing with small puzzles, games, and toys. Self-reliance tasks—buttoning coats, tying shoelaces, and so on—are also important for coordination and control. Such activities are generally part of the center's overall educational program and are discussed in Chapter 5.

For a four-year-old, 8 A.M. to 6 P.M. can be a very long haul. All of the full-day programs we studied set aside an average of an hour for nap time, a chance for children to rest and adults to regroup. In one center, older children could choose between lying down and playing quietly, but for most programs, nap time is sleeping time. Many centers found that a period of quiet play just before nap time helped prepare kids for sleep. Soft music, dim lighting, backrubs, and bedtime stories help children settle down and doze off. Easy-to-stack child-size cots or sleeping mats are most generally used, and some centers had separate nap rooms or areas set aside for this quiet period.

Meeting Emotional Needs

A child is emotionally healthy when his basic trust in people, the world, and himself outweighs feelings of fear, suspicion, and helplessness. Kids in the quality child-care centers we studied seemed basically happy, cooperative, and self-reliant. We saw little crying or withdrawal, and parents generally reported that their children were at least as happy as they had been at home. What was outstanding about our centers was not merely the fact that they were conscious of children's emotional needs but that staff members gave greatly of themselves in the process of addressing those needs. Our observers associated positive adult behavior (things like praise, one-to-one attention, constructive redirection) with happy children, and negative adult responses (coldness, hostility, intervention without redirection) with unhappy children. In quality centers, we saw very little negative adult behavior and a great deal of tender loving care.

While we can't cover all the emotional needs a child may have, most parents, child development specialists, and psychologists would find it important for a day-care center to try to help children with these broad kinds of needs: the need for security and a sense of belonging, for self-expression, for independence, and for guidance.

Security and Acceptance Moving from the security of home to the larger, outside world of the day-care center is a big step for a child. Sensitive handling of this transition can help a child adjust to his new life at the center with a minimum of fuss. Parents can be encouraged to bring their children with them to look over the center while admission interviews and enrollment paperwork are conducted. When a child has been accepted, many centers find it helpful for a staff member to visit the child's home; the child can meet his future teacher in familiar surroundings, and the teacher can learn about his family, his likes and dislikes, and his special needs. This visit can also give the teacher conversational topics to ease a child into the center's life. Kids feel more secure during the first few days at the center if a parent can be present. Some centers suggest that new children attend for half days until they're comfortable. Separation from parents, when the time comes, is usually difficult and requires plenty of reassurance from both teacher and parent. Some children never do get used to letting their parents go.

Children can feel secure in a center where they are cared for by people they know and trust. This takes time, of course, but it's important for children to be able to depend on the same teachers being there every day. High staff turnover makes it difficult for children to form stable relationships with their teachers. In the same way, a predictable daily routine—with playtime, story time and snack time in a fairly regular order—helps foster security feelings.

Making sure each child feels he belongs at the center is another way to reinforce his sense of security. At most quality centers, teachers greet children and parents by name as they arrive and guide children individually into activities. Kids can be given their own personal storage space or cubbies, their own cots or cribs, their own places at the lunch table. Labeling items with a child's name is also useful. Here is how the Greeley Parent Child Center in Greeley, Colorado, promotes a feeling of belonging:

As you enter the Greeley Parent Child Center, in the small foyer you discover a series of hooks for the children's coats. Over each hook is a color Polaroid picture of the child with his name written under it. This had just been inaugurated. . . . The children had not yet gotten over the excitement of seeing themselves and finding their names when they arrived.

Self-Expression Kids feel things fiercely—love, anger, fear, pride, the whole range of emotions—and need to be able to express these feelings in constructive (or at least nondestructive) ways. Self-expression can take many forms: painting, singing, dancing, coloring, making music, playacting, any kind of creative production. A teacher's praise and encouragement of such self-expression will help bolster a child's sense of his own worth. There are no "rights" and "wrongs" in creative expression: a child's production should be considered worthwhile and valuable whatever his level of skill or his choice of medium.

Language is another avenue for self-expression. Teachers in quality centers make it a point to listen to children as well as to teach. When a center serves children of two or more cultures, it's obviously important to have staff members who can speak the children's languages. An upset child finds additional comfort in being reassured in his familiar language.

Forms of self-expression may vary from culture to culture and

should be respected. At the Ute Indian Tribe Day Care Center in
Fort Duchesne, Utah,

The center runs smoothly and quietly, with a quiet born not of
fear or passivity, but because the children seem naturally tuned to
a world in which words play a secondary role for the young. This
is hard to describe to someone who has not seen and felt it. Children will be very intensely involved in single or small group pur-
suits. There is little or no competition or aggressiveness of the kind
one sees in other centers. Long periods of time may go by without
a word or sound . . . from any of the 23 or so children in attendance.

In contrast, the children attending the 5th City Pre-School in
Chicago swarm through the building singing and chanting the
school's songs. Many of the songs are designed to promote the
children's self-images, to help kids understand who they are and to
feel good about themselves. "Hold your head up! Hold it up high!/
5th City Pre-School is marching by!" rings down the corridors as
the kids march from place to place. After meals, another ritual
goes, "Who are you? I'm the greatest! Where are you? In the universe! Where are you going? To bend history!" The majority of
5th City's children are black, and heavy emphasis is given to
strengthening black pride. The closing verse of a 5th City song
says,

People of 5th City
Are black and that is great,
We're gonna give our blackness to the world
And the world will celebrate.

Many of the centers we studied were working hard at enhancing
children's views of themselves and their cultures. In New York
City, the predominantly black West 80th Street Day Care Center
taught African dancing to its children and community members.
The Ute center mentioned previously has a strong program of
ethnic education in which children learn traditional Ute skills,
legends, dances, and rituals. The Northwest Rural Opportunities
Child Development Centers in the state of Washington serve the
children of migrant farm workers, most of whom are Spanish-

speaking. NRO curriculum includes Mexican songs and games, educational materials in Spanish, a Mexican Cultural Heritage program, and many other features to promote self-image.

Independence In addition to the self-reliance skills—dressing, toileting, and so on—taught to most preschoolers, many of our quality centers made a special effort to let children do things for themselves. Children helped prepare, serve, and clean up after meals, set up their own cots at nap time, and cleaned up after themselves when they finished with activities. Even if you know you can do a faster and better job of something, give kids a chance at it. Their pride in taking care of themselves is worth the extra time, and you can always step in to help if frustration levels get too high. A child-size environment really helps. Child-size tables, chairs, equipment, and facilities, things placed at child's-eye level, will help kids help themselves.

At the Haight-Ashbury Children's Center in San Francisco,

. . . there is a strong feeling of independence among the kids: they are proud of it and are encouraged in it by the staff. Hurt children sometimes seek teachers for comfort, but more often work out their own problems. A five-year-old girl knocks over her milk, calmly saunters over to get a sponge, mops up, and with a "Here," tosses it to another youngster who has knocked over his milk in the meantime.

At Haight-Ashbury, even the curriculum structure is designed to foster self-reliance. Teaching staff are used as resource people: the kids decide who and what they wish to work with each day.

Guidance Kids need help—some more than others—in accepting and living with the center's rules. Your rules for behavior must be clearly and simply expressed if children are to understand them. Some kids require more repetition than others. But when a child goes beyond your limits, it's important to let him know that it's his *behavior,* not him, you disapprove of.

Hostile or aggressive behavior can be treated in a positive way. In our quality centers, a typical routine was first to talk with a child who was having problems and attempt to redirect him or her to a new activity. Often, a sharing problem between two children could be mediated by an exchange of toys or introduction of new toys. If this was unsuccessful, one child would be taken aside and started on something different. If the problem continued or was disrupting other children, a child might be removed from the room until tempers cooled. In the centers we studied, we saw almost no instances where children were physically disciplined: in fact, this was generally contrary to center policy. Teachers seldom yelled at kids: they found it more productive to address problems on an individual basis. This one-to-one interaction also lets a child know he's considered a worthwhile individual.

Many centers encourage their children to dissipate aggressive energy in pounding activities (pegboards, toy hammers) or large-muscle games. One of the centers in Kentucky's Rural Child Care Project even has an adult-size "sock-it-to-me" doll for children to hit when they're angry or frustrated.

Kids should never be shamed or ridiculed in an effort to make them conform. Our centers found it better to reward appropriate behavior and withhold rewards for inappropriate behavior. Rewards were commonly candy (although parents often disapproved) for younger children, special treats or privileges, or, for older children, simple praise. Reinforcement of positive behavior is an incentive for children to keep behaving in positive ways. Praise and attention are also important for self-image: they can mean the world to a child who is ignored at home.

These are some of the ways our quality centers were trying to meet children's emotional needs. Perhaps most important, though, is a warm, supportive atmosphere where children know they are accepted and appreciated for themselves, where they can cry and be comforted, laugh and be smiled at, or just plain *be*.

Promoting Readiness for Future Learning

The preschool years are critical ones in which kids may or may not develop the skills and attitudes they'll need in the larger world of grade school. We're speaking here about skills like cooperation and sharing, self-control, self-reliance, language and communication skills, and curiosity and motivation to learn. While children whose first language is not English may need extra help to succeed in our educational system, all kids can benefit from the basic socialization skills a center promotes. An only child, for example, may need to adjust to the give-and-take of group life. Overly-protected children may need to feel more independent, more self-reliant. Kids who haven't had much stimulation at home can benefit from a center's educational materials. After all, children learn through play: providing a variety of toys, games, and experiences for children will automatically start them on the road to new concepts.

Every child needs a chance to discover the world. Letting them explore that world and giving value to their experiences make learning the fun it should be. Regardless of their feelings about how children should be raised, parents expect child care to begin teaching the skills and attitudes necessary for future learning. Quality day-care programs take this educational component very seriously and regard their task as more than simple baby-sitting. Chapter 5 discusses in detail how various centers help their children discover the world and themselves.

Letting Kids Be Kids

This need may seem obvious, but we include it because there's a real danger that children cared for in groups may be oversupervised and overregulated. Letting kids be kids means allowing them to do things their own way, even though it's messier, slower, or less skillful than the adult way. It also means letting kids cry now and again, laugh, shout, sit quietly, run around wildly, join in, or watch from the sidelines. Given a chance for self-direction and energy release, a child can be more relaxed, more able to identify his own needs, interests, and skills, more him- or herself.

In our quality centers, adults seldom interfered in children's activities unless they were needed. Several centers even saw to it that children had places of their own where they could get away from it all. For instance, in the Rural Child Care Project, which serves several counties in Kentucky,

In some of the centers, observers were very impressed with the housekeeping corners, not only set to a child's scale, but so arranged with openings and screens that it would be difficult for an adult to squeeze into the space, thus giving the children a feeling of privacy and possession. . . . There's a tree house inside one center, accessible only by ladder, with an entrance only children can get through easily. It's a quiet spot with its own small library.

These are some of the basic needs our quality centers were trying to meet. But day-care centers can't replace parents. Nor should a center compete with a child's family for his loyalty. Day care is a cooperative venture in which a center is temporarily sharing responsibility for children and providing another place where kids can feel at home and be themselves. If you can do your job with imagination and warmth, you're on the way to providing quality care. The fact remains, if day care is to serve the community, if it's to serve parents, it must first serve kids.

I like the way they love the children first, and then teach them
things.

Parent, Central City Head
Start Day Care Center
Salt Lake City, Utah

Nine of the staff members are white and eleven are black. Of the
thirteen teachers and aides, four are men who fill the very important male roles for children, most of whom come from mother-
headed families. Two staff members are parents themselves, and all
the staff relate well with the center's young parents. Average age
of the staff is twenty-five. Several teacher assistants are community residents with a lot to offer the children. . . . Staff members have an informal style: some are long-haired, most are dunga-
reed, and all have a strong presence. They are direct, warm,
actively opinionated about child development and each other, and
have unusual rapport with and respect for the children. Teachers
often spend their own money to buy materials and equipment
they feel the children need.

Haight-Ashbury Children's
Center
San Francisco, California

A day-care center is only as good as its staff, and by staff we
mean all the people who come in contact with kids—cooks, house-
keepers, bus drivers, nurses, directors—not only teachers. Many of
the people involved in quality day care go far beyond the call of
duty in caring for and loving children. Hugging, holding, patting,
kissing, comforting, praising, rocking, and rubbing backs isn't in
any job description, but there's a lot of this kind of contact and
reassurance going on at good centers. There's also a lot of sensitivity, of knowing when a child needs to be alone and when he
needs to begin learning how to deal with others. There's a great
deal of patience at quality centers: teachers take time with each
child and try to let kids proceed at their own rates. And finally,
there's guidance. When behavioral problems come up, children are
redirected in positive ways—shown something else to do or an
easier way to accomplish what they want.

All these things take extra time, devotion, and energy. The brunt
of it falls on the teaching staff, who spend most of their time with
the kids and who can be a center's greatest asset. In our quality

centers, we were most struck by the real dedication of staff members. People were often working for low pay, for long hours and on weekends for no overtime, in centers that could offer little job security and few fringe benefits. Staff members donated materials and services and took pay cuts when funding difficulties arose. Time and again we were told by teachers that they simply loved to work with children, and in many centers we found great loyalty to the programs themselves.

A common theory about child-care staff is that if you offer enough money and hire enough people with degrees, you'll automatically have a good staff. We don't think this is true. Degrees are certainly nice, but they don't *ensure* a good program. It's just as important to have *enough* people to care adequately for the children as it is to have well-qualified people. Moreover, some of the warmest and most successful operations we saw were centers where nonprofessionals played vital roles. What's important is finding staff who really enjoy kids and who have skills and lots of love to offer.

Finding Good Staff
Since there aren't any neat formulas to determine who will be good with children, directors (or parents, if they do the hiring) must rely on their own judgment and intuition as well as on past experience. One helpful guideline, however, is to look for people who have a variety of experiences under their belts, experiences they can use to make the program and the lives of the children richer and more fulfilling. Choose a varied group of people: men as well as women, senior citizens, teen-agers, people from different ethnic and cultural minorities. While it's obviously important for non-English-speaking children to be able to communicate in their own language while they're learning English, it's also a benefit for English-speaking children to learn about other languages and cultures.

Until recently, day-care staffs have been decidedly homogeneous: day care has traditionally been the province of young and middle-aged women. The presence of men in child care, while not altogether new, is an important trend. They offer children new

role models, a particularly strong asset for children from families
with no father at home. Teen-agers from high-school child development courses, older brothers and sisters of children in day care,
Neighborhood Youth Corps workers, and other young people have
done good jobs as teaching assistants in many centers. College and
graduate-school students can often get credit for their work while
they're helping your program. Another resource recently tapped
has been senior citizens. Foster Grandparents programs have added
new dimensions to several center staffs. A warm grandmotherly or
grandfatherly person can work on a one-to-one basis with children
who need extra attention, and these older people are often the
ones who are sought out by children for comfort. At the same
time, child-care work can provide senior citizens with a sense of
their own worth, which is often difficult for them to attain in our
society.

We saw a special vitality in centers where there was staff diversity. At the Avco Day Care Center in Boston, Massachusetts, each
of the six staff members has a special way of dealing with the kids:
together, they're an excellent team.

Sally, one of the center's codirectors, is tall, attractive, a sharp
dresser. Hip, she knows where it's at but isn't pushy about it. She
has a Master's in early childhood education, is young, somewhat
Afro in style, and has good relationships with her codirector and
other staff members. She started as a teacher and was moved up to
codirector. As with many others in the day-care field, her qualifications could allow her good positions with much higher pay, but
she is very interested in working directly with children. Like her
codirector, she handles what administrative chores she must, but
she also spends a good deal of her time with the children, particularly the preschoolers.

Her codirector is Mary Lou, the only white who is a regular staff
member, and petite where Sally is tall. Mary Lou worked in a
Bedford-Stuyvesant day-care center while she was completing her
nursing training. She was instrumental in getting the center going
and has been with the project since the planning stages. She is
young, rather an idealist, and very soft spoken. (At first one thinks
this is a disadvantage, but in practice it turns out to be a suitable
style for her and for the way she handles the job.) She doubles as
the [Avco] plant nurse and spends much of her free time with the
infants in the center.

Cynthia and Shirley are the women teachers and, like the men, are parents of center children. Shirley is warm, easygoing, kindly, and really cheerful—a loving, motherly figure for the children and an uplifter for the staff. Her personality is complemented by Cynthia's, who is full of humor, flashy, funny, and quite creative. Cynthia does a lot of work with the children on art projects and other small-group activities—dress-up parades, rhythm bands, group learning sessions. She has a knack for holding children's interest.

. . . the center is very lucky to have two men staff members. Both in their early to mid-twenties, they are attractive men, good role models for the kids. Walter has been with the project for some time and is a real strength to the rest of the staff. He's hip, tender, and loving with the kids but able to be a stern figure when it's needed. He's often heard telling kids to "get themselves together." He works out a compromise between what he wants them to do and what they want to do. Ronnie, who is new to the center, was referred to the program by Walter. Sincere in his hopes for the kids, he's somewhat quieter than Walter but is smiling, friendly, and has his own kind of strength. He had hoped to be a probation officer, but a lung ailment prevented it, and day-care work seemed ideal. The observers found him fitting in well with the rest of the close-knit staff, and the children seemed to accept him easily.

The center's staff has achieved a friendly and informal style of operation that gets the job done with a minimum of fuss. Teachers work on staggered shifts and are rotated daily so no one has the same shift for too long. The place is small enough so that children, staff, and parents all know each other. Because they roam from group to group during the afternoon, staff members are able to exchange roles and work well with any age or activity group. Although the administrative duties can be weighty even for a center this small, the directors feel strongly that it is important for both of them to participate as teachers as much as possible, even if the paperwork suffers.

Planning How Staff Will Be Used
Staff/child ratios and the amount of time staff spend on non-care duties are critical issues in day care and should be determined before the program begins.

Staff/Child Ratios A staff/child ratio is simply the number of staff you have to care for the number of children you serve. Often, the staff/child ratio isn't a matter of choice: regulations vary from state to state, and there are also federal interagency guidelines that require certain minimum staff/child ratios for programs receiving federal funds. Current federal ratios are 1 staff member to every 5 three-year-olds; 1 to every 7 four- and five-year-olds; and 1 to every 10 children over six years of age.

Just how many staff you *should* have for a given number of children is a widely debated issue, but our observation was that as the number of children per staff member rises, quality in a number of areas suffers. There are several ways of arriving at a staff/child ratio, and it's important to know the method used when evaluating the final ratio. For instance, for the child figure, some programs count the total number of children enrolled in the center, while others estimate the average daily attendance. Since the number of children actually in attendance is usually some 12 percent less than total enrollment, we think using the average daily attendance estimate will give you a more accurate staff/child ratio. Some programs count only teachers as staff, while others include administrators, support staff, and volunteers. If you include people who are not directly involved in caring for the children, the staff/child ratio will be higher, but it will also be deceptive if you're trying to find out how many staff are directly involved in working with how many kids.

Staff Time Spent on Noncare Duties Another related issue to consider is the proportion of time spent by staff on nonteaching duties—clean-up, paperwork, meetings, and a host of other tasks. If a great deal of time is spent in these nonteaching activities, the staff/child ratio will tend to exaggerate the amount of teaching and supervision the children really get. The more support staff you have (paid or volunteer) and the more you can streamline your nonteaching operations, the happier your staff is likely to be.

One way to determine actual child-care time is to compute the staff/child *contact hour* ratio, which measures how much adult time is actually spent with children. You get this ratio by counting the number of hours adults in the center are actually in contact with kids: this way you account for administrators who spend part of their time teaching and also for teachers who spend time in noncare duties. The staff/child ratio and the contact hour ratio may vary a lot. For example, at American Child Centers, Inc., in Nashville, Tennessee, the staff/child ratio was 1/6.5 while the contact hour ratio was 1/9.4. At Amalgamated Day Care Center, however, the difference was much smaller—1/4.5 staff/child ratio and a 1/4.9 contact hour ratio.

Working with Staff

Once you've found and hired your staff, it's important to see that morale is high and that individual teachers can be effective in their work. One way to do this is to make sure that all staff members have well-defined jobs, time enough to do them, and some time left over for themselves. Many center directors have found that job descriptions are a big help here. A brief and concise job description should list all the duties a staff member is expected to perform and state which supervisory person he or she is responsible to. Good job descriptions can mean that staff aren't saddled with more than they can handle and that jobs and responsibilities don't overlap. Directors also use these descriptions to evaluate staff performance for promotions and staff development.

Scheduling is also important for staff morale. Full-time staff, who spend eight or often nine hours a day in the center, are under constant pressure from children, parents, and other staff. If at all possible, teachers should have at least an hour during the day to themselves. A staggered schedule, with teachers arriving and departing at various intervals, will allow some staff to cover for others during the day. Most centers also rotate schedules so no one has the earliest or latest shift all the time. Floating staff members can also be used to relieve the burden on individual teachers: these people simply move through the center and help where and when they're needed.

Your staff roster can be supplemented by parent or community volunteers who will fill in competently when teachers are absent or when funds just aren't available for full-time, professional staff. Many centers in our study used support staff (the cook or a housekeeper, for example) as substitute teachers. This may work for emergencies, but it quickly becomes too demanding for these people, who have other jobs to do. The center with a pool of resource people in the community has a great asset. Volunteers

needn't be only teachers. In the Holland Day Care Center in
Holland, Michigan,

Volunteers from the community serve on the board of directors,
the policy advisory committee, personnel, finance, and other
policymaking bodies. They also assist in all phases of the center's
operations. They are aides to the two cooks and to the teaching
staff; professionals volunteer their services as pediatrician, dietitian, and social workers, as dental consultant and career development counselor; volunteers from the community are baby-sitters
for center parents, laundresses, field trip aides, fund-raisers, clerical help; they assist at parties for the children and parent social
events, provide homemade food, repair and mend toys, make
sheets, bibs, blankets, mittens, caps, and other clothing for the
children, and so on. They are indispensable to the program.
 The assistance represents more than a financial saving for the program. Extra adults in the classroom means that teachers can give
more individual attention to the children. Inside the center, they
allow staff more time for meetings and in-service training; outside
the center, they provide services to families that they could not
otherwise afford and allow parents to attend meetings and be
involved in the center's programs.
 The program has a roster of 7 nap room aides, 6 professional
volunteers, 26 cook aides, 104 laundry volunteers, 45 teacher
aides and 50 baby-sitters. . . .

Volunteers can really lighten the load on both teaching and support staff. Many centers find it useful to appoint a volunteer to
recruit other volunteers, coordinate their use, and generally act as
a liaison between the center and the community. Remember also
that people who donate their time and services need to be thanked
now and again. Let your volunteers know you appreciate their
help.
 Good staff communication is very important for staff morale
and the smooth functioning of a program. A director can't see that
improvements are made if he or she can't get feedback from the
staff. Staff, for their part, need to know about policy changes,
planning (if this is done by others), new goals, and so on. They
also need a chance to work out problems with individual children
and their jobs by talking to each other and their supervisors. Most
centers hold meetings at least once a week for all staff members,
with an agenda that typically includes:

1. Announcement of new center policies or procedures
2. Discussion of current or upcoming problems, or ideas for making things work better
3. Planning for the next week's program
4. Discussion of individual children, evaluation of their needs, setting up new goals for them
5. Brief talks by various staff or by visiting speakers on topics of interest to all personnel (child development, parent services, community resources, etc.).

Often, there just isn't time to cover all these topics in one meeting. Issues (3) and (4) are so important they may require a separate meeting. Staff sessions can be held early in the morning before the kids arrive or after they've left in the afternoon. Some centers hold meetings during nap time, although if no volunteers are available, it means some staff must miss out. Many programs find evening meetings unavoidable, but no one particularly likes giving up this time after they've spent a long day in the center.

Staff Training
New staff members, whether professional teachers or community members, need an orientation and training period to introduce them to the program, its philosophy, its goals, and its procedures. Most of the programs we saw set aside a week for this preservice training. New staff spent the first few days observing in the classroom or working alongside other staff members. Some centers also provide an orientation manual, which describes the center's organization and staff, how it operates, and several procedures all staff must know (how to deal with sick children, how to work with parents, how staff are promoted, and so on).

In good programs, training usually doesn't stop after preservice training: it's an ongoing process for all staff in the center. Sometimes in-service training sessions are incorporated into regular weekly staff meetings when outside speakers come in to discuss issues such as child development, curriculum, and goal-setting. Many of the centers in our study also made arrangements with colleges and universities in their areas to offer credit courses to staff on a part-time basis or at reduced cost. If your program can afford it, you might also consider giving staff time off with pay occasionally so they can attend educational seminars or meetings or conferences of various child development or day-care service organizations, or to visit other day-care programs in your region. The techniques and ideas teachers bring back from such sessions can be invaluable for solving problems in your program.

The Northwest Rural Opportunities system of nine rural day-care centers in the state of Washington has an extensive teacher training program. At NRO,

... 70% of the system's staff is drawn from the Chicano migrant community. In the early stages of the project, the Chicano staff were performing menial tasks while Anglos did the teaching. The training program was initiated, along with new curriculum, to make sure that Chicanos would have the chance to move up in the system.

Training is done by [a child development specialist in the program] and a team of VISTA volunteers with child development training, supervised by an outside consultant. The program is broken down into units, each dealing with a specific aspect of the curriculum used in the program and the methods for implementing it. Every six weeks, teachers attend workshops covering one of these aspects and two associated teaching strategies. Between workshops, the trainers scatter to the centers to observe and help teachers use the strategies. . . . The system also tries to deal with the uncertainties felt by new staff. Center coordinators, many of them Chicano, make a point of bolstering trainee confidence.

[Already] about 10% of the staff have been promoted because they have increased their skills. Inside the centers, aides have been promoted to assistant teachers or lead teachers. Some have left the centers to become teacher aides in other schools, secretaries, and welfare department paraprofessionals.

In addition, all center cooks and aides attend nutrition workshops four times each year. The system conducts these sessions in cooperation with the Washington State Cooperative Extension Service, Washington State University, and USDA Consumer and Marketing Service in San Francisco. In-service training includes menu planning, food purchasing and preparation, and inventorying.

Career Development for Staff
Good in-service training programs usually go hand-in-hand with career development opportunities. Career development plans help

staff members get the skills they need to move up in the child-care field and in your own program. What you're doing is offering staff training opportunities not only for the jobs they're currently holding (through in-service training) but also for related responsibilities they might like to assume in the future.

The best way to define career development is to describe a program that really does the job, like the one at Central City Head Start Day Care Center in Salt Lake City:

From the beginning, career development was considered crucial to the needs of growing children. The original director strongly believed that disadvantaged children would be more likely to achieve if they could experience successful adult models from their own racial and cultural backgrounds. So a real effort was made in the initial hiring to bring in paraprofessionals who not only cared about children, but who also cared about themselves and where they were going with their lives. All staff who had any contact with the children were and are considered "guidance teachers" (including the bus driver), and special attention was given to the recruitment of males. Of the original staff of twelve, four were men—despite the facts that the salary ceiling is low, lower even than day laboring, and that men are seldom easily convinced that working with three- to five-year-olds is a manly job.

All paraprofessionals were given in-service training, not only to prepare them for their jobs, but also to encourage them to attempt more. In addition, several parents were drawn into the center as classroom volunteers and were offered full-time work as guidance teachers when vacancies developed, rather than being held at the volunteer level while outside personnel were brought in. This policy proved important both for aiding staff career development and for increasing and strengthening parent involvement in the center program.

During the center's second year of operation, funds were made available for individual college credit courses or group workshops carrying college credit, through the OEO Supplementary Training program. Paraprofessionals can receive full tuition through the B.A. degree. An economic incentive is added in the form of a $5/month salary increase for each full five credits completed. Professionals on the staff are reimbursed half their tuition costs. University extension classes are given at the center during the children's rest periods or in the evening for interested center staff. Subjects such as child development, Spanish, sociology, and psychology are taught for college credit.

Most of the staff members interviewed revealed strong positive feelings about themselves and the work they were doing. Part of this feeling undoubtedly results from the supportive atmosphere of the center, but a more emphatic confirmation comes from the history of the program itself. Asked how far she felt she could go in the program, one guidance teacher replied, "All the way to the top." The system proves that kind of confidence is justified: Ed Owens is a case in point. . . . Ed became director of the Central City Day Care Center through the center's career development ladder. He started as a bus driver-guidance teacher, become a head teacher, and then was chosen over several outside candidates for the position of director.

Other advancements within the program since it started include five parents from volunteer status to guidance teacher (in addition to the director, the parent coordinator, and the administrative assistant). Recently, one of the guidance teachers was promoted to head teacher, and the head teacher she replaced has become teacher-director in a new northwest day-care center. In addition, another Central City guidance teacher will soon move to a head-teacher position in that new program.

Staff have also moved upward and outward to other agencies and career positions in the larger Salt Lake educational and business community: a parent who moved from volunteer to guidance teacher to head teacher to the Family Planning Agency to State Community Services; a bus driver-guidance teacher to the Kennecott Personnel Office to salesman for Mobil Oil; and a guidance teacher to the University of Utah on a full scholarship.

What seems to make Central City's career development program work is the staff's unthreatened attitude. Four components contribute to the success of the Salt Lake City program:
1. A genuine belief on the part of staff members in the ability of people to succeed if they are given the opportunity;
2. Careful screening and hiring procedures to insure potential;
3. In-service training and maximum use of all available educational facilities and resources;
4. Positive promotion practices.

Other examples of good staff training and career development can be found in the case studies of the Kentucky Rural Child Care Project and of the Family Day Care Career Program in Part IV of this book.

[Our director] is the drive behind the center, not for herself, but mainly because she loves these children. She's a very perceptive, compassionate person with a superhuman job.

> Staff member,
> Casper Day Care Center
> Casper, Wyoming

Directors

The director is the linchpin of the day-care center, pulling together all aspects of the program and personnel on the inside as well as gathering the resources, services, and people the program needs from the community. The director administers the program, supervises staff, and more often than not is the guiding spirit of the enterprise. The directors we met were typically dynamic, warm, and capable of juggling an awesome number of tasks simultaneously. Here are a few center directors:

5th City Pre-School, Chicago, Illinois:
The director, at present, is Lela Campbell, the most dynamic force in the Pre-School. . . . Lela works at a helter-skelter pace, involved in a thousand and one things at the same time, and managing to get at least the most important ones done. . . . She spends considerable time fund-raising. She also substitutes in the classroom, helps with lunch, works with parents and the community organization, and fulfills additional responsibilities to the [sponsoring] Ecumenical Institute. Two years ago she and one of the leading parents in the community went out and knocked on doors to get children enrolled in the center. Now there is a waiting list of about 50 kids and no recruiting effort is necessary.

Casper Day Care Center, Casper, Wyoming:
Helen Dawson, director of the Casper Day Care Center, is a fighter. She fought to start the day-care center operation and is fighting to keep it alive—against very real odds. Money is an incessant problem. There is less than $700 to spend for each child each year. This means scrambling to get donated labor, facilities, and services, which provide another estimated $750 for each child. There is wide agreement among board members, staff, parents, and volunteers that the center wouldn't have begun without Helen and wouldn't be the same if she left. . . . Helen took the observer team to the [center] early on a Monday morning in late November. She was met immediately and warmly by a number of children as we entered the attached church building. She returned this warmth and

gave her undivided, though necessarily short, attention to each. Then she plunged into a hectic Monday. . . .

Central City Head Start Day Care Center, Salt Lake City, Utah:
Paul Edward Owens—Ed—is Central City Head Start Day Care's director. He's a tall man, well above six feet, weighing perhaps 210 pounds. He's an ex-football player who came to Central City after a season with a Texas pro team. Watching Ed work in the center, one is struck by the sense that he has decided that his job is people, and thus he directs his energy to staff, parents, and children. His style is nondirective and supportive; the kids love him and he loves them back. . . . Ed Owens became director via the center's career development ladder. He started as a bus driver-guidance teacher, became a head teacher, and . . . was chosen over several outside candidates for the position of director. He was already known and respected in the parent community, and as a black, his appointment served further to bolster the self-image of the mixed racial community.

West 80th Street Day Care Center, New York City:
Dorothy Pitman Hughes founded and organized the center. She is responsible for all the administrative work and community education. When we visited, she was flying from a speech in Philadelphia to a hearing in Washington, busy laying groundwork for the many projects she's always got in her head. She is indefatigable, militant, and highly effective. . . . Her full-time organizing and fund-raising efforts have initiated dozens of other child-care projects, improved state laws, launched many self-help projects in her own community and the city. In three years, she and the community have raised over $400,000 to buy a building shell and renovate it as a new center. The community, with her help, has successfully fought for city acceptance of community residents without formal qualifications as center teachers.
  Grace Richmond [her codirector] is primarily in charge of skill education, working the same 12-hour day as Dorothy Hughes. She is tiny, quick, elegant. She pays the way for kids going to the zoo out of her own pocket. . . . She agonizes every month to get the center bills paid. She spends hours a day with parents, on the phone and at her desk. She is, throughout, a gracious, occasionally flustered, competent professional.

  It takes a very special kind of person to be a good center director. While directors report little difficulty recruiting and hiring teaching and support staff, boards of directors seem to have a hard

time finding day-care directors. Salaries for directors generally
range from $8,400 for a center with an average daily attendance of
25 children to $10,450 for a center serving 75 children. And most
boards want people with early childhood education degrees or a
great deal of experience in the field of child care.

What's it take to be a good director? Patience, tenacity, unflap-
pability. Strong commitment to your work, to children. The ability to do public speaking, fund raising, public relations. Rapport
with and availability to your staff. Attention to detail, from budgeting to admissions procedures to ordering supplies. You have to
like people and be able to work with them. You need to be a
statesman with parents and boards of directors, an administrator, a
good listener. You have to be able to cope with crises and with
day-to-day routine. If your program can't afford certain services,
you'll have to be willing to make the effort to get them, which
may mean cajoling and wheedling free medical and dental examinations for children, emergency food for a family in need, counseling for parents. You may have to be a teacher trainer for your
staff, and you'll certainly have to be a morale booster. An understanding friend to kids. A curriculum planner, a grant proposal
writer, a lobbyist. You need to be able to do all these things effectively and with warmth. Maybe what you need most is a sense of
humor and a lot of stamina. Directors in good centers often put in
60-hour weeks.

How Directors Spend Their Time
Directors in our centers spent, generally speaking, between 70 and
80 percent of their time on administrative duties, much of it in
training and supervising center staff. Anywhere from 6 to 40 percent of a director's time may be spent on fund raising and public
relations activities. If your program is funded by the community
or is dependent on federal or state funds, the director will probably have to spend more time fund raising than if the program is
privately financed or part of a school system.

Rarely is more than 15 percent of a director's time spent teaching children. In those cases where considerable teaching *is* done,
there are usually codirectors who share administrative responsibilities, or the center is part of a system of child-care centers in
which administrative functions are handled in a central office.

Every director approaches this job differently, depending on her or his own style and the day-care setting itself, but the figures presented here may give you some idea of the way directors spend their time. Figures 3.1-3.4 represent time spent by each of the codirectors of a privately funded center (Avco). Figures 3.5 and 3.6 break down the duties of the director of a parent-owned corporation (Greeley), a very poor center that relies heavily on volunteer staff. Finally, we include the activities of a center director in the Berkeley, California, school system (Figures 3.7 and 3.8).

Briefly, here are the administrative tasks most of our directors were handling:

Setting Policy This means establishing an overall set of operating procedures for the center and includes setting up personnel policies for recruiting, hiring, and promoting staff. Similarly, there must be policies for child admissions, program content, staff training and career development, budgeting and financial reporting, and for basic center operations, such as hours open, fees, referrals, and so on.

Program Planning and Budgeting Determining the goals of the program, projecting its growth and needs, and developing a budget to cover the staff, facilities, and equipment needed are all part of the director's job. When centers receive grant funds, proposal writing and follow-up also become part of this planning process. Planning and budgeting are done not only annually but for longer periods of time as well. Boards of directors, directors, and their staffs should ask themselves where they want to be two or even five years from the present and should plan for these long-term goals.

Mobilizing Resources A director helps identify the resources the center will need to carry out its plans—resources such as staff, money, equipment, or other support—and then works to bring them into the program. Often, this means applying for grants from federal agencies or groups like the United Fund or securing in-kind donations of facilities, staff, equipment, and food from center parents, volunteers, and the community, which often involves some scrounging and cajoling.

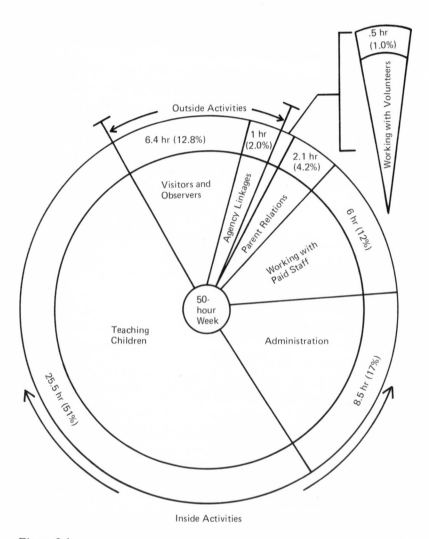

Figure 3.1
Breakdown of administrative duties of one Avco Day Care Center codirector

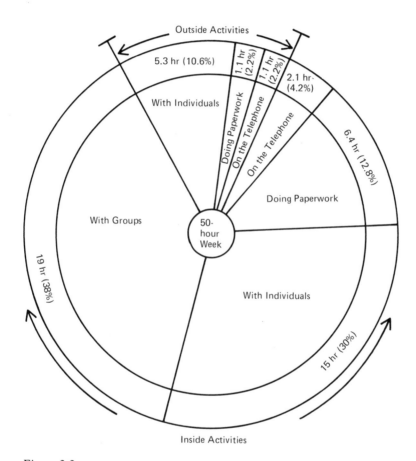

Figure 3.2
How one Avco Day Care Center codirector spends her time in the performance
of her administrative duties

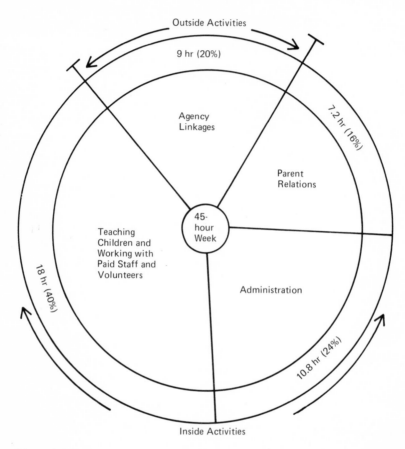

Figure 3.3
Breakdown of administrative duties of other Avco Day Care Center codirector

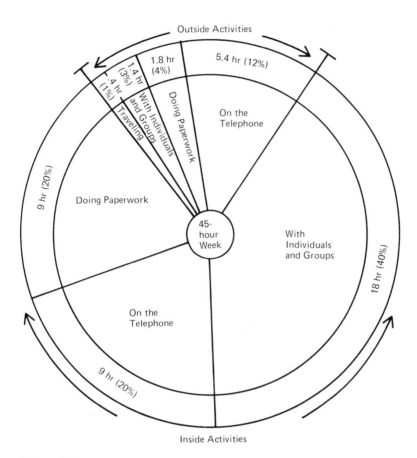

Figure 3.4
How the other Avco Day Care Center codirector spends her time in the performance of her administrative duties

Figure 3.5
Breakdown of administrative duties of Greeley Parent Child Center director

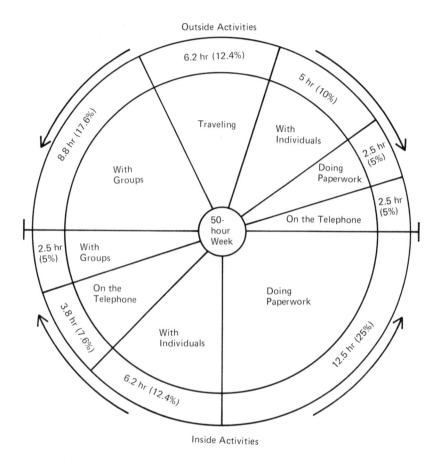

Figure 3.6
How the Greeley Parent Child Center director spends her time in the performance of her administrative duties

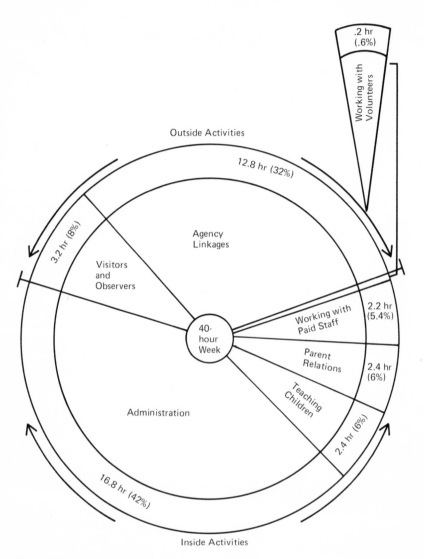

Figure 3.7
Breakdown of administrative duties of West Berkeley Day Care Center director

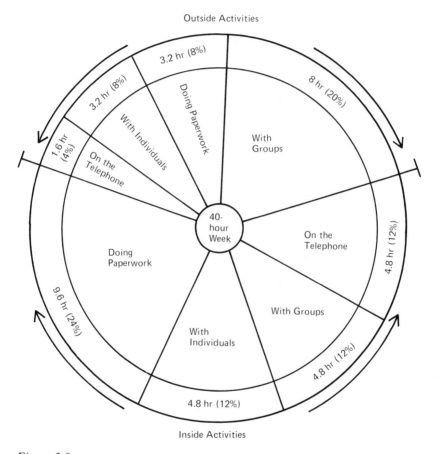

Figure 3.8
How the West Berkeley Day Care Center director spends her time in the performance of her administrative duties

Personnel Development Directors are usually responsible for everything associated with the growth and development of the center's
staff, particularly recruitment and hiring, setting salaries, training,
supervision and promotion, and firing.

Ongoing Program Management This is the day-to-day management
of the center and includes planning curriculum, activities, and
daily schedules; anticipating equipment needs; organizing staff
schedules; supervising staff to make sure the program is being
carried out as effectively as planned; and arranging for parent
meetings and participation.

Parent Relations Directors conduct or help with the admissions
interview, set up periodic conferences with parents about child
progress, and help refer parents to services outside the child-care
program. Good directors take the trouble to locate and set up
working relationships with various agencies so that parents in need
can be referred. They also follow up the referral to make sure
parents have gotten the help they needed.

Program Evaluation This involves determining how well the program is meeting its goals: how well it cares for children, relates to
parents, develops its staff, deals with the community, and improves as an organization. In quality centers, directors often ask
their staff and parents to evaluate different aspects of the program, formally and informally. Sometimes outside professionals
are called in for evaluation.

Boards of Directors
Center directors seldom carry out all these tasks by themselves.
Most centers have boards of directors, which assume legal responsi-
bility for the overall program and help formulate its policies.
Board duties differ from center to center, but typically, boards

Approve the annual budget developed by the center

Establish personnel policies that specify the qualifications required
for different jobs in the program and confer with the center director in hiring, firing, or promotion of staff (the board itself usually
hires the center director)

Establish the center's admission policy, which involves determining child or family eligibility for the program

Set other major center policies, such as hours of operation, fees to be charged, general program content

Review the director's administration of the center, its budget, and its personnel.

These represent the more formal kinds of duties, but there may be informal ones as well. Board members can be very helpful in mobilizing resources for the program—locating volunteer staff, finding equipment to be donated, or soliciting financial contributions from the community. Individual board members (professionals in social services, law, medicine, education, or management, for instance) often donate their own skills and time to help the center.

Who Sits on a Board
Board composition is usually closely related to the kind of operation you have. For example, if your program is a parent-owned cooperative day-care center, the board will most likely be composed entirely of parents. Centers that operate under umbrella agencies such as Community Action have boards that are half community representatives and half parents. This is the pattern called for by Head Start and many other OEO-funded programs. A third membership pattern occurs with United Fund or other social service organization sponsorship: here, boards are made up mostly (75-80 percent) of community representatives—social workers, educators, businessmen, and so on.

Boards heavily weighted toward community members are often supplemented by parent advisory committees to make sure parents have an adequate voice in the policies that will affect their children. Such committees commonly have the power to consider staff candidates, veto budget proposals, and suggest changes in various aspects of center operation. Similarly, when boards are heavily weighted toward parents, a professional advisory committee is often formed to help the staff and the board with certain technical functions, such as budgeting, grant applications, etc. Professional advisors can also be a great help to parents in locating sources of revenue.

Whichever membership pattern is chosen, the total size of the
board is generally between 15 and 20 members: our centers
found that too many members made boards unwieldy, and too
few participants meant a possible lack of representation for some
concerned group. Quite frequently, the director or one or more of
the professional staff of the center also sit on the board but do not
vote. Our observations indicated that staff representation on the
board is a good idea: it keeps communication channels open between teachers and policy makers, and there's less feeling on the
part of staff that decisions made without them are being imposed
on them.

Not all day-care centers have boards of directors, however. The
board system is not usually used by private profit-making corporations, employer- or union-subsidized day care, or in public school
systems that operate child-care programs. For instance, the Avco
Day Care Center, sponsored by the Avco Printing and Publishing
Division for its employees, receives most of its financial support
from and shares many of the benefits of the Avco Corporation.
Although the codirectors are responsible for center operations and
make the decisions about staff, curriculum, and so on, the overall
plans and the budget are set by the Avco management. Parents and
community play almost no role in the program.

We found very different administrative styles in our study.
The Haight-Ashbury Children's Center and the Berkeley Unified
School District Children's Centers are at opposite ends of the
spectrum when it comes to policy-making structures. Haight-
Ashbury is a parent-owned and controlled corporation, while the
Berkeley system is part of that city's Board of Education. At
Haight-Ashbury,

Parents have a real financial stake in the center. The Parents' Participation Share Plan was designed to help meet the center's expenses while involving parents in the center's operation. Parents
are required, instead of paying fees, to purchase shares in the
Haight center as long as their children are enrolled there. (When
children are withdrawn, installments for incomplete shares are
refunded, less a small handling fee.) Share purchases are made on a
monthly installment basis of $25, until the half-share price of
$250 has been attained. For those who cannot afford the monthly
charge, adjustments can be made.

When a parent has paid $250, a half-share is issued that pays interest each year. After three years, the entire balance of the half-share is paid off to the parent. Through this plan, the center is buying its property and buildings, and meeting day-to-day expenses. Parents, moreover, have a tangible stake in the center, and the director estimates that 50 percent of the parents are actively involved in the center's programs.

Policy-making authority and responsibility lie directly in the hands of center parents, through the board of directors (eight parents, four community members) and the parent governing board that elects it. Parents plan the program, develop the budget, administer funds, hire and fire staff, and oversee all aspects of the program. There are also various subcommittees, which are formed when called for: at present they cover finance, health, maintenance, and staff screening.

Very few of the center's parents have much experience running anything, even their own lives. Given this, many people have, out of their helplessness or habit, looked to the board and the director for decisions and leadership. Others want to seize the opportunity to tell the rest what to do. Parent meetings are often passive-aggressive, push-me/pull-you sessions. Some people are too shy to speak up. Others are more aggressive and of these, some are sincere—they really want to get things done and assume responsibility. . . . Bear in mind, too, that this is a young center in many senses of the word. Because it is rich and energetic, its potential for problems is bound to be on the same order as its potential for productive impact. True crises occur instead of mere problems; there are miracles instead of mere effectiveness. . . .

In contrast, the Berkeley Children's Centers are a system of seven day-care centers operated by the Berkeley Unified School District. Parents here do not exercise a formal voice or policy-making control in this system, and parent involvement has been very low. The governing board of the system is the Board of Education of the school district: final control of program planning, staff hiring, firing, and promotion lies in the hands of the Board and a Superintendent, whom the board hires. A Coordinator of Early Childhood Education, who works under the Superintendent, assists center staffs in some of their day-to-day operations. Teachers in the centers determine the daily program activities. Parent involvement in the policy-making process is limited to suggestions to the board or center staffs. The study team describes the Berkeley system:

But what struck us most about Berkeley's Early Childhood Education effort was the system itself. It is an established, efficient, progressive, and humane system, one that tolerates diversity and creativity and has attracted a first-rate body of teachers. . . . The District provides all basic services for the centers . . . many of these being routine administrative matters, which can be time-consuming at the local level. Their centralization has freed staff energies for other things. As in any system, there are ordering and purchasing delays, some red tape, some inflexibility, but ECE seemed freer, more receptive to change than most systems.

Association with the Public School District also allows the centers to share in the higher salaries and employee benefits, specialized staff (such as special education, project development, accounting, maintenance, food services, etc.), information resources, personnel services, stability, and community support garnered by the larger system. In Berkeley, these are all significant.

Another advantage of the system is the stable financial atmosphere. . . . Center directors are not required to divide their time and attention between their centers and fund-raising. The latter, in many of the centers we visited, took up a considerable portion of the director's energy. When a center doesn't know where its next financial shot-in-the-arm is coming from—or even if it will come in time—there is invariably a kind of tension, a "Will-we-be-here-next-month?" feeling, which can result in short-range planning and staff apathy and insecurity. . . . While stable funding can also breed complacency and lack of innovation, we found neither at Berkeley. People were simply able to do their jobs with hope and enthusiasm.

Administration and management at Berkeley are efficient and well coordinated, not at all hectic, as they can be at Haight-Ashbury. But on the other hand, Berkeley's parents, community, and staff can't exercise the direct control over the program and its operations that Haight-Ashbury parents have. Although very different in style, both places have good programs. Figures 3.9 and 3.10, which show the organization of both programs, reflect the different operating styles.

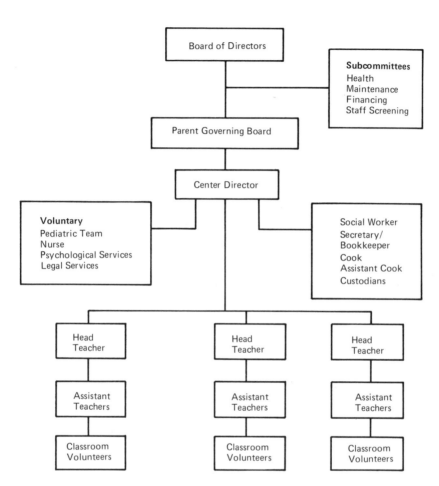

Figure 3.9
Organization chart of Haight-Ashbury Children's Center

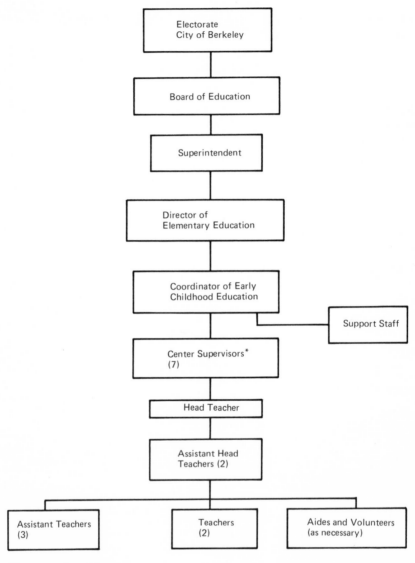

*Representative of 7 centers

Figure 3.10
Organization chart of Berkeley Unified School District

I've learned to continue the work of the center at home and that makes what happens at the center better.

I never realized before I brought my children here that they are people too. I understand them better now . . . you get along so much better when you understand them. I understand myself better, too. The atmosphere at home is happier—our family life is better. I'm not under pressure all the time wondering why my kids are behaving the way they do.

> Parents, Central City Head Start
> Day Care Center
> Salt Lake City, Utah

If kids are to keep the gains they make during the day in your center, if they're to continue to learn and grow, they need acceptance, support, and understanding at home, too. That's why it's important for teachers and parents to work together to help children develop. If teachers have one set of ideas about caring for kids and parents have another, children get caught in the middle. Good day care really *is* a cooperative venture, and parent understanding and support of your program can make it far more effective.

Parent participation in day care is one way to make sure parents understand and approve of center policies. When parents work in the classroom, for instance, they can see firsthand how the center is educating their children and how teachers deal positively with problem situations. Parent teachers, aides, or classroom volunteers can reinforce a child's learning at home. In addition, many good centers consider parent control of center operations essential: parents, after all, have the biggest stake in seeing that their kids are being treated properly and are learning the skills and values that will facilitate their entry into the larger society. Parent participation in staff selection, administration, admissions policies, center hours, and other areas means that staff are more likely to respond to their needs and wishes. We found that in centers where parents had decision-making authority, parent involvement was generally quite high: where they had no voice, their participation tended to be lower. The staff's attitude toward parents is crucial. If parents aren't encouraged to participate, they won't. If they don't feel comfortable or particularly welcome at the center, they'll stay away. If staff members are condescending toward parents or even hostile because they feel threatened, parents will get the message very quickly and opt out of involvement.

We noticed an engaging kind of vitality in centers where parents were really involved. Staff and parents seemed to like and respect each other; people pitched in unselfishly with their time, money, or services to make sure things got done; often, a dialogue between two races was established where there had been only suspicion before. As a parent at 5th City in Chicago put it, "The school has helped enlighten us all."

Of course, not all parents can or want to participate in center activities and policy making. Most parents who need day care have jobs, and they're tired after a full day's work. Often, too, they have several kids to care for in the evenings. Many people using day care are single parents who haven't got a spouse to baby-sit while they attend center functions. (Several of our programs maintained a pool of community volunteers who would baby-sit while parents attended center meetings and social events: this service helped promote parent involvement.) But nonparticipation by some parents doesn't mean they're not interested in the program or their children's welfare: it means they're human and have multiple demands to meet.

In its commonest and most basic form, parent involvement with the center is really just communication: it's the staff and the parents sharing information about children, first in the admissions interview and later in regular parent-teacher conferences about child progress. Many centers go a step further and offer parents a chance to participate in the program in ways they'll feel comfortable with and that are meaningful to them. Finally, many of our quality centers served parents as well as children by making social services available for the benefit of the whole family. Let's look at these kinds of parent involvement more closely.

Sharing Information about Children
Parents need information about how their children are doing in the center and a chance to work along with the staff on child progress and problems. For their part, teachers need insights and

information from parents who, after all, have been caring for their children for years and know them best.

The center director usually takes the first step, at the time the child enters the program, by arranging an enrollment interview with his or her parents. In this interview, the director typically

Explains the program and makes sure parents understand what the child will be doing in the center

Discusses any special needs parents feel the child might have (a handicap to be overcome, a special need for love, attention, or discipline, special dietary needs, and so on)

Outlines the importance of parent involvement in the program and tells parents how they can participate

Asks parents about the child's life at home to see if there might be some special needs they've overlooked and to see if parents can use some of the center's social services

Makes sure the parents (or the child) meet the program's formal eligibility criteria (if any) and understand the fee system (if any)

Asks parents for all the information the center needs in such areas as child health, family profile, how to contact parents for emergencies, and so on.

In this interview, the director, or interviewer, should make sure the parents understand that their child's growth and development in the program are closely tied to his or her life at home. Parents should be genuinely encouraged to get involved in the center's activities and informed about the ways they can keep in touch with the staff—through daily contact and regular parent-teacher conferences in which their child's progress will be discussed.

Often a teacher or other staff member will want to visit the family at home before a child is enrolled. We think this is a good idea. It allows the teacher to meet different members of the family, to see how the child behaves when he's secure and happy, to see his favorite toys, to learn his likes and dislikes. These visits help make the child feel more comfortable with his teacher when his parents must eventually leave him at the center, and the teacher will be able to talk to the child about his family and home.

If their working hours and transportation permit, parents should be encouraged to bring their children to the center each day and to pick them up each afternoon. This system allows working parents to get at least a glimpse of the program in action, and it gives staff a chance to chat about the child and any parent concerns. Some centers designate particular staff members to greet children and talk with parents.

Regular individual parent conferences can also maintain contact between home and center. These conferences may be handled by the director or teaching staff and are usually held every month or every three months. Teachers bring to these conferences their written comments about a child's behavior and activities in the center and discuss them with the parents. Changes that have occurred since the last parent conference are also discussed, and parents have a chance to explain their feelings about how their child is doing and where he needs extra help. If they're held in the center, parent conferences must be scheduled at a time when parents are able to attend, and this often means in the early evenings or on Saturday. At some centers, teachers visit children's homes for these sessions.

Opportunities for Parent Participation

Whatever form parent involvement takes, centers usually provide one person to help parents coordinate their activities. This person might be a parent who serves as a liaison between parents and staff. Some centers form parent groups, which get started with social get-togethers or discussion groups and then later become more involved in actual center operations. Once parents are organized, they participate in the center's program in various ways.

Parents as Staff In many centers, parents are paid members of the staff—teachers, teacher aides, transportation aides, cooks, and so on. Some parents already have background in these areas, and some centers offer training for specific jobs. It can be extremely valuable for a child's self-image to see his mother or father in a position of authority and responsibility in the center. Parents who speak foreign languages can provide bilingual and bicultural activities for the program. Some centers prefer to have parent teachers work with groups that don't include their own children. This way, staff members can treat the parent teacher's child like any other, and feelings on all sides are less likely to be ruffled. Our parent interviews indicated that parents who had worked in the center often felt they'd learned a great deal about their children and child development in general, and they were able to apply these insights and skills at home. Direct carryover like this is ideal.

Parents as Volunteers If their regular employment permits, parents can work as teacher aides one afternoon a week or month or supervise Saturday or evening baby-sitting where the center offers this service. Although parents may not be able to serve as regular or full-time volunteers, their assistance for special events or field trips can be very helpful. Here, it's often up to teachers to involve parents in creative ways. A father who works in a bakery, for instance, might be able to organize a trip to the bakery for center children. A parent in the nursing profession might come to the center to talk to the kids about hospitals or good health habits. Parents can help the center at home by making toys or other educational materials for the program. Parent groups can really get things done: several centers set aside weekends when parents work together to clean up, repair, or repaint the center building. This kind of cooperative work is more than a financial help to the center: it's a way to bring people together in a mutual—and tangible—enterprise. It gets people talking and it often leads to friendships. Kids benefit too. Seeing their parents really contributing to the center is a fine way for kids to understand that their parents care, that they consider the center an important and worthwhile place. It closes the gap between home and school.

In the centers of the Rural Child Care Project in Kentucky, parents have done an excellent job of providing their centers with equipment:

The list that follows is only partial, but it is indicative of the care and imagination parents, staff, and volunteers have applied to a real center problem: that of low-cost play materials. . . . Large telephone cable spools have become trains (or whatever the children want them to be), with huge building blocks for coaches. Discarded milk crates are stepping stones, swings are made of old tires, lumber has been fashioned into small cars (with real steering wheels) and horses (with horse heads and broomstick tails). Board ladders are attached to the walls of another center, each rung a different color to help children devise their own climbing games. Hard-surfaced playgrounds are covered with sawdust to soften falls, but at one site, the ground was too rocky for equipment to be anchored. So a "sliding board" was fastened to a tree trunk, and braided rope ladders dangled from its limbs. After thorough sanitation, outdoor privies have been converted to playhouses.

Parents have cut triangles, squares, rectangles, and circles in the sides of a huge old barrel so children could learn their geometric shapes as they crawled in and out. Another center has a derelict car and worn-out parking meters for its children. One parent donated some pipe and made hand-walking bars; others built anchored balancing ropes. Donated oil barrels, with tops and bottoms removed, were covered with dirt to make tunnels; there's a gate free-swinging around a pole. Pieces from an old dinette set magically became a horse. The chairman of one policy advisory committee made an ingenious bouncing device out of a gaily painted pole, an old tire, and a washing machine chassis. A parent made his center a play motorcycle out of scrap materials and then donated a crash helmet. Another took the panels off an old washing machine and made a slide.

Parents as Mobilizers of Resources Good day care is expensive, and many of our programs were constantly searching for additional supplies, equipment, or money to help them stay in operation. Parents at many of our centers canvass their communities for such contributions or hold fund-raising events. The Holland, Michigan, day-care center raises funds each year by holding a Mexican fiesta for the whole community and by selling Christmas cards. The Greeley, Colorado, center netted $1,500 with a fund-raising Chicano-style dinner. The Central City Head Start center, which serves a mixed racial community, held a Multi-Color Elephant Sale. And the parents at the West 80th Street center in New York helped raise $400,000 in three years for a new building for their program.

Parents as Advocates of the Program Another important role for parents is advocacy—their active support of the program in its relations with other agencies and the community. Strong parent support is usually helpful in getting the center funds from public programs. Parent support also helps where a center has problems with licensing, establishing relationships with public agencies, or getting along with its neighborhood, if racial tension exists. Strong parent support leads to strong community support in many cases, and community support has enabled the West 80th Street center to hold out successfully against and change city regulations it felt were either demeaning or inappropriate to the black community it served. In the same way, the Haight-Ashbury Children's Center was able to count on its parents and community when its city refused to release desperately needed funds that had been promised the center. Parents led the community and their children on a march and sit-in at city hall: the funds were released. Parent advocacy like this is usually the result of a strong community organization program at the center. You don't find much parent advocacy when parents aren't involved with or participating in a program.

Parents as Learners Centers often organize parent education classes and workshops in child development to help parents understand the program's philosophy and methods. Many of our centers saw their jobs as much more than this, however. Child needs were often synonymous with or related to overall family needs, and these centers let parent needs and interests guide their parent education programs. The Holland Day Care Center offers courses in health, sewing, toy making and repair, consumer and sex education. Parent requests to the Rural Child Care Project in Kentucky have generated instruction in such diverse subjects as quilting, sewing and clothing alteration, upholstering, furniture refinishing, home repair, carpentry, plumbing, landscaping, picture framing, automobile maintenance and repair, family planning, nutrition, canning and food preserving, personal hygiene, health education, child behavior, sanitation, driver education, drug abuse, first aid, home safety, vital statistics and the census, income tax, FHA and low-cost home loans, and food stamps.

Aside from dispensing purely practical advice to help parents improve their standard of living by their own—not outside— efforts, these discussions can also help parents overcome fear and embarrassment due to misinformation and inexperience and can help them take advantage of the community resources at their disposal.

The Central City Head Start Day Care Center has instituted a cross-cultural education program for parents and children from this racially mixed Salt Lake City community. According to one parent, "One thing I feel is really important. I've learned not to fear others. In our parent meetings, we've learned so much about each other. [My daughter] Annie was ashamed of being half Mexican. Now she's not. She used to be afraid of Indians, too— you know, T.V. Now she's not. . . ." The center's rich ethnic and racial mix has been emphasized in monthly cultural and social programs planned and presented by the parents, including a Soul Brothers' Ball, an Indian Powwow, and a Mexican supper. "The children learn more about the world, and each child gets a sense of identity and pride in his own culture when the parents bring experiences—food, music, stories—from the different race or culture groups," a parent told us. At Central City, the racial mixture has become a positive experience. "This is what I call a small United Nations," is the way a black parent summed it up.

Making Social Services Available to Parents

Most day-care programs don't have the staff or facilities necessary to offer social services directly to parents. But through the admissions interview and daily contact with parents, as staff and parents get to know each other, you'll often discover that parents need services that are available in the community. Many of our centers developed linkages to those services and referred parents to them for help.

Usually, the center director or a social services coordinator (often called a social worker or community worker) has the task of forming linkages between the center and the community's services. He or she finds out what services are available and then contacts people in the agencies to find out who is eligible for such services and whether the agency will accept center referrals. The latter is important to make sure parents aren't put to the trouble of trying to deal with an agency that can't help them in the first place.

Throughout this process, social services must be offered in a
sensitive way so parents or families are not slighted. Tact and
respect are required, particularly for families whose self-esteem has
been bruised in previous brushes with cold or unresponsive social
service personnel. When the center serves families with limited
English, social workers are often bilingual. They provide transportation, accompany parents to agencies, and remain with parents to
translate and generally smooth the way. They also follow up to
make sure parents have gotten the services they needed.

Many social services, including employment and housing referrals, are handled by staff in the center itself. Direct services commonly offered by day-care centers are described in detail in Chapter 7, Supplemental Services. For a description of an excellent
social services program, see the case study of the Rural Child Care
Project of Frankfort, Kentucky, in Part IV. The section entitled
"Homemakers and Social Services" treats this aspect of the project.

A Comprehensive Parent Involvement Program

Certainly most programs can't offer all the parent services and
activities mentioned here. The services you offer will depend on
the needs of the parents you serve and the resources at your disposal. The Central City Head Start Day Care Center, for example,
uses the Salt Lake City community resources to the utmost,
thanks to Alberta Henry, the center's first-rate parent coordinator.
Alberta is what a parent coordinator ought to be:

Like Ed Owens [center director], she is black; like Ed, she moved
from guidance teacher to head teacher to her current position. She
has a phenomenal amount of energy, which works as a catalyst in
calling forth energy from parents. Every social event she organizes,
for example, is laced with purpose: breaking down cross-cultural
suspicions by opening up, demonstrating, using the culture. . . . On
the side, Alberta runs the Alberta Henry Foundation, which raised
over $9,000 in 1969-70 to provide scholarship assistance to 23
college students of all races from disadvantaged backgrounds. In
addition, she continues to work on her own B.A. at the University
of Utah under the center's career development program. And all
this when she is only ten years from normal retirement age.

Thanks to Alberta Henry and the center's enthusiastic staff,
Central City's parent involvement program is both real and effective:

Although it began as a dutiful response to OEO policy regulations
for Head Start operations, when Alberta Henry was promoted to
parent coordinator the program gained impressive impetus. It has
been going strong ever since. Every teacher considers parent involvement essential and productive, and every teacher identified
Alberta Henry as the most influential person at the center.

The primary objective of this program has been to get parents into
the center to see—and become a part of—what is happening to
their children. The staff feels that unless the learning that begins in
the center is carried on at home, many of the benefits to the children may be lost. A secondary objective of the program is to encourage parents to enhance their own lives—themselves—by providing information about and access to resources of the larger
community. This objective is achieved by counseling, guidance,
education, information about employment opportunities, etc.
Alberta Henry makes extensive use of a directory of community
services published with United Fund money by the Salt Lake
Community Service Council. The services of the parent coordinator are available to all center families.

Classroom educational programs for adults have evolved so that
learning at the center becomes a family affair. Parents also get
together in parent meetings held once a month. These are lively
sessions where Chicanos, whites, blacks, and Indians exchange concerns, hopes, suggestions, and information about themselves and
their cultures.

Parent involvement in Central City affairs has provided benefits to
the center as well as to the parents themselves. Five to ten parents
serve as volunteers in the classroom regularly from two to five
hours a week; they have constructed curriculum materials; they
have raised funds to buy a water-play table; they are currently
improving the center's playground and its equipment. Parents are
also currently involved in setting up a small profit-making corporation. Their first project has been capitalized through a loan by
the parent committee to purchase the materials for making and
selling aprons.

Complementing this parent involvement is enthusiasm for it on the
part of the center staff, who look on it as a benefit, not as an
annoyance or interference. One Central City teacher responded to
a question about the participation of parents as volunteers this
way: "I think it's great. There are so many ways they can relate to

other parents when I can't. They also have more insight into the children's problems. For this kind of program, it's essential." This kind of attitude explains why parents are deeply involved in the center's operations: they are, quite simply, wanted and welcome.

Part II   **The Program**

[My son] is in the oldest group. They study letters, numbers, the geography of Berkeley—a regular instructional program, real challenging. He goes on trips almost every day. When they come back at 2:30 they have a discussion period.

Parent, Berkeley Unified School
District Children's Centers
Berkeley, California

Curriculum

Walk into the average day-care center and ask a staff member what curriculum is used and you'll probably get a blank stare. Most of the programs we visited didn't consciously follow a formal curriculum methodology—for example, the Bereiter-Engelmann model, or the New Nursery School model. This doesn't mean these programs weren't helping children learn in a systematic way. They were, but their curriculum approaches were more evident in their actions than on paper. We learned what brand of curriculum a center was using by spending a day or two in the classroom, rather than by reading about it or listening to someone talk about it.

Wherever we went and however the centers were organized, each center had specific goals for its children, which it met through its educational program. The most commonly identified goals were

Educational development: language and communication skills, concepts (time, number, similarity, etc.), and perception (shapes, colors, sizes, etc.)

Socioemotional growth: handling feelings and emotions, getting along with others (sharing, cooperation), and self-reliance and independence

Self-image enhancement: strong sense of identity and self-esteem, ethnic and cultural pride, feeling of competence, and ability to make choices

Imaginative and experiential growth: creative expression and concrete experiences (field trips, community events).

In addition, all programs were trying to meet physical needs for exercise, good nutrition, and health care.

All of these goals are desirable and interrelated to some extent. For instance, centers used field trips not only for the experience they gave children with the outside world but also for some specific goal: a trip to the docks was part of a study of transportation. Creative expression through storytelling can also aid language development. Dancing is exercise and can also be part of an ethnic program that enhances a child's view of his own culture. Artwork can teach perceptual skills while improving small-muscle coordination. Let's look at each of these categories and the ways our centers handled them.

Educational Development

Language and Communication Skills The most commonly used formal tool here was the Peabody Language Kit. Some centers adapted it for their own needs, and some simply used selected units. Other centers trained volunteers in the kit's use and had these people work with individual children who needed extra help. Language development activities can be structured (group games, such as lotto, flash cards, songs, and stories) or done individually. Characteristically, in good centers language instruction goes on all day, whenever the occasion arises. Children are encouraged to speak (and this requires that teachers *listen*), to complete sentences, to name the objects around them, to tell stories, to ask for the things they need. "Sesame Street" was often part of the curriculum if the center had a television set. Tape recorders, records, and typewriters were also used for language activities, while pre-reading skills were taught with a wide variety of books, alphabets, and magnet-board games.

At centers where children came from severely isolated environments or non-English-speaking families, language development was of paramount importance. In the former case, the problem was simply to get kids *talking*. Often, children were withdrawn, unused to social contact, and as they became more comfortable in the centers and joined in activities, they learned quickly from other children. In this case, the need was more for basic socialization. For kids whose primary language was not English, good centers found it necessary to include bilingual staff who could translate for children and who could relate to kids in special ways. These centers found it particularly useful to label classroom objects in both languages, to use bilingual records, tapes, flash cards, games, and songs. It's especially helpful if English-speaking teachers make a real effort to learn the children's language. It can be very encouraging to a child struggling with English to hear someone struggling with *his* language. English-speaking children in the classroom can certainly benefit from exposure to another language and culture as well.

Concepts and Perception Children learn through play, and good centers provided an assortment of toys and games to help kids understand concepts such as time, number, similarities, and differences. These toys included stacking toys, puzzles, blocks, picture games, beads, felt-board pictures, drawings, and so on. Younger children were guided in the use of the items but were also allowed to discover relationships for themselves during free-play activities. In the same way, centers provided a wide range of perceptual toys of various sizes, shapes, colors, and textures to stimulate interest and promote sensorimotor skills. Ann Heiman, the director of the Greeley Parent Child Center in Greeley, Colorado, worked with the Denver-based Kennedy Development Center to create an exciting stimulation kit for her center. It's a brightly colored suitcase crammed full of soft cloth bags. Inside each bag are things to play with, feel, put together, puzzle over, and otherwise enjoy.

Older children typically move on to more advanced relationships and concepts, using more complex building blocks, Lincoln logs, Erector sets, train sets, and so on. Cuisinaire rods for mathematical skills were widely used. Science corners are wonderful discovery places for older preschoolers. Many centers have pets, plants, aquariums and terrariums, magnet sets, scales, magnifying glasses, and science libraries. The Haight-Ashbury curriculum is particularly creative in its offerings:

All children meet each morning with the teaching staff to map out the day's activities. Teachers who have special projects or outings planned (it is rare that a teacher leaves the center for anything without taking a group of children along) describe them at this time and let children know when and where they will be happening and what kinds of things they can expect. At the end of this meeting, staff pinpoint some of the children on their choices before breaking up and getting down to work.

At the Haight center, the staff feel that kids can teach other, often as well as staff can teach. This interaction between children can occur on a one-to-one basis, with one student teaching or helping another, or in small groups of children engaged in some kind of problem solving. Although it is not necessarily part of this process, the practice of mixed age groups is often used—either in terms of years or skill development—where groups of children are working together. This kind of family grouping, as it's called, is used at the Haight center, and it seemed to be working well at the time of our visit. Children were helping each other, and within these groups, children appeared to be gaining a good deal of independence. . . .

. . . A child dictates a story to the teacher at the typewriter, then moves the teacher aside to type her own name; Cuisinaire rods move among ten hands at the math table; fifteen kids are outside with a teacher, all of them climbing on the play structure; five kids strike off for the market with a teacher who is buying vegetables for an afternoon cooking class. The animals must be fed and loved, plants watered, a picture painted, a puppet house nailed together for the puppets being made in stitchery.

. . . Small groups of kids meet in the halls to chatter or bother each other, then reconstellate, one child wandering off to play with the instruments in the music room, a handful drawn into the science room to squeeze berries for tomorrow's shirt dyeing project. . . . Afternoon snack is pumpkin pie made by the kids in cookery. As kids wind down, they drift to quieter activities. In one corner, a teacher turns the pages of a book to illustrate a recorded story. One boy puts his head on the table and listens. During a pause the teacher rubs his head and says softly, "Did you go to reading class today? You know your letters so you'll enjoy it. Try it tomorrow. When I go to your house next week to visit, I'll tell your mother all about the letters and numbers you've learned. . . ."

Socioemotional Growth

We've discussed this aspect of child development in Chapter 1. Most programs try to help kids learn to handle their own feelings and emotions without using their fists. Staff members settle disputes by positive redirection. Sharing and cooperation are essential and are promoted in positive ways as children begin to learn how to get along with others in groups. Self-reliance and independence are also important and are fostered through the systematic teaching of self-help skills such as toileting, feeding, dressing, cleaning up after activities, and so on. At Haight-Ashbury Children's Center, the curriculum is designed to teach not only basic educational skills but also self-reliance and independence:

The center uses a modification of the British Infant School system. The philosophy is that each child is an individual and as such is given the freedom to set his own pace and to choose those activities that interest him within an overall developmental framework. The center and its staff are resources from which each child can choose to learn at his own pace.

This system, as adapted at the Haight center, has a strong relation to the developmental concepts of Piaget, with a focus on the child doing things rather than watching or listening. This involves open classrooms, student control of their own programs, and a good deal of peer interaction and teaching. Kids wander from room to room, class to class, at will. They can put down one activity when they tire of it and move on to something else. Each staff member specializes in one area and plans his or her own program around that area, developing materials to fit his needs. The Haight staff offers math, dramatic play, cooking, blocks, writing, stitchery, art, carpentry, music and body movement, discovery science, reading, and language development. Quieter activities for younger children include water play, sand, play dough, and painting. Students learn quickly which teachers are responsible for the various activities and where they will be happening. Teachers spend extra time orienting new children to the resources and staff.

Self-Image Enhancement

Letting children choose activities also enhances their view of themselves. Some centers let kids determine what they'll eat with a cafeteria feeding setup; some go further than that with open snack times, 40- or 50-minute periods when food is available and kids can drift in when they wish to eat. If they're not hungry, they skip the snack. At some centers, older children can choose whether or not they'll nap (although if they're cranky, their teachers may use some persuasion).

More often, self-image enhancement is a matter of letting kids know they're worthwhile, valuable human beings. Teachers in good centers do this with praise and love, encouragement and support. Children are not shamed or humiliated into "good" behavior at the expense of their self-esteem. They're accepted and made to feel welcome and wanted. They're never threatened or physically abused, and they get one-to-one attention instead of an order yelled across the room. As we said in Chapter 2, the kind of people you hire as staff is crucial to the kind of care you give. Staff members have to like and respect the kids they're working with. Kids take their cues from the people around them. If they feel that adults hold them in low esteem, they'll hold themselves in low esteem.

A positive self-image is also the aim with ethnic and cultural programs where parents want their children to develop pride in their own ethnic heritage. Bilingual programs go hand-in-hand with bicultural programs that stress ethnic values, traditions, and history. Such programs often rely heavily on staff- or parent-created materials and curriculum:

An integral part of the Ute Indian Tribe Day Care program is the stress the center places on Ute Indian ethnic identity. . . . Emphasis on ethnic identity plays an important role in social development, educational development, as well as the nutrition program. Many of the Indian children come to the center with a poor self-image. The center employs mostly Indian staff. . . .

Indian foods are frequently served. Children help to make Indian bread. Lesson plans for the spring and summer units on Indian foods include field trips to gather fresh berries, preparing dishes from them, and learning how to dry and preserve these native berries.

Children will also gather the wild onions and other roots for use as dye in basketmaking, thus learning the basic principles of the age-old art of basketmaking while enriching their pride in their own Ute culture.

Other activities include playing Indian music, Indian dancing, and reading books on Indian life. The center asks Indian storytellers to come in and tell kids legends. The children also make Indian costumes and take field trips to local schools for Indian culture programs. The center children are taken to the Ute Bear Dance in the spring. Field trips are also taken to tribally owned businesses and offices.

Not only does this program give children a sense of pride in their heritage, but it also helps the Anglo children gain a better understanding of their Indian neighbors.

At the West 80th Street center in New York, the lobby displays a black solidarity poster and portraits of famous blacks. The center's emphasis is on black pride: children learn African dancing, and the center uses ethnic materials and a predominantly black staff to reinforce the children's pride in their heritage.

Particularly in centers that serve black children, the theme is self-determination. Children are encouraged to make decisions for themselves rather than let circumstances dictate to them. This is the aim at the 5th City Pre-School in Chicago. The Ecumenical Institute, which owns and operates the center, is in the process of trying to revitalize the Chicago ghetto in which the school is situated. The Institute's community organization efforts are dedicated to helping people help themselves, and preparing children for this role is seen as an integral part of the overall community project. But first, children at 5th City are encouraged to feel good about themselves:

Rituals and songs play a significant role in the content of the curriculum and in the time structure. They are used to open and close the day and are used throughout the day as transitions from one location, activity, or curriculum area to another, within the time design. For example, the opening ritual in all of the classes includes various songs and chants that point out to the child that he is now in school and about to begin a new day. He has a choice of "living this day or throwing it away." He is told that he is part of a universe with many cultures ("Universe Man") and that he lives in a bustling city ("Drum of the City").

Here are some of the songs and chants used at 5th City:

Opening Ritual

"Drum of the City"
This is the drum of the city,
This is the drum of the city,
It says to us that we can live,
Let's be the drum of the city! Yeah!!!

"Universe Man" (Tune: "This Land Is Your Land")

We are the black man, we are the red man,
We are the brown man, we are the yellow man,
We are the tan man, we are the white man,
This is the land for you and me!
(Chanted) Black man! Red man! Brown man! Yellow man!
Tan man! White man! Universe man!

"We Are in 5th City Pre-School"

We are in 5th City Pre-School,
Out in Chicago West,
We sing our song to greet each brand new day,
We dream our dreams and dance our YES!
(Chant)
This is the day we have,
This is the day we have,
We can live this day or throw it away,
This is the day we have,
So pick up this day and LIVE!

Closing Ritual

"Drum of the City"

"Chicago Is a Wonderful Place"

Chicago is a wonderful place,
The west side's where we live, yeah, yeah, yeah!
Chicago is a wonderful place,
The west side's where we live.

So sing all you people, life is here to love,
So sing all you people, life is here to live.
Oh, Chicago is a wonderful place,
The west side's where we live, everybody,
The west side's where we live, everybody,
The west side's where we live, yeah!

Meal/Snack Ritual

Leader: Food is good, right?
Children: Right!
Leader: Life is good, right?
Children: Right!

Leader: All is good, right?
Children: Right!
Leader: What do you say? ⎱
Children: It's OK!   ⎰ (repeated three times)

Chants:

1. Hey, hey, what do you do?
   The whole world is watching you!
2. John, John, he's an iron man,
   You can do it, John, you can! you can!
3. Hey, hey, I'm alive!
   I just got back from City Five!
4. Hold your head up! Hold it up high!
   5th City Pre-School is marching by!

Song:

"I Love 5th City" (Tune: "I Love the Flowers")
I love 5th City,
I love the planet earth,
I love this day and time,
I love the universe,
I'm always ready to see this world of ours,
I'll tell you, man, I like it here,
I'll tell you, man, I like it here. Yeah!

Good centers also reinforce children's feelings of self-esteem by making sure they can feel successful and competent. Praise is important here, as this Haight-Ashbury parent knows: "My son built a block bridge that was real special. The teacher made a big thing of it and left it for others to see. My son was so proud. This kind of approach is fantastic." Be sure the goals you set for children are within their reach. Continued frustration will kill a child's motivation to learn.

Imaginative and Experiential Growth
Dramatic play (or "pretend" activities), where a child can assume many different roles, can be an important psychological outlet as well as an educational experience. This is why so many of our

centers had housekeeping corners, dolls, dress-up clothes, tree houses, makeup kits, and all kinds of make-believe toys for their kids. Free-play periods were chances for children to let their imaginations roam: staff intervened in activities when kids were fighting or needed assistance but generally gave them this chance to be who or what they pleased.

Young imaginations can also be stimulated through more structured activities, such as artwork, music, dancing and body movement, playacting, and so on. Creative expression activities are not contests for the "best" picture or performance: they're opportunities for children to depict the world as they see it, and one child's product should be regarded as just as valuable as the next child's.

Finally, our centers tried to give their children concrete experience with the world through field trips. At the Holland, Michigan, center, kids have gone to the library, grocery stores, department stores, the zoo, the museum, fire and police stations, a local 7-Up plant, and a blueberry farm. At the West 80th Street Day Care Center in New York City,

Field trips are used extensively in this curriculum. Children learn about the world by going out and seeing it. They study transportation by visiting a bus depot, an airport, and the shipping docks. In studying the letter B, they might take a bus trip, and for F they can visit the fish market. Children study families by visiting the zoo to see parent and baby animals, and then go to community homes where they can see newborn babies. Children also visit museums, special exhibits, the Hayden Planetarium, the Brooklyn Aquarium, libraries, plays—anything useful in adding to their concrete knowledge and experience.

At West 80th Street, the community is very much a part of the center's curriculum. Staff feel that school and real life need not and in fact should not be separate realms of experience. The center, therefore, tries to establish links between what kids see in their classrooms and what they experience outside the door, in a West Side ghetto. The children are encouraged, for example, to reject drugs. They aren't just told—the job is done graphically, with photographs. A teacher says, "See this guy on the street? See

what's in his hand? Yeah, a sugar cube. If some guy tries to give
you a sugar cube, you take off. . . ."

Whatever goals a center chooses for its children will guide the
curriculum's emphasis, and the curriculum, in turn, determines the
program's organizational setup—the grouping patterns, space
arrangements, schedules, and staff deployment used. For example,
centers that emphasized self-esteem gave kids a good deal of freedom of choice and movement: they were less concerned with
fixed schedules and formal curriculum. All centers, however, have
to deal with several major organizational decisions.

Grouping of Children

Decisions about how to group kids are usually determined by such
factors as the layout of the center building, the number and ages
of the children, the number and kind of staff, and, of course, the
program and philosophy of the center. We found several arrangements in the centers we studied.

Grouping According to Age Most often, centers group children according to age. They separate younger, middle, and older preschoolers (two to three years, three to four years, and four to five
years) in different classrooms or areas. These divisions aren't rigid:
some allowance is made for the maturity of the individual child.
The average size of the groups is usually around 15 children, although younger children are sometimes divided into smaller
groups and older kids into larger ones. Each group typically has
two or three staff members responsible for it. Centers using this arrangement feel it offers a child a secure and predictable environment. They feel individuality is stifled in overly large groups and
that kids feel more confident playing with others who are at
roughly the same level of competence.

Grouping According to Activity In this system, children choose
the activity they wish to pursue and join a group working in that
area under staff supervision. This is the case at the Haight-Ashbury
center described earlier. Staff members offer activities, and children select whatever they want to do. This system is also used at
the Syracuse University Children's Center in Syracuse, New York.

Designed for toddlers sixteen to thirty-six months, the Family
Style program allows children to choose among various learning
experiences, which are arranged along the lines of their home situations, with older children helping the younger ones. In such programs, the emphasis is on self-reliance and independence: the children at Syracuse, for example, choose whether they wish to snack
(an open snack-time, where a snack area is open for a certain
period of time and kids serve themselves) or skip the snack and
play in the gym or playground. Older children provide leadership
for younger ones in peer teaching situations and serve as role
models for decision making.

A Combination Approach There's no reason why these broad approaches—grouping by age and by activity—can't be combined. In
fact, as the Haight-Ashbury program has evolved, the staff has
found it useful to incorporate certain aspects of age grouping into
its approach. Because some of the younger children had trouble
making choices in an unlimited situation, morning meetings remain an institution for the older kids, with younger ones invited
to attend. If they choose not to, more structured activities are
available for them. In the late afternoon, when kids are tired and
any program is most likely to dissipate into cranky disorder, the
activity grouping is suspended and students are divided into three
age groups with activities appropriate to the attention levels of
each.

The Use of Space
It's not how much you've got, but how you use it, we discovered.
Our centers ranged from those with shiny new facilities and plenty
of room to those housed in old and crowded buildings, in factories, churches, storefronts, and even trailers. Interestingly
enough, shiny new centers may have as many problems in using
their space as do programs with fewer resources and smaller facilities.

   Take, for instance, the Amalgamated Day Care Center in Chicago. Termed "a Rolls-Royce of day care" by a union official, ,
this center is provided by the Amalgamated Clothing Workers of

America Union, AFL-CIO, for its members and is very well funded.
(A complete description of this center is included in Part IV.)
Building plans were initiated with the idea that this would become
a model day-care center upon which future centers could be based.
A brand new one-story building was erected, specifically designed
for day-care use, although not entirely successfully. The front and
back walls of the center are almost all glass with swinging glass
doors to divide the classroom areas. When the center opened, the
kids, unaccustomed to any kind of away-from-home situation,
lacked internal controls and the limits and direction necessary for
working and playing with adults and other kids. The freedom of
the building design intensified this chaotic state of affairs, and the
open glass space was a little too much for the children to handle.
Movable partitions about six feet high have been added in an attempt to alleviate the confusion.

A similar problem was encountered by the Greeley Parent Child
Center in Greeley, Colorado. Located in what was formerly a
church, the center's main play area is the old sanctuary. Many of
the more active kids tend to treat the building as a carpeted gymnasium. Their first instinct as they enter the large, open, high-
ceilinged room is to run. The staff hopes to hang movable canvas
curtains from the pipes running across the ceiling to divide this
large space into smaller areas.

Space Divisions The Woodmont Center in Nashville, Tennessee,
has no walls, but it works. This center is one of a chain of private,
profit-making day-care operations run by American Child Centers,
Inc.

The center building was especially designed by an architect for
ACC, Inc., after careful research into existing child-care facilities.
The center is basically one large floor for the children, with no
permanent dividers, but lockers, cabinets, and other equipment
used to define smaller play areas. There are windows all around
and some nooks to which children may withdraw to be by themselves. Each play area has some large play equipment for climbing.
A multilevel carpeted amphitheater faces a television set, where
the children can gather for television, stories, or music. A row of
sinks lines one wall and a small hooked door leads to the kitchen.

A Dutch door was installed between the hallway and the play area
as an afterthought, as children wandered into the entrance area
too frequently.

The second floor is an open balcony where teachers can meet,
observe, and relax. It is also used for parent meetings and training
sessions. The director's office is also on the balcony, glassed in on
three sides so there is a view of almost the entire floor area
below. . . . The total floor is divided roughly into three activity
groups—Red, Yellow, and Blue, for [the various age groups].

The Red Group uses one end of the center, which is fully carpeted, with bathrooms leading off to one side. Child-sized sinks
with mirrors, a playhouse, climbing equipment, steps, and a platform are available. . . . There is also a home/living area with child-
sized sink, stove, refrigerator, cupboard, tea tables, bed, and dress-
up clothes. Other subareas are set up for art activities, table toys,
and books. Folding cots are stacked on a rack in the area for nap-
time use.

Space for the Yellow Group, in the center of the main floor, is
likewise divided into interest areas. One portion is used for very
active play, another for block-building. The Yellow Group's area
has the television well and stage where musical instruments are
kept. The third portion of the center main floor is for Blue Group
activities: this has a sizable uncarpeted area for a large variety of
art activities. Finger painting, brush painting, cutting and pasting,
and other creative play are encouraged here.

Although teaching and child-care techniques require adjustment to
the open-floor plan and although noise levels may be higher than
in some centers, the Woodmont Center generally works quite well.
Most teachers and parents felt that the extra effort and noise involved paid off in freedom for the children to develop.

Dividing your space into smaller activity areas is also a way of
providing structure for children. Each room or partitioned area
can contain different kinds of equipment, and one teacher can organize the activities within each space. Typical areas might include
a housekeeping area, blocks and toy area, books and play, water
and/or sand play, an art corner, and a music area.

At the Syracuse University Children's Center,

Kids can move freely from room to room. . . . Children are re-
minded, however, that certain activities go on only in certain
rooms, and materials must be left in their appropriate rooms and

be respected and cared for. Teachers move from child to child and group to group. There are usually two teachers in each room, while one or two float from room to room.

The creative-expression room has housekeeping and art materials, such as play dough, clay, paints, sand, and water. Here teachers spend a great deal of time distributing and replenishing materials. They participate in make-believe games and encourage and reinforce the spontaneous labeling children often devise during water play and pretend activities. . . .

The sense-perception room is for listening and looking. There are books and filmstrips to look at, stories and records to hear, and flannel-board presentations. There are teacher-devised touch and feel boxes and other materials designed to provide discussion of basic concepts such as heavy/light, rough/smooth, high/low, and so on. The room is arranged with corner table and chair set-ups to allow for individual reading and language-master work. Teachers also organize cooperative games—language lotto, felt-board activities, and others—and initiate storytelling and songs.

The most difficult area to keep in order is the small-muscle room, with its sorting materials, puzzles, Montessori equipment, magnifying glasses, crayons, etc. The great variety of materials is distributed along open shelves. Children select their materials, play with them, and then replace them on the shelves before leaving. At the moment, staff feel that the children do not have the internal controls to use this room to its best advantage, so a different group of activities is made available each day.

Concepts such as high/higher/highest, round, left and right are taught in all the rooms, but in the large-muscle room children use their bodies in games and dances to understand them. Teachers may use activities such as throwing and running to teach "far" and "fast," but most of the action in this room is free-flowing and boisterous. Loud talking, singing, and yelling are permissible, and body contact is encouraged. Equipment includes climbing bars, large blocks, cardboard boxes, steps, riding toys, and balance boards. . . .

Kids also learn to take behavioral cues from different activity areas: in the book corner, you need to be quieter; in the water-play area, you can be messy; in the gym, the sky's the limit.

The Northwest Rural Opportunities system of day-care centers has a special kind of facility. Their centers are located in trailers and serve migrant families. Today there are 21 trailers (each serving about 22 kids) scattered over eight permanent sites.

. . . They were constructed inexpensively (between nine and ten thousand dollars apiece) and in accordance with state health and fire regulations. Each trailer measures 60 by 20 feet and meets federal and state space requirements for children. They provide clean, compact, and legal space in an area where the project had been unable to find decent buildings to convert.

Trailer units are adapted for various uses, but they generally contain two classrooms, a director's area, storage space, a kitchen, and a lavatory (child-size). Kitchens have typical institutional equipment, such as portable or commercial grills, and some have freezers. One kitchen area serves several adjoining trailers. . . . Children eat in the classrooms at small tables and chairs, and nap cots are neatly stored when not in use.

Much center equipment is built in, and all trailers seemed clean and orderly—there is literally a place for everything, and everything is kept in its place.

Creative Use of Space Some of the centers we saw did a fine job of using limited space or creating something lovely out of an aesthetic liability. Most centers have outdoor playgrounds or access to parks with large-muscle equipment—swings, slides, see-saws, jungle gyms—kids need to let off steam. But at the Haight-Ashbury center,

. . . Outdoor space is barely adequate, and it's in little chunks between and alongside the buildings. It's awkward for children to play in and teachers to supervise. So a local sculptor/carpenter was commissioned to design and build a structure that would offer as many activities as possible within the bounds of space and safety. The resulting structure of driftwood, telephone spools, tires, boards, and branches was quite successful. Whole groups of children can use the structure at the same time. Different parts of it are good for climbing, hanging, dancing, playing house in, and so on, and nobody seems to get in anyone else's way. A ship's funnel is still to be incorporated as a slide.

The Kentucky Rural Child Care Project has also done a good job with their space. In Chapter 4, we described how parents worked to make center playgrounds marvelous places for kids to play, despite lack of funds and surfaces too rocky to support anchored equipment. The project's funds are too limited for it to build its own centers, so they've had to take any space they could get. The

centers are housed in churches, abandoned schoolhouses, basements, storefronts, community centers, old hotels and rooming
houses. Creativity and ability to make do is shown by the way one
center approached its pipe problem. Large structural pipes were
exposed throughout the center and were considered quite dreary.
With a little imagination, those pipes have become trees, with paper
branches hanging down for the kids to refurbish with different-
colored leaves as the seasons change.

One final note about space: teachers and kids need a place to get
away from each other. Your center should try to provide a room
where staff members can relax, talk, or have a cup of coffee when
they're not teaching kids. In Chapter 1, we mentioned some of the
ways centers made sure children could be by themselves when
they needed to be: these were tree houses, child-size play areas,
special housekeeping setups. Other retreats can be a tent set up
outside, an old overstuffed chair, or any of the nooks and crannies
found in old houses.

Figures 5.1 and 5.2 are floor plans of two of our centers: the
Syracuse University Children's Center, located in a church, and
the Ute Indian Tribe Day Care Center, set up in an old house.

Schedules

A daily schedule introduces a degree of regularity so that staff and
kids know generally what to expect next. It also ensures that activities and experiences take place in a balanced sequence. The actual
form of the schedule, how detailed it is, and how closely it's followed vary widely. Certain events, however, do recur daily in all
programs, so most schedules are built around these events:

Arrival (followed by free play at least until most kids have arrived)
Midmorning snack
Lunch
Rest period
Afternoon snack
Clean-up and preparation for departure

Among these major events, centers fit in periods of outdoor play,
free play, directed play or organized games, creative expression,

First Floor—Infants (5½-16 months)

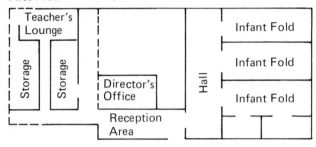

Basement—Toddlers (16 months-3 years)

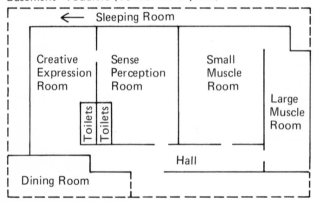

Space: Indoor 11,322 sq ft (123 sq ft/child)
Outdoor 1,413 sq ft (15 sq ft/child)

Figure 5.1
Floor plan of Syracuse University Children's Center

Figure 5.2
Floor plan of Ute Indian Tribe Day Care Center

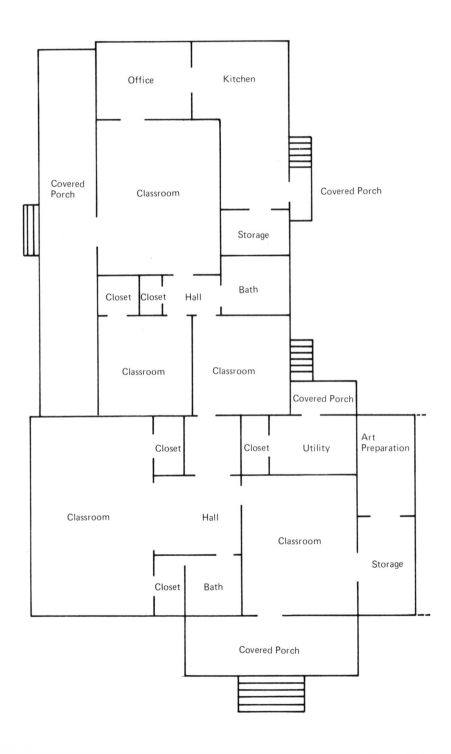

stories, lessons, demonstrations, and occasional field trips or excursions.

How best to order these activities involves several considerations. It's important to alternate noisy and quiet, strenuous and passive, individual and group activities so you can maintain a child's interest. Flexibility about activities is crucial: you ought to be able to give a child who doesn't want to join in the main activity an alternative. Providing transition periods between activities helps kids who have trouble "changing gears." For instance, if the children have been very excited and active, it's a good idea to have some quiet play before lunch.

The amount of time you allot for each activity depends on your own program and philosophy. Many centers, particularly those with fewer staff, emphasize a great deal of free play time, while others stress directed play and structured lessons. Some operations are based on organized group activities; others believe in individual self-directed play.

Table 5.1 gives a typical daily schedule at the Central City Head Start Day Care Center in Salt Lake City, Utah. The schedule lists activities as well as teacher assignments to each project.

Equipment

In the course of our study, we ran across well-funded centers that had invested a great deal of money in special educational equipment, and we also saw centers where almost everything had been donated. We noticed that centers with expensive new equipment spent a lot of time worrying about maintaining that equipment and making sure children respected those shiny new toys. Centers with well-worn, donated materials didn't worry so much, and it seemed to us they were doing just as good a job of meeting their own educational goals. Homemade equipment is often better appreciated because of the work that goes into it, and built-in equipment, added to make an old building more serviceable, can often fit the center's specifications perfectly. Shelves can be constructed to fit the dimensions of an odd-shaped room, cabinets can be designed for unusual spaces, and so on.

We're not against expensive new equipment: we're saying that it doesn't ensure good day care any more than a new building or a staff composed strictly of people with Master's degrees. Again, like

Table 5.1
Typical Daily Schedule at Central City Head Start Day Care Center

Time	Activity	What the Activity Teaches	Teacher
7:30-8:00	Preparation and room setup		Janis
8:00-9:00 Free play indoors	Paper, crayons, scissors; collage Animals in the block area Lego blocks Color lotto	Creative experience Fantasy play Small-muscle development	Sondra Janis
9:00-9:30	Outdoor play		Janis
9:30-10:30 Work groups	1. Snack and story time (use zoo animals for story) 2. Writing letters of names 3. Object lotto	Improve pencil skills Matching size and shape	Minnie Sondra Janis
10:30-11:15	Token store (Free play items in the closet, which children are allowed to buy with tokens)	Buying and selling	Minnie Janis Sondra
11:15-11:30	Chalk-drawing story on rug		Janis
11:30-12:30	"Sesame Street" Set up lunch and cots		Sondra Minnie Janis
12:30-1:00	Lunch in classroom		
1:00-1:30	Clean up after lunch and get ready for rest		
1:30-2:30	Rest on cots		All teachers
2:30-3:00	Quiet activity in room, puzzles, books, crayons		
3:00-3:10	Clean up after rest		
3:10-3:20	Afternoon snack		
3:20-3:30	Get ready to go home		

the space factor, it's not how much you've got, but how you use it: how your staff help kids use equipment, how they settle disputes over it, how accessible it is to the kids.

Child-size equipment is a real advantage. Small tables, chairs, and toilet facilities help kids help themselves: cupboards, shelves, coat hooks, and mirrors at child's eye level help kids feel that the center is really theirs. These things are also important in seeing that kids learn the self-help skills they must acquire. A child can learn to wash himself, set a table, and put away his toys more easily if he can reach things.

If you don't have the funds for new equipment, you can involve parents, teachers, and community members in building what you need. Many centers have found that the process of involving people in their operations this way is as important as the final products. And those final products can be just as sturdy and useful as store-bought items. In fact, programs with new equipment have decided to develop some of their own materials as well, not because of financial restrictions, but as a training and involvement technique.

Nutrition

The school has a rabbit, which is a special friend of the cook's. Together, they make the back kitchen-storeroom-office a friendly
place, especially for the occasional sad child. . . .
                                          West 80th Street
                                          Day Care Center
                                          New York, New York

Your nutrition program will be keyed to the needs of the children you're serving. These needs are determined during the routine
health examination each child gets before he enters the program.
If children are getting adequate and well-balanced diets at home,
your nutrition program will likely consist of a hot lunch plus midmorning and midafternoon snacks daily. This is called maintenance nutrition.

Health examinations may reveal, however, that children are
anemic or chronically undernourished: in such cases, your center
will have to provide compensatory nutrition. Compensatory nutrition can range from extra protein and vitamins to a second full
meal, depending on need. When children travel long distances to
the center or when the program opens very early in the morning, a
hot breakfast is often added to the schedule. Programs that operate until late in the day and/or those that serve school-age children
who may stay after 6:00 P.M. often serve an evening meal of sand-
wiches, fruit, and beverages.

To make sure the nutrition program is meeting child needs,
many centers hire dietitians or dietary consultants to supervise
menu planning. Meal preparation is usually done at the center by a
cook who may be a part- or full-time employee, depending on the
scope of the program. Many centers use volunteers as aides for
meal preparation, serving, and clean-up. These people may be parents, community members, or center staff whose duties don't conflict with mealtime tasks (part-time teacher aides, for example).

Some programs go beyond the child and reach out to the whole
family in an effort to improve child nutrition. They feel it's important to educate kids and their families about different foods,
food buying, and meal planning and preparation so nutritional
deficiencies can be prevented in the future. Through its extensive

homemaking service and its in-center nutrition program, the Rural
Child Care Project in Kentucky (described in Part IV) has made
real gains in this area.

The Mecklenburg County Department of Social Services Day
Care Centers in Charlotte, North Carolina, offer an extensive nutrition program, which is unique in both style and scope. As the
administration itself says, food seems to be the easiest way to
reach both parents and children. Many of the children in the department's centers suffer from malnutrition, anemia, low blood
count, and a variety of psychological anxieties about food, which
are the result of chronic hunger. Each center has a cook who
works closely with teachers, parents, and children to promote and
introduce new foods. Centers plan their own menus, and parents
are encouraged to come in and eat meals with the children.

While surplus foods are used extensively, menus are not planned
around them, except that hot homemade bread, rolls, or muffins
are served every day. All children are given a hot, well-balanced
lunch and midmorning and afternoon snacks. In addition, children
who have not had breakfast get an early-morning snack, and those
who must stay late have another light snack if they are hungry. It
was pointed out to the observers that cooks almost double the
amount of food served on Monday, when children are hungry
from the weekend, and that older children tend to stuff themselves on Fridays in anticipation of two days at home.

A good nutrition program can make a tremendous difference not
only in general health and well-being but also in basic socialization. Many of the children had never eaten regular meals before
they entered the centers. One child in a family of four children
had never sat at a table and cried if he were not served last: it
seemed that at home he had to make sure his brothers and sisters
had enough to eat before he could eat. After eight months in the
program he still insisted on being served last, but he was no longer
crying with anxiety. Other children could not take time to chew
their food unless their plates were piled high so they could be sure
there was plenty to eat. Children who formerly snatched food off
plates and wolfed it down have been patiently and kindly reassured and have responded dramatically to the program.

When one four-year-old girl was enrolled at the center she weighed
only 28 pounds. An extremely thin, anemic child, she ate only
bread and milk. Within a year she had gained nine pounds and was

eating everything on the table. Like many of the program's children, she gained weight and height, and her skin began to take on a healthy tone.

Center kitchens are set up so that children will feel free to come and go, as they do at home. In one center, the kitchen is between two playrooms, and the children are able to watch meal preparation. Often, a cook will let a new child or one who is having problems visit with her for a morning and help out. . . . Meals are taken in a relaxed atmosphere, with staff and children eating family-style at small tables. Children are encouraged to help set up and clean up, and in some centers they help with the serving.

New foods are usually introduced once a week. To prepare for this, teachers talk about the food in the classroom, describing the color, texture, and growth cycle of the dish.

Children find magazine pictures of the food, and a tasting party is organized. For example, when carrots were about to be introduced to the menu, children read a story called *The Carrot Seed,* then planted seeds, had carrot sticks as a snack, and watched carrots being cooked in the kitchen for lunch.

Some centers have gardens. In one, children grew enough tomatoes to feed the entire center and enough turnip greens to serve the center twice. There are also flower gardens, which provide blooms to decorate the tables. The children with gardens are terribly proud of their work and take great pains to instruct new children on the care of the plants.

The centers make a special effort to hire cooks (they are called Food Service personnel) who can work well with children, will take time with them, and who are interested in expanding their skills through nutrition workshops held periodically by the department. Children tell their mothers about the center foods, and the mothers are now coming into the centers to get recipes. Children are also being taught the importance of a balanced diet—one family of children described the good lunch they'd had at the center, but felt they should have something different for dinner.

The department has no problems to report in its nutrition program and is delighted with its success. Many other centers could replicate this program with sensitive staff selection and good planning. Children do not have to be severely deprived to benefit from learning about the foods they eat. . . .

Mealtime should be a happy and relaxed time for your children. We felt that in centers where children had a role in preparation, serving, and clean-up or where staff members ate and chatted with the children rather than simply standing and supervising, a pleasant, relaxed atmosphere was built in. Many teachers used mealtime conversations to reinforce classroom learning but in an unobtrusive way. Child-size tables, chairs, and utensils help kids help themselves.

Children aren't forced to eat or clean their plates in most quality programs, but centers typically make an effort to introduce new foods to the children from time to time and to see that picky eaters get a balanced diet. Many of the parents we talked to were pleased that their children were learning to eat many different kinds of foods. In addition, centers serving different cultural groups usually include ethnic specialties on the menu—soul food, Mexican food, Indian food, Italian food, and so on—to make children feel comfortable and to reinforce cultural pride. Tables 6.1 and 6.2 show two sample weekly menus from centers we visited.

Health
A good nutrition program goes hand-in-hand with a good health-care program. Regular health examinations can detect nutritional deficiencies and can also help you evaluate how well your nutrition program is meeting children's needs.

Health care in the centers we studied ranged from simple referrals to outside agencies all the way to comprehensive medical care for the whole family through community organizations. But, at the very least, our centers found it necessary to

Arrange for preadmission physicals for all children and compile complete health histories

Make sure that all children had the proper inoculations and immunizations specified by the program

Provide emergency health care for children in the center and instruct various staff members in first-aid and emergency procedures

Refer sick children (after checking with parents) to appropriate medical personnel outside the center.

Most centers employ a full- or part-time nurse or doctor who may visit the center anywhere from once daily to twice a year. Center staff members routinely check children as they arrive in the

Table 6.1
Sample Weekly Menu at Haight-Ashbury Children's Center

	Monday	Tuesday	Wednesday	Thursday	Friday
Breakfast	Orange juice Rolled oats Raisins Milk Toast	Grapefruit juice French toast Orange sauce Milk	Orange juice Cold cereal Strip bacon Milk Toast	Grape juice Scrambled egg Buttered toast Milk	Orange juice Farina, cooked bulgur Toast Milk
Snack	Whole wheat sandwich Pineapple juice	Banana bread Cream cheese Grape juice	Ribbon sandwich Olives Mixed juice	Orange toast Apple juice	Raisin bread Pineapple juice
Lunch	Spaghetti & meat & cheese Cabbage carrot slaw Buttered French bread Peach crisp Peanut butter cookies Milk	Braised beef tongue Creamed corn Harmon salad Buttered toast Apple/pineapple sauce cake Milk	Corned beef Mashed potatoes Buttered asparagus Apple, celery, raisin salad Cornbread/butter Tapioca cream pudding Milk	Roast turkey & gravy Savory rice bulgur Carrot-zucchini sticks Buttered hot biscuit Apricot halves Milk	Fish stick with lemon Hard-cooked egg Spanish green beans Lettuce/spinach salad Buttered bread Fruit gelatin & banana Milk
Snack	Cinnamon roll Apple wedges Milk	Peanut butter brownies Vegetable stick Milk	Bologna sandwich Sweet pickle slice Milk	Half tuna sandwich Radishes Milk Cucumber sticks	Peanut butter pinwheel Apricot Milk

Table 6.2
Sample Weekly Menu at the Ute Indian Tribe Day Care Center

A.M. Snack	Lunch	P.M. Snack
Monday		
Cold cereal and milk	Roast beef and gravy Whipped potatoes Celery sticks Rolls and butter Milk Jello and fruit	Oranges
Tuesday		
Toast, butter, and juice	Lunch meat sandwiches Vegetable soup Crackers Milk Cookies	Bananas
Wednesday		
Oatmeal and milk	Weiners and wraps Mashed potatoes Lettuce wedges Carrot sticks Vanilla pudding	Apple wedges
Thursday		
Graham crackers and juice	Meat patties Tomato sauce Rice, butter Assorted veg. sticks Milk Applesauce	Hard-boiled eggs
Friday		
Cream of Wheat and milk	Salmon loaf Buttered carrots Pickles Mixed vegetables (canned) Milk Fruit cocktail	Peanut butter cookies Juice

morning to make sure they're well enough to participate. Many of our centers set aside an isolation room with a cot where sick children could wait until parents arrived to take them home. All centers have established emergency procedures, which generally involve locating parents and taking children to private physicians, clinics, or nearby hospitals. Staff members in many of our centers visit sick children at home, and some programs provide baby-sitters to look after children so parents can continue working.

Many day-care centers go beyond the minimum in providing health services. Most often, centers make extensive referrals to community health services to see that children get the help they need. Referrals are made by the director, the nurse, or social worker. Follow-up referrals are also made, in conjunction with carefully kept records. Centers with a formal link to an outside health service or those with access to medical services provided by their sponsors are particularly successful in referrals. Other programs use consultants or volunteer professional staff (often members of the board of directors).

It's important to keep records on the children's medical histories and to record any health services or referrals that are used by the children and their families. Table 6.3 is the comprehensive medical form used by the Mecklenburg County Department of Social Services Day Care Centers in Charlotte, North Carolina.

The Northwest Rural Opportunities system of day-care centers in Pasco, Washington, works hard to get services for its children:

. . . Physicals are donated by area doctors, and there has recently been some drop-off in donated time. Center coordinators spend part of their time drumming up help in this area. Public Health Department personnel are used for vaccinations, immunizations, and hearing tests. The most common health problems among the children are anemia, parasites, and malnutrition.

A number of different organizations may cooperate on a single case. Through a Department of Public Assistance program for the blind, a child received eye surgery, and a local Latin American association then provided eyeglasses. This effort and many others like it are coordinated by NRO child development specialists and the child's center.

A dental hygienist from the State Department of Health examines teeth and makes necessary referrals. Some centers hold their own

Table 6.3

Medical Record Form Used by the Mecklenburg County Department of
Social Services Day Care Centers

Form Ca—1965	**CHILD'S MEDICAL RECORD** Face Sheet	Number_____

Name   Sex   Date of Birth   Nationality { Father_____   Race of: { Mother_____

Family History:				(Refers to members of family and relatives)
Father	Age	Living	If dead, cause of death	Miscarriages _____
Mother				Month _____ Cause _____
No. of Children				Tuberculosis _____
				TBC Contacts _____
				Allergy _____
				Mental Disorder _____
				Diabetes _____
				Convulsive Disease _____

BIRTH AND DEVELOPMENT

Term _____ Delivery _____
Condition at birth _____ Birth Weight _____
Condition first week _____ Feeding _____
Cyanosis _____ Sat up _____ Stood _____
Convulsions _____ Walked _____ Words _____
Jaundice _____ First tooth _____ Short sentence _____
_____ Bladder _____ Bowel _____

FEEDING HISTORY

Breast _____ Formula _____
Vitamins _____ Soft food _____
Present diet _____ Feeding habits _____
Appetite _____ Likes _____ Dislikes _____
Vomiting _____ Stools _____
Sensitivity _____ Hives _____ Hay Fever _____ Asthma _____

HABITS

Sleep adequate _____ Regular _____ Meals adequate _____
Regular _____ Bowel movement regular _____
Constipated _____ Urination normal _____ Enuresis _____
Nocturnal _____ Diurnal _____

NERVOUS HABITS

Nail biting? _____ Tic? _____ Masturbation? _____
Other? _____

BEHAVIOR

Any special problems? _____

IMMUNIZATIONS AND TESTS					ILLNESSES		
	Dates			Comments	Pertussis_____	Other Operations_____	
Vaccine					Measles_____	Glands_____	
DPT					Rubella_____	Rheum. Fever_____	
D T					Mumps_____	Otitis_____	
Diphtheria					Chickenpox_____	Colds_____	
Pertussis					Scarlet Fever_____	Tonsillitis_____	
Tetanus					Diphtheria_____	Convulsions_____	
Typhoid					T & A_____	Constipation_____	
Polio					Appendix_____	Diarrhea_____	
Smallpox							
Dick Test							
Tuberculin							
Hemoglobin							
STS							
Stool							
X-ray of Chest							

Accidents, Injuries, Operations,
or Illnesses other than above _____

CHILD'S MEDICAL RECORD
EXAMINATIONS AND RECOMMENDATIONS

Form Cs

Name _____ Birth Date _____

Any Complaint?			
Height			
Weight			
Temperature			
Head Measurement on Infant			
Skin			
Scalp			
Eyes – Pupillary Reaction	Rt. Lft.	Rt. Lft.	Rt. Lft.
Vision Without Glasses			
Vision With Glasses			
Eyegrounds			
Other			
Ears – Otoscopic			
Hearing	Rt. Lft.	Rt. Lft.	Rt. Lft.
Other			
Nose			
Teeth – Number			
Condition			
Occlusion			
Other			
Throat–Pharynx			
Tonsils			
Adenoids			
Glands			
Thyroid			
Chest			
Heart			
Lungs			
Abdomen			
Secondary Sex Characteristics			
Genitals			
Deep Reflexes			
Superficial Reflexes			
Extremities			
Feet			
Spine			
Posture			
Nutrition			
Menstrual History since last			
visit on adolescent girl			
Signs of Endocrine Imbalance			
Signs of Vasomotor Instability			
Other			
Urinalysis-Color, Reaction, Sp.G.			
Sugar, Albumin, Micros.			
Blood Pressure			
Blood Hemoglobin, Count, etc.			
Other Tests			
Impression and Advice			
Examining Physician	Dr. Date	Dr. Date	Dr. Date

ISSUED BY CHILD WELFARE LEAGUE OF AMERICA — 100M-6/66

For recording subsequent medical examinations, another form (Cb) may be secured from the Child Welfare League of America.

evening clinics for children and have had 100 percent participation from parents.

All centers have consulting MDs on call. A Licensed Practical Nurse, an RN, or a member of the teaching staff—it depends on the center—gives each child a routine inspection every morning. (All centers with children under two-and-a-half must have an RN present for at least 16 hours per week, and where infants under one year of age are cared for, an LPN must be present the rest of the time, under state regulations.) Children who seem in questionable health are sent home with their parents or isolated from the rest of the group until parents can come for them.

Health records are kept for each child at his center. These are given to the parents before they depart for new points in the migrant stream.

Many of the centers we visited provided extended health services, which fell into the following general categories.

General Medical Services These include physical examinations, diagnostic testing, and inoculations and immunizations. They're most commonly provided through referrals to a local clinic or health service and occasionally to a private physician. If such services are provided for all children, it's generally more practical to have medical personnel come to the center.

Special Testing Special testing is most often provided for children who are suspected of having hearing, vision, speech, sensorimotor, or other special problems. It may also be included as part of the regular preadmission or annual physical required of all children in the program. We feel it makes sense to test all children: if special needs and problems can be recognized and treated early enough, handicaps that might surface later on can be prevented or at least minimized. In some programs, trained personnel come to the center to administer special tests; elsewhere, students or members of private, civic, or charitable groups may be willing to help administer these screening tests.

Dental Examinations and Treatment This may be part of the regular check-up procedure, or it may be provided only as the need arises. Dental services are usually offered through referral.

Psychological Services Provided on an individual basis, as necessary, psychological services are usually through referral to local mental health clinics. In some instances, mental health workers may come into the center and work through play therapy or may observe particular children and instruct staff in the most effective ways of dealing with emotionally disturbed children.

Special Services for the Handicapped These may be provided by referral to special service agencies. Center personnel usually help parents get necessary attention and equipment from outside sources (braces for a physically handicapped child, for instance). Centers that serve a number of handicapped children may want to use a special curriculum and provide extra staff training.

Most child-care programs with extended health services also provide transportation for the child and his or her parents to and from the health service. In addition, staff members often help parents make appointments for children with special service agencies. Where center parents do not speak English, aides or staff members may accompany parents to make sure things go smoothly.

The Central City Head Start Day Care Center runs a fine health program:

Thanks to the broad social skills and widespread nursing experience of Lily Grobstein, Central City's part-time nurse, the center has an outstandingly good health-care program. Lily's years of experience in Salt Lake have given her extensive contacts with the medical community, which have proven invaluable to the center. She uses her resources fully, and her warmly supportive personality has helped her establish good relationships with both children and their parents.

Each new child accepted to the center undergoes a physical examination, paid for, if necessary, out of center funds. Shortly thereafter, the child also has a dental examination, and arrangements are made for dental care if needed. (Children have been found to have as many as 26 cavities needing attention.) Eyes and hearing are checked, inoculations brought up to date, and special problems (such as a need for orthopedic shoes) attended to. The nurse also sees that special clothing needs are met through items donated by the Salvation Army and other agencies.

The style in which these medical services are given supports self-image and a sense of dignity. The nurse does not give inoculations although she takes temperatures. She does not wear a uniform, feeling that many children fear that "differentness" and associate it with unpleasant experiences in the past. Whenever a child goes to a doctor or a dentist, the nurse accompanies him in a supportive and educational role. She has learned that many of the parents and children she works with distrust "professionals," and in all her dealings she takes care to be open and honest about methods and consequences. She takes great pains not to violate parent dignity. (Any used clothing offered to families, for instance, is clean and in good repair.) Comprehensive medical records are kept on all center children, and copies of these records go to the school and the parents when the child goes on to kindergarten. In addition to her regular duties with center children, the nurse provides health counseling to mothers and will often arrange for medical care of other children in the home.

Lily Grobstein also regularly teaches basic health and nutrition in the classrooms. The subjects she covers include:

1. How to wash hands and face thoroughly (demonstration and class practice);
2. Which foods are healthy, which are not; the beginnings of a balanced diet;
3. How to brush the teeth (demonstration with large plaster model—each child has his own toothbrush at the center);
4. How the doctor helps (she uses a bandaged doll, a doctor doll, and a nurse doll to instill healthy expectations about medical services. Children help bandage and play with the dolls).

While the observers were at Central City, Lily and a teacher were in the middle of a nutrition-health unit. The first morning, the nurse weighed and measured each child and talked to the class about good food for growth, emphasizing the extra energy provided by breakfast. The following day Lily and the teacher brought a hot plate and cooking utensils and supervised while the children prepared their own breakfasts of orange juice, cereal, bacon and eggs, toast, and milk.

The exemplary health care provided at Central City is replicable, objectively, at any center that can afford a part-time nurse (Lily spends approximately 25-30 hours a week working for the center). But the quality achieved again has a great deal to do with Lily's experience and personality. Her widespread knowledge of and connections in the local medical community are immense, intangible assets to Central City. Her warm and honest manner in dealing with disadvantaged children and her diplomacy and sensitivity to parental concerns are hardly less of a benefit to the center.

The Amalgamated Day Care Center in Chicago, sponsored by the Amalgamated Clothing Workers of America, has a unique health program. The union has extended its comprehensive health program to include all the center's preschoolers as well as center staff who become ACWA members. The union's well-equipped medical, dental, and pharmaceutical clinic located next door to the center provides free medical service and prescription drugs as well as glasses, braces, orthopedic shoes, and so on. All center children are given an examination and inoculations, and a medical record is begun. A pediatrician visits the center three times a week, and a pedodontist performs all necessary dental work, including fillings and extractions, at union expense. Finally, a psychiatric social worker visits the center one day each week; severely disturbed children are referred to other agencies for help, again at union expense. Amalgamated's health-care program is a tremendous asset to its center and its parent-employees.

We see ourselves as responsible to the families in terms of any kind of help we can offer.

> Staff member, 5th City
> Pre-School
> Chicago, Illinois

Supplemental services, while not necessary for a program's survival, do help supplement its goals. The career development programs we've already discussed are supplemental services, as are social services, community organization, and transportation. Which of these services you offer—if any—will depend on the need for them, the scope of your program, and your financial and manpower resources. Your overall philosophy may also influence your decision: if you serve children from disadvantaged families and feel you can only help children by helping the whole family, you may want to expand your program to include social services or community organization activities.

Social Services

Typically, social services are offered to the families of children enrolled in your day-care operation, but they may also be extended to the larger community. Social services most frequently offered are counseling, education and training services, and material assistance.

Counseling Usually, this means offering advice on a one-time basis to a parent who's concerned about a specific problem. Counseling is commonly about child problems, family and marriage problems, family planning, and, less frequently, psychological problems. It can include tips about meal planning, cooking, nutrition, budgeting, health, and other practical matters as well. Sometimes, counseling simply lets parents know which community agencies can provide help on a continuing basis.

Day-care programs with limited resources have to make do with regular staff for these services. The director or qualified teachers will usually provide counseling at the center when parents request help. When staff members haven't the time, training, or knowledge to offer advice, parents are referred to counselors in various community social service agencies.

Some programs hire a social worker, counselor, community aide, or a parent coordinator to provide in-center counseling. This person may be a professional or nonprofessional community resident familiar with the area and its resources. The counselor may meet with parents as often as once a week or may be available only on request. Once again, this person may be able to handle most counseling him- or herself or may simply direct parents to outside sources. All social service programs, no matter how extensive, rely to a certain degree on referrals to outside help. In the Neighborhood Centers Day Care Association in Houston, Texas,

Great emphasis . . . is put on delivery of services. Easy communication with the parents allows troubles to be spotted early and referrals made. The larger Neighborhood Centers Association is well connected for welfare work within the Houston area and works closely with NCDCA personnel in solving problems. There is a full-time supervisor of support services in the parent organization, as well as a staff of counselors and assistant counselors who work with NCDCA.

NCDCA takes good advantage of Houston's relatively comprehensive and accessible social services. Medical, psychological, and job counseling are supplied on a regular basis. Most referrals stem from the problems of one-parent families and low income levels. . . . Clients have been referred to various area employment services. NCDCA runs the in-school NYC (Neighborhood Youth Corps) program and makes referrals to it. As the Texas Employment Commission is housed in a NCDCA settlement house, referrals are also made to them. Several parents have been sent to the Houston WIN (Work Incentive Program).

The Neighborhood Centers Association has a heavy referral load to health and welfare services, rehabilitation services, legal services, and social work services. Follow-up of referrals has proved to be very delicate; many parents become frightened when someone checks up to see if they have received satisfactory service.

In general, the referrals are made at the same time as the child is enrolled in day care, or placed on the waiting list, as part of the total agency function. In the case of medical services, the agency will often send the mother to a private physician and agree to pay some or all of the fee. . . .

Education and Training Education is most commonly provided to small groups of interested parents at informal center meetings or monthly parent group sessions. The majority of these programs center around child development and early childhood education, and many centers use this opportunity to explain their curriculum and teaching methods to parents. Other popular discussion topics are similar to those mentioned in connection with counseling: nutrition, family planning, budgeting, health, and so forth. The difference here is that counseling is a one-to-one response to an individual situation, while informal education in parent groups is more general.

Parent interest should guide parent education programs. Where these services were available, parents were pursuing a great variety of topics, including consumer education, grooming, home economics, preparation for childbirth, drug and alcohol abuse, home maintenance, car repair and maintenance, housing and tenants' rights, problems of working mothers, first aid, exercising, and driver education. The Kentucky Rural Child Care Project described in Part IV offers extensive parent education opportunities.

Some programs offer formal academic training, usually adult basic education, General Equivalency Degree, and so on. Where parents speak a language other than English, centers may offer English classes taught by their own staff, a volunteer parent, or a community resident. Parents may also be referred to existing adult education programs in the area.

Job training is seldom handled exclusively by an individual center, but many child-care programs help community agencies by using student teachers and trainees from programs like WIN (Work Incentive Programs), NYC (Neighborhood Youth Corps), and New Careers as staff members. These people usually take the center's in-service training course and work alongside experienced staff members. The Casper, Wyoming, day-care center, for instance, uses 13 NYC workers as full-time staff members.

Sometimes job training is provided by an organization associated with the center (often the program that helped start the day-care center in the first place). The Northwest Rural Opportunities program offers parents and community residents 9- to 12-month courses training them to be welders, mechanics, secretaries, nurse's aides, beauticians, etc. This center also provides General Equivalency Degree and regular staff training for parents and employs them as staff members. After they are trained, they are encouraged to move out into jobs in the community. They are particularly well-suited to become teacher's assistants and bilingual aides in the public school system.

The Ute center offers parents job training through their tribal organization. The tribe owns a motel and recreation complex and a furniture factory, and there are training programs for employment at the motel and in the factory.

Another way some centers encourage parents to enter job training is through an admissions policy that takes children of parents in school or job training. The most common and, it seems, practical way of providing job training for parents is by referring them to community training programs such as New Careers, WIN, and others.

Material Assistance and Other Services These are generally offered to the entire family. Material assistance can be emergency clothing, food, medicine, housing, food stamps, and surplus food furnished by local individuals, churches, the Red Cross, government agencies, or similar groups. Health services include testing, treatment, therapy, and check-ups for medical and dental problems, as well as mental health, services for the handicapped, family planning, prenatal and well-baby care, and so on. These services are usually not handled in the center but are offered through referrals to local clinics, hospitals, public health agencies, and visiting nurse programs.

Additional services deal with housing problems (tenants' rights, financing, locating adequate housing, building inspections, etc.), legal aid and advice, vocational rehabilitation, job placement, and public assistance. Again, these services are generally provided by steering parents to local resources.

Some counseling and services are offered in home visits. At the Syracuse University center program, a mother enrolls before the birth of her child. Community women trained in child development visit each mother weekly both before and after the birth of her baby and offer advice about nutrition for mother and child, infant education, and any other questions or problems that might arise. As mentioned earlier, the Kentucky Rural Child Care Project (see Part IV) has an extensive homemaker service. The program's families live in isolated areas, and few services are available in the region. The project's solution has been to train parents and community members, who then offer counseling and services in the homes. The program has been successful, thanks in large part to the project's sensitivity and tact about the way these services are offered.

A more typical example of an active social services program is the one at Central City Head Start Day Care Center, where the director, parent coordinator, and nurse all take a role in referring parents to services and following up.

Administrative staff members pull in help from their own circles of influence, and these resource people then pull in others, creating ever-widening circles of commitment and concern. The Policy Advisory Committee has proved to be an invaluable source of aid. There is community prestige in serving on the board; community members respond by donating professional advice and services willingly and inventively. These people represent a wide range of professions—health, vocational, housing, welfare, legal, social, and educational:

Health: Each year the center refers most of the children and about 10 percent of parents to a general health clinic. Each child receives a dental examination shortly after entering the center, and there is follow-up care at a dental clinic for those children who need it (some 30 percent each year). Individual children are referred for hearing, vision, and orthopedic care as required, and arrangements are often made for siblings not enrolled at the center. Both parents and children are referred for counseling as needed to the local hospital's mental health clinic.

Family planning and maternity health services are also available to mothers by referral. Nutrition counseling, including food stamp information, can be obtained in the same building that houses day care. In emergencies both medical help and food can be gotten with center assistance.

In general, health care, counseling, and referral service is done by the center nurse. Need is the primary determinant of response. The service is comprehensive and sensitively rendered.

The remaining social service counseling and referral is handled principally by the parent coordinator and also the director.

Vocational: Referrals for training and placement are made through the Employment Security Office to such programs as WIN and the city's New Careers program, which trains and places people in various city departments, by making jobs available to parents at the center, and by word-of-mouth. The Central City center has also used NYC and is about to employ Job Corpsmen. About 40 percent of parents are assisted in this manner yearly.

Housing: The center makes use of two local realtors and Community Action Program neighborhood aides to help locate housing, both rental and purchase, for some 25 percent of the parents every year.

Welfare: The center personnel help parents on welfare (about 75 percent of center families) in their dealings with the Welfare Office.

Legal: About 5 percent of the parents are referred to the Legal Aid Center and to private legal services.

Social Service: Thirty percent of center families receive direct counsel from University of Utah graduate students in social work.

Educational: Discussions and lectures for parents have been held at the center, using outside "teachers" on topics such as sex education, child development, nutrition, behavior modification, and health.

The Holland Day Care Center in Holland, Michigan, works mostly with migrant and ex-migrant workers. Here, the center director and two staff members called community aides act as liaisons among parents, the center, and local agencies. There is a parent education program, which offers, among other things, instruction in English. The center relies heavily on volunteers to teach parent classes, to provide transportation and translation for parent social services appointments, and so on. The program emphasizes the need for parents to get to know and understand the community and their rights as well as to learn where to find housing, jobs, and medical aid.

Your attitude toward parents will be critical to your social service program's success. While people may need help, they also need their self-esteem and dignity. There's a middle ground between condescension and cloying solicitousness. Most of our programs aren't interested in ministering to the disadvantaged. The emphasis is on helping people help themselves.

Community Organization
Day-care programs that are active in community organization work see themselves as the advocate of the family in the political and economic context of the wider community. Community or-

ganization activities are usually found where the child-care program is affiliated with a larger organization devoted to making
positive changes in the quality of people's lives, particularly the
disadvantaged and low-income members of the community. Programs associated with Community Action Agencies or Model
Cities are examples.

Community organization works best when the community is a
clearly defined one, with commonly identified needs and interests.
The community may be a physical one—a black ghetto, a Chicano
barrio—or it may be a cultural entity—a migrant population scattered through a region. Typically, centers get involved in community organization efforts because of the need for more child
care in their communities. The demand for extended child care
often introduces parents and community people to the political
arena.

Generally speaking, the center's administrative personnel—the
director and assistant director, if there is one—are most heavily
involved in community organization, although teachers and aides
may also be involved if the activities require extensive community
outreach. The most common community organization activities
are technical assistance advice; lobbying support for better housing
and for physical improvements, such as street lighting, flood protection, paving, traffic lights, sidewalks, and gutters; and advocacy
for improved service from community agencies, such as departments of public welfare, public health, and local schools.

At West 80th Street, where the community controls the center,
people have found they can stimulate change.

If a day-care center in a New York City ghetto provided only child
care and only for its own child list, so few problems would be
touched that there would never be any discernible difference in
the community. West 80th Street wants to make a difference.
Staff feel that it is not enough to help a child recognize that he is a
worthwhile person with some choice in his life, if he then goes
home at night to a family victimized by social circumstance and
the system in which it lives. The center is dedicated to helping
its people learn to deal with the system and use it for their own
benefit.

Many center efforts are tied to the West Side Community Alliance—the original parental organization for West 80th Street. The

Alliance and the center have, for instance, been involved with
Operation Move-In, which provided 150 families with better
housing—one of the most pressing problems in the area. The Alliance has "liberated" housing by exposing racial discrimination and
generated publicity to make others aware of the poverty in the
area. The Alliance has also championed community control of
schools, and other neighborhoods have been encouraged to adopt
this approach.

The center has helped other groups to get funded by the city
and has brought pressure on the city government to effect changes
in its early childhood education and care programs. It has organized job fairs, participated in city hall demonstrations, and conducted voter education and registration.

The center is active in almost everything happening in its community. Center administrators spend hours daily on the telephone,
counseling individuals and groups, explaining how to get things
done, who to see, how to deal with government agencies and city
officials. They have a great deal of experience in these matters,
which is particularly helpful to other centers and schools.

The center has also had a lot of experience helping people in
emergency situations—every day. In November 1970, it organized
reception and emergency education for over 200 children evicted
from substandard housing—not just for overnight but for the fore-
seeable future. At least 100 of these "extra" children [were] cared
for all winter by the Alliance and the center.

At 5th City the sponsoring Ecumenical Institute is trying to revitalize the Chicago ghetto in which it's situated. The 5th City
day-care operation is only a small part of the community effort,
which is a highly organized plan to develop structures responsive
to the needs of the community, operated and staffed by community members. 5th City has

recruited and held classes for a General Equivalency Degree program, graduating five community members. It secured work on a
$1.5 million Federal Housing Authority loan and increased its
"Health Outpost" staff from one to two doctors in the past year.

The community has established a federal credit union, a community housing rehabilitation corporation (run by community members), an employment referral service, and a garbage control and
rat extermination program, in addition to the Health Outpost (two
part-time doctors, a registered nurse, and a direct relationship with
a city hospital). . . . The community organization structure also

supplies advocacy personnel to follow up on referrals, which include those made to the Social Security Office, private business, Employment Security, city housing agencies, Family Planning Service, public schools, neighborhood legal aid, neighborhood centers, city police department, hospitals, the Department of Public Works, property managers, job training programs, and city hall.

Obviously, a center involved in community organization must have strong parent support as well as community support. Programs most active in this area are programs controlled directly by parents who are concerned about their communities and willing to work to make them better.

Transportation

Roughly one-third of our centers were truly neighborhood centers: they provided no transportation service because children and parents were able to walk to and from the building. This was particularly true when programs were located in inner-city neighborhoods or housing projects.

But not all centers are so accessible to the families they serve. In rural areas and smaller cities, public transportation systems are decaying or nonexistent, and people must rely on private automobiles. Lower-income families who don't own cars often have a difficult time taking advantage of day-care services. Parents sometimes form car pools for transporting children, with gasoline costs reimbursed by the center when funds are available. Staff members may pitch in and pick up a few children each day. However, many of our centers mentioned that eligible families could not be served because of transportation problems.

Another third of our centers provided some form of transportation, either by buses, vans, or cars, which they leased or owned. The Kentucky Rural Child Care Project has an extensive transportation system because children live in scattered, isolated areas. At the Syracuse University Children's Center the nature of a long-term research project makes it essential that children stay in the program, even when they move to the outskirts of Syracuse.

Most of the children are transported to the center in three buses. (Two buses hold 14 children each; the other carries 13.) Special

seats have been installed for the infants, and a teacher or aide rides
in each bus, leading songs, pointing out places of interest, and generally keeping children safe and amused. As well as morning and
evening shuttles . . . the buses make noontime runs with infants in
the half-day programs, taking one group home and picking up the
afternoon children.

Parents must notify the center if children cannot attend or are
to be picked up or dropped off someplace other than usual. While
observers were in the center, this telephoning was taking up a good
deal of the center director's and secretary's time. . . . One of the
bus drivers works part-time, and the other two help in the kitchen,
do errands, and fill in any of the odd jobs that may be required
during an operating day.

Busing allows many children to participate in day care who
otherwise could not attend, but it can also mean limited parent-
center communication. When parents bring their children to the
center and pick them up at night, they have a chance to chat with
staff members, to voice their concerns, and to see the program in
action. The Holland Day Care Center in Michigan is housed in two
buildings in different parts of town.

Since Holland has no public transportation system and few parents
own cars, the centers must provide transportation. They have two
buses, each with a capacity of 17 children, and 90 percent of the
center families use this service. Although it means parents are not
in and out of the centers during the day, without this busing many
children could not attend. The program has one part-time bus
driver. The other bus is driven by the secretary/bookkeeper.

Teachers rotate bus duty, supervising the children, leading songs,
and generally keeping kids occupied. Community aides provide
extra transportation services for children and parents who must be
picked up late, for medical appointments, and other special occa-
sions.

...It seems to me they care for the babies as much as it is possible.
> Parent, Syracuse University
> Children's Center
> Syracuse, New York

The main thing I like about the center is that Jeff is treated normal, is never teased.
> Parent, Casper Day Care Center
> Casper, Wyoming

So far, we've generally been referring to care for preschool children between the ages of three and five years. But depending on the demand for care in your community, you may want to extend your services to other children—infants, school-age children, and children with special needs. The availability of day care for these children in many cases determines whether or not a parent can work.

The needs we discussed for preschoolers apply, of course, to infants, schoolchildren, and special children as well. But there are also special requirements for these other groups. Infants (a few months to one-and-a-half years of age) need a great deal of physical care. Because they have limited mobility and physical resources, they are more dependent than older children on adults for stimulation and social contact. Toddlers (one-and-a-half to three years of age) require somewhat less physical care but are still very dependent on a maternal figure for emotional support, comfort, and approval. For both age groups, emotional and intellectual growth requires a stimulating and interesting environment, adequate opportunities for exploration and physical activity, and a great deal of face-to-face human contact.

School-age children (six years of age and older) who spend most of the day in school require a minimum of physical care. For them, the center must offer a broad spectrum of enriching and skill-enhancing experiences geared to the maturity and experience level of older children. Well-designed child-care programs for school-age children expand the child's world view, increase his appreciation of his own and other life styles, build his sense of confidence and self-worth, and provide him with relevant models for adult behavior. Older children also require greater responsibility and control over their own activities.

Infants and Toddlers
Quality day care for infants and toddlers is a complex issue and a
highly controversial one. Some experts in the area of cognitive and
affective development argue that no infants should be cared for in
child-care centers. They feel that the needs of infants are so
numerous, intense, and individualized that they cannot be met in
the kinds of group situations centers normally offer. Others, accepting the fact that some parents must work and that infants are
going to be cared for in the day-care setting, feel it *is* possible to
provide quality care for infants and toddlers if some important
standards are met.

First, the physical environment you offer must be clean, warm,
and free of hazards. Good programs provide brightly-colored surroundings, varied objects and things that are interesting to feel,
look at, and listen to. Walls are decorated with pictures and cut-
outs of brightly colored objects, and toys are placed on open
shelves, accessible to an exploring child. The aim is to provide a
stimulating and challenging environment. Care should also be
taken to avoid chaotic, noisy, and disorganized conditions, which
can startle or disrupt playing toddlers and infants.

There'd be little point in having those stimulating surroundings
if children were confined to cribs or playpens all day. Good centers make it a point to give infants a chance to interact with various people in different areas of the center. For instance, part of
the day the children move about on the floor in exploration; at
other times, they can be placed in high chairs or at play tables.
And for at least part of the day, they're allowed to mix with older
children who can often be quite helpful at amusing the younger
ones.

A consistent and predictable daily routine of meals, naps, and
playtimes is also desirable, but your responsiveness to specific
needs such as diapering and affection should be keyed to the
child's expression of need rather than rigid routine.

The most important element in the care of infants and toddlers,
and the most difficult to prescribe or control, is the way staff provide care. While no single list of practices is likely to be applicable
to all children or acceptable to all adults, there are a few basic
standards for adult behavior on which staff in quality programs

agree. Infants and toddlers need to have a feeling of security in their environment and a sense of trust in the adults around them. They require a consistent and warm relationship with a maternal figure. The staff behaviors listed here address these needs and are practiced in quality programs:

Nurturance Staff members talk to and hold infants a great deal while performing routine activities such as diapering, bottle or solid feeding. They comfort and talk to infants when the children express a desire for contact. At times of special stress, such as arrival and departure, staff members are on hand to help a child cope with his distress.

One-to-One Attention For the very young, the human face is the most interesting, pleasurable, and varied object in the environment. For older infants and toddlers, sustained socializing with adults is a powerful learning experience. Staff members in quality centers spend a significant amount of time with one child, playing games, babbling, leading, and following the child's lead.

Guidance As we mentioned in Chapter 1, simply interrupting a child engaged in a dangerous, frustrating, or disruptive activity is an appropriate but incomplete response; mere intervention only adds to his sense of helplessness and frustration. Staff members must also offer interesting alternatives to engage a child's energies along constructive and more satisfying lines. This enhances a child's feeling of competence. Children can also be taught, through praise, to recognize their own accomplishments and thereby bolster their own self-esteem.

Consistency Staff members find it important to be consistent and predictable in their daily routines so children know what to expect. Similarly, most center staffs feel that a consistent relationship with one adult over an extended period of time is a very important characteristic of quality care for young children.

To meet these goals, your day-care program must have an adequate number of staff. In most of our centers, staff/child ratios for

infants and toddlers ranged from 1:3 to 1:5. And once again, the
kinds of people used as staff are critical. Good programs give priority to people with warm and responsive personalities, people
energetic enough to extend themselves right to the end of a long
and active day.

The Syracuse University Children's Center is both a day-care
center and part of a long-range research project. Mothers are
brought into the program when they're three months pregnant,
and special center personnel make home visits from this point until the child is about five months old and starts coming to the center half-days.

The Infant Fold program meets the young child's emotional needs
for attachment to a special person by making each teacher responsible for the care, loving, and lessons of only four babies. Piagetian
sensorimotor skills and language enrichment are used. Specific
Piagetian tasks are tools to identify where an individualized program will be helpful. Such programs are carried out with loving
contact and enjoyable physical experiences for the child.

Teachers try to stimulate each infant to respond to the goals of a
given task and to devise ways of modifying a task presentation,
being sensitive to each baby's performance level. For example, a
toy rubber cat might be used as a hidden-object task. If the baby
does not search for the hidden cat at all, then only part of the cat
might be hidden and the uncovered part made more interesting.
Thus the toy cat becomes a partially-hidden-object task with a
red and white striped tail left uncovered to attract the baby's attention. Task sequencing is also stressed.

Language skills are strongly emphasized as well. Teachers are encouraged to enjoy books with the infants and to sing to them.
Objects, feelings, and actions are labeled not only during structured learning times but also as an integral part of diapering, feeding, bathing and other caretaking routines. The Early Language
Assessment Scale (ELAS) was developed, simplified, and is now
routinely used by staff as an achievement test for infant language.
ELAS also furnishes an additional incentive for a teacher to promote her infant's vocalization and language skills.

In each room, mirrors have been placed at ground level so infants can see themselves and also learn, for example, to imitate
facial expressions, which are normally invisible. Floor rugs help
children arrange their own toy and task areas. Large wall charts in
the infant rooms outline tasks, including Piagetian items, in ten

curriculum areas. Teachers initial tasks each child has worked on during the week, and the overall chart indicates child growth in various cognitive and skill areas. . . .

One way to evaluate how well infants are cared for in your program is to look at their behavior. If they function physically and emotionally in your program the way their counterparts do in a positive home environment, you're probably doing an adequate job. Infants in quality centers are physically active, alert, and interested in what's happening around them. They reach out to explore and manipulate objects, express themselves by babbling and talking, and show delight in eliciting responses from adults and other children.

School-Age Children
After-school programs are another thing entirely. They have to take into account the maturity of the children involved. If your program is irrelevant to them, dull, or too highly regimented, school-age children simply won't attend on any regular basis.

Centers with after-school programs usually serve kids ages six through twelve. The needs, capabilities, and interests of children within this age range vary considerably. The younger kids (six to eight years old) need plenty of physical exercise to let off steam after being confined in school all day. But they're still very much interested in toys and make-believe play. Nine- to eleven-year-olds often want to participate in the decision making about activities. At this stage, the peer group becomes more influential and is an important source of learning and satisfaction. Adolescence (twelve to sixteen) brings dramatic physical, emotional, and intellectual changes. It's often a critical period for the formation of adult identity and the development of boy-girl relationships, life philosophies, goals, and ideals. Concerns about sex, peer group acceptance, personal relationships, and personal adequacy become all-important.

Programs for school-age kids entail flexible and extended schedules to accommodate parent and school schedules. Most of the groups we studied operate between 3:00 P.M. and 6:30 P.M. on school days, and some are also open from 6:00 A.M. until school begins. Kindergarten children may be part of the regular preschool program on a half-day schedule. Our programs also provide full-day care on school holidays and throughout the summer.

Because of these schedule demands, after-school programs often rely heavily on volunteer help. However, fewer staff members are required for adequate care of these children than for preschoolers. Staff/child ratios for school-age children in our study ranged from 1:8 to 1:13. Obviously, the ability of staff members to relate well with kids becomes increasingly important with older children. Centers make a special effort to match staff racial and cultural backgrounds with those of the children and to provide male staff members, as well as women, for this age group.

Services for school-age kids cover a broad range.

Recreation A variety of recreational opportunities is commonly provided—swimming, basketball, handball, baseball, and so on. If facilities aren't available at the center, arrangements are made to use other community resources (YMCA, community centers, city recreation department).

Education Tutorial programs are typical where centers wish to be more than a chaperoning service. In addition to tutoring in various subjects, some centers provide courses not offered in conventional school curricula, such as black history, foreign cultures, or inter-personal relations. Subjects must be relevant to the environment, culture, and family styles of the kids and should be guided by student interest.

Social Services If a program is able to offer social services to its preschoolers, it usually extends those services to after-school kids as well. Some centers offer health services and diagnostic testing for learning problems and provide eyeglasses, hearing aids, adequate clothing, and so on.

Broadening Horizons Programs often take advantage of outside resources and events as learning opportunities for school-age kids. These include field trips to museums, libraries, factories, department stores, concerts, and different neighborhoods.

Career Preparation Quality programs for older children typically make an effort to familiarize kids with a broad spectrum of careers and emphasize individual capabilities for career achievement.

School-age day care is more often found in day-care systems rather than at single centers. An exception is the 5th City Pre-School in Chicago. It accepts after-school children ages eleven and twelve, who assist in the care of younger school-age children and, occasionally, preschoolers. The program, called the "Jets," has its own staff and the use of a multipurpose community building as well as the gym facilities at a nearby YMCA during the school year. In the summer, when the program expands to full-day sessions, kids use the recreational and educational facilities at the community's Malcolm X. College. Throughout the year, the program offers tutorial classes as part of its basic curriculum.

The Mecklenburg County Department of Social Services in Charlotte, North Carolina, operates nine day-care centers and five day homes. (It also contracts out a large Extended Day Care program to the local YMCA.) The day homes are an experimental project to provide after-school care for some 25 children. The homes operate four or five hours a day during school months and ten or eleven hours daily in the summer and on school holidays. The department carefully screens families who wish to take in after-school children and provides training and supervision to ensure good care.

Cooking is a favorite activity at several of the homes—in addition to food preparation, it involves science, nutrition, hygiene, home economics, math, and sensory experiences. Children help in meal planning, grocery shopping, food preparation, and table setting. Even the older ten- and eleven-year-old boys in the program seemed very proud when they served the . . . supervisor a piece of pound cake they had made.

A big activity in summer is gardening. Children have learned about plant needs, pest control, and growth cycles and have made vegetable soup from the gardens they help tend. In other homes, science projects have included building terrariums and aquariums. In addition to various trips to amusement and local facilities, one mother has taken her children on a fishing expedition. Other special activities have included, in the summer months, tutoring ses-

sions, dance classes, arts and crafts, as well as organized team
sports through the Model Cities enrichment program.

Children with Special Needs

In the past, almost all children with special needs (physical disabil-
ities, emotional problems, learning problems) have been segregated
from regular school programs and educated instead in specialized
settings. Teachers felt these children couldn't fit into regular
groups, that they needed special staff, equipment, and expertise.

Recent research, however, has shown that these segregated facilities can be damaging to a child's overall development. By isolating
children with special needs from the rest of society and from other
kids their own age, we deny them the chance to lead a normal life.
Day-care programs that have integrated special children into their
regular classes have shown that these children are able to adjust to
and benefit from these settings. Special children get a chance to
emulate other children's behavior, and they can also develop a
more positive self-image in an environment that focuses on potential, not disability. All of the children in the group can learn, at an
early age, to work and play with different types of children in
preparation for the larger outside world.

The director of the Casper Day Care Center in Casper, Wyoming,
has recognized that emotionally disturbed and mentally and physically handicapped children need the stimulation of daily association with other children their own age. After much discussion,
the center's board of directors agreed to include in their day-care
groups one special child for every five "normal" children.

Activities are generally the same for all children, except that
those with special needs may receive speech therapy and special
attention at mealtimes. Presently, there are four children enrolled
who have emotional problems and six children who are mentally
retarded, one of whom is also deaf. Two full-time women, one
deaf and the other mildly retarded, are also part of the center's
program, as special aides. Parent interviews indicated that everyone is pleased with the program. It does require extra work on the
part of the director and staff, but the benefits to children, staff,
and parents are evident. One staff member put it this way. "This

center gives a lot of children an opportunity that can change their paths. As an example, we have one child whose parents thought he was a borderline retarded. He really isn't. He was disturbed because of a home situation. We've been able to work with him, and we see great hope. It's so important to nip these things before they get to the point of no return."

Part III   **Costs and Models**

Money (or the lack of it) is the core of most of our problems.
Director, Casper Day Care Center
Casper, Wyoming

Perhaps the most frequently voiced comment we heard in our study of the 20 good day-care operations was the need for more money. The fact is, it's expensive to provide good, organized child care, wherever you're located and whomever you serve. In our survey, child-care programs ranged in cost from $1,200 to $4,000 per child per year. Moreover, no center in this study cared exclusively for infants, who are, as a group, even more expensive to look after.

The quality of your program depends on the number of people you hire as well as on their quality. It's important to have people who like children and work well with them, but it's also important to have enough staff to ensure that each child gets personal attention when he or she needs it. Not surprisingly, then, three-fourths to four-fifths of the real costs of child care are personnel costs. Variations in per-child costs are highly predictable: they vary pretty much as staff costs vary. Knowing the staff/child ratio at a given center and where in the country it's located allows you to predict within narrow limits how much a given arrangement will cost. (Tables for adjusting for regional differences are included on pages 166-169.) For instance, for a center serving 25 children, if the staff/child ratio is 1:5 and the center is located in New York City, you would multiply New York salaries by five: the resulting figure will account for three-fourths to four-fifths of the value of resources used in that center. (Of course, some of these resources may be volunteered or donated, so the resulting figure will represent *true* costs, not necessarily cash costs.)

Functional Budgeting

Like most programs, day-care centers and systems account for their costs and develop budgets by line item—so much for personnel, for fringe benefits, for consumable supplies, and so on. Our study took all centers and system budgets and program descriptions and turned them into functional form. To do this, we determined what percentage of the budget of each center was spent on major functions—child care, administration, feeding, rental, health, transportation, and supplemental programs. For the sake of clarity, expenditures are divided into four major categories. Together, the first three make up basic child-care costs:

I. **Standard Core** (This category shows costs incurred in all day-care operations.)
    A. *Child care and teaching*—personnel, curriculum, and general classroom supplies
    B. *Administration*—personnel, equipment depreciation, office supplies, staff travel, telephone, insurance, audit
    C. *Feeding*—personnel, foodstuffs, other food-related expenses

II. **Varying Core** (This category shows costs for optional programs, which can be assumed by the center, by parents, or both.)
    D. *Health*—personnel, supplies, health-related services
    E. *Transportation*—personnel, operating expenses, maintenance, insurance

III. **Occupancy** (This category includes rental value of property, utilities, taxes, property insurance, custodial personnel, and supplies. Because occupancy costs vary widely, they are shown separately.)

IV. **Supplemental Services** (This final category includes programs that go beyond basic care and that have significant dollar costs or revenues associated with them.)

Standard Core As we've mentioned, a very substantial portion of the standard core costs are for personnel. In our 20 centers and systems personnel costs average 76 percent of total standard core costs. Personnel costs account for the major part of three functional categories—care and teaching, administration, and health—and are a substantial fraction of feeding. Only in the occupancy category are personnel costs overshadowed by other components.

"Care and teaching" generates more than half of the total costs for most programs—rightfully so, since this is the function child-care centers exist to perform, and most staff members are engaged in this work. Administration is the second most significant cate-

gory in terms of percent of budget, accounting for 22 percent of
the total. The ratio of costs of administration to costs of care and
teaching is about 1:3, on the average. Although the amounts spent
on administration and care and teaching varied considerably in our
study, about 80 percent of this variation was due simply to differences in staff/child ratios and differences in prices around the
country.

Feeding usually accounts for about 12 percent of a program's
budget, assuming at least one meal and two snacks daily. Where
extra meals are added to the daily nutrition program, foodstuff
costs per child may be slightly higher, but a second meal or compensatory nutrition doesn't seem to increase overall costs signifi-
cantly. In some cases, regular staff help with the nutrition program
without additional wages. Elsewhere, day-care programs may be
eligible for food subsidies and surplus food. Even to the extent
that compensatory programs require the substitution of special
foods to supplement dietary deficiencies, costs may not be signifi-
cantly increased. When professional nutritional advice is needed,
centers can sometimes call upon community resources at no expense. Where a dietitian's services must be paid for by the program, the additional expense is, again, minimal in terms of increased cost per child.

Varying Core Most centers have at least a basic health program
consisting of a part-time nurse who checks to see that children
have had dental and medical check-ups, inoculations, and so on;
refers them to these services if they haven't already received them;
checks children regularly for illness; trains staff in first aid and
emergency procedures; and maintains health records on all the
center's kids. Our study determined that this kind of basic health
program usually consumes 1 percent of a center's budget, or,
across our centers, $38 per child or less.

Providing comprehensive health care beyond this basic level en-
tails a considerable jump in expenses. More comprehensive health
programs range from $95 per child to $516 per child, with an average cost of $192. The wide range in costs here is a reflection of
variation in needs. The more health problems children have, the
wider the scope of services necessary and the more expensive the

costs. A low-cost, basic health service provides for regular medical and dental check-ups and the services of a consulting psychologist. A high-cost, comprehensive service, like that provided by the Ute day-care center, employs a half-time nurse for 22 children; offers regular medical and dental check-ups; provides donated services from a pediatrician and a psychologist; provides special clinical examinations and treatment for eye, speech, and hearing problems; and uses the facilities of a local clinic for special medical and dental services.

Here, too, personnel costs account for most of the expense associated with health care, with very little going for supplies. In our study, most health services were donated. The general rule seems to be that the poorer the center is financially, the greater the proportion of health costs that are covered by in-kind contributions. Either the director raises funds to cover such services or he or she spends a great deal of effort searching for in-kind aid.

While many programs don't provide transportation, where it *is* provided it's vitally needed (large rural areas, for example). Transportation costs in our study averaged $141 per child, but the range of costs was great. With the exception of centers using parent car pools, in-kind donations accounted for a very small portion of the total cost of transportation. If your center plans to offer transportation, it's likely that you'll need to cover the full cost of this service. Parent car pools where parents are reimbursed for vehicle expenses seem to be the least expensive kind of transportation.

The cost of providing transportation derives from driver's salaries and operating cost of the vehicles. Driver's salaries, on a full-time equivalent, annual basis, ranged in our study from $4,400 to $5,700, with an average of $5,000. As a percentage of total transportation cost, salaries averaged 62 percent. As for the number of personnel required, we found that one half-time driver is usually provided for each 25 children. The position of driver is rarely more than part-time (although it can be combined with another part-time position, such as teacher, secretary, or custodian, to create a full-time job). Only if pick-up and delivery times are staggered will the position of driver be full-time.

Operating cost of vehicles includes gas, oil, servicing, maintenance, insurance, depreciation, and taxes. If the center owns its own vehicles, these expenses are covered in its budget; if vehicles are leased, all expenses except gas and oil are usually included in the rental price. If the center reimburses the driver for the use of his own vehicle, the reimbursement should be sufficient to cover these vehicle costs. At the center in our study using such an arrangement, the reimbursement rate was 8 cents per mile, well below the Federal Highway Administration's estimated cost of 13.7 cents per mile for operation and maintenance.

Of these three arrangements, the driver-reimbursement plan seems to be the best. It's probably the least expensive, and the driver assumes responsibility for vehicle performance. The second choice would probably be center ownership of vehicles, since it's less expensive than leasing. This means, however, that the center must raise the money to buy the vehicles. Vehicle costs on a per-child basis ranged from $51 to $76, with an average of $67. As a percentage of total transportation cost, vehicle costs averaged 38 percent.

The cost of transportation per child remains the same regardless of the size of your center: we discovered no economies of scale. Center planners should bear in mind that the figures we've given are merely guidelines. Costs in a specific program will vary depending on the number of children needing transportation, the nearness of the children to the center, and the drivers' salaries. Also, alternatives such as parent car pools can considerably reduce a center's expenses.

Occupancy Occupancy costs in our study, on the average, represented 13 percent of a center's budget. This included the rental value of the property, utilities, taxes, property insurance, custodial personnel, and supplies. Only in this category are personnel costs overshadowed by other factors.

Whether your building is purchased, rented, built, or donated, the price of land and facilities will affect operating costs (and, therefore, the price of service). The greatest outlay of resources comes in the start-up phase of a center, when capital must be found for the costs of land, building, and equipment (see Chapter

10). For centers already in operation, however, costs are prorated across the operating year, and a rental value is put on facilities considered to be in-kind donations.

Supplemental Services The most commonly provided supplemental services include social services, community organization, and staff training. Adding social services to a child-care program raises center costs if special staff are required. Virtually all of the additional costs of providing social services are attributable to personnel. This isn't to say that center resources aren't used: the center is the physical base of operations, and office and other building space and the telephone may be needed during the evenings and on weekends. But for the most part, these resources are used anyway in the day-to-day operation of the center. Additional demands on these facilities for social services usually add very little to costs.

Social services are typically provided by center personnel—a social worker, parent coordinator, community aide, the director, or various staff members trained for this purpose. Annual salaries for social workers in our study of child-care programs ranged from $6,500 to $7,800, with an average salary of $7,000. Annual salaries for parent coordinators and community aides ranged from $4,000 to $6,300, with the average at $5,200.

Yearly costs per child for supplemental services ranged from $16 to $310 with a great many such services donated. Again, this wide range of costs is due primarily to differences in the scope of services provided, which depends in turn on the needs of the families involved and the center's own financial ability to provide these services. Extensive social services depend on in-kind contributions: in some of the programs we studied, all social services were volunteered.

Where centers are involved in community organization, substantial staff time is usually devoted to these activities. Because community organization activities tend to use existing center resources, it's difficult to determine costs for them, but it's evident from our study that extensive community organization work is a significant drain on center resources. In the one program in our study where these costs could be estimated, they appeared to re-

quire approximately 40 percent of the director's time and 50 percent of the assistant director's time, implying a cost to the child-
care program of $300 per child per year. On the other hand, effec-
tive community organization may lead to increased donations of
in-kind labor and supplies as a result of community involvement
and support of the program.

Cost per child for staff training ranged from $20 to $160, with
an average of $71 per year. Staff training costs are only rarely met
by donations—usually where a center is near a university. Large
variations in the personnel costs associated with staff training reflect differences in the scope and content of various programs.
Training can also be a cost-saving device if it allows centers to hire
competent people without formal educational credentials. The
costs of training are usually offset by the increase in salaries necessary to recruit and keep more formally qualified staff.

Donated Goods and Services

One way directors lighten the burden of child-care expenses is by
recruiting volunteers and donations. Even well-financed centers
use donated time and labor, and almost a quarter of all resources
used by all centers and systems in our study were not paid for.
Most of these volunteered resources are people: directors working
overtime, professionals donating their skills, volunteer staff. (We
did not compute the cost of the very extensive inputs from members of boards of directors, without whom many centers could not
exist.)

For people who want to estimate the value of their donated
goods and services (particularly important for those trying to replicate other programs), we've developed some definitions and guidelines for valuing in-kind donations. A donation should meet the
following criteria:

It has a measurable commercial value.

It is truly helpful to the day-care operation.

It is furnished directly to the program and under its administrative
control and is not routinely provided to all children as a community service. (Thus, public schools, tax-supported transportation,
or scouting and recreation facilities are not counted as donations.)

Generally speaking, donated personnel services fall into three classes: unpaid volunteers who do program work; people who receive substantially less than the commercial rate of pay; persons who work for the center but are paid by an outside organization other than the parent organization. In your estimations, reasonable reductions from fair market value (not to exceed 75 percent of fair market value) should be made when the program did not seek or has no appreciable use for donated goods but at the same time can't afford, for one reason or another, to reject such items. Because of the highly individual nature of donated goods, the amount of such reductions must be left to the judgment of the specific center. To help clarify things, here are some definitions: *Volunteers* may be parents of children in the center and/or other people who help out in the center but do not provide professional service. *Professional donated services* cover specialists' services that the program would otherwise want to or have to pay for. This includes firms and individuals who would otherwise be paid on a retainer fee or on an individual contract basis.

Donations of services should be valued at whatever it would cost the program to obtain those services if you were forced to purchase them in the local community. In some cases, donated services will be roughly comparable to services currently being purchased by your center (that is, volunteer teacher aides working alongside paid teacher aides). Elsewhere, as in the case of professional services, the center may be familiar with standard rates in the community. In general, use your own best estimates of local wage and salary scales. For programs that can't develop their own estimates, we've included a list of rates in Table 9.1, drawn from current market conditions. Individuals or firms donating fewer than 12 hours of service per year should not be reported. Volunteer services in general should be computed at at least the federal minimum wage plus FICA (since federal minimum wages may soon be expected to cover child-care centers).

Since most professional staff members expect to work more than 40 hours a week or have some understanding of this when they continue in a job, we don't generally recommend imputing a cost to overtime as a donated service. Nonprofessional staff work-

Table 9.1
Guidelines for Computing Value of Donated Services

Staff Position or Profession	Number of Programs	Average Enrollment	Hourly Rate
Director	1	Under 30	$ 4.00
Director	1	30 - 99	4.50
Director	1	100 and over	5.00
Director	2	—	5.00
Director	3 or more	—	7.50
Asst. director and/or business manager	1	Under 30	3.25
Asst. director and/or business manager	1	30 - 99	3.50
Asst. director and/or business manager	1	100 and over	4.00
Asst. director and/or business manager	2	—	4.00
Asst. director and/or business manager	3 or more	—	5.00
Head teacher or division supervisor	1	Under 60	3.25
Head teacher or division supervisor	1	60 and over	3.50
Teacher	1	All sizes	3.00
Teacher aide	1	All sizes	2.00
Trainee and all other nonmanagerial	1	All sizes	1.65 +
Medical doctor, psychiatrist, lawyer, banker, stockbroker, architect	1	All sizes	10.00
Management consultant, accountant, educational consultant, psychologist, therapist, social worker, nurse	1	All sizes	7.00

ing overtime are usually given compensatory time off or are paid
for their extra time. Only in cases where staff members are paid
less than the minimum wage guidelines recommended for full-time
teaching or child supervision activities or where overtime assumes
heroic proportions (over 50-60 hours per week) should the difference between the recommended minimum hourly wage and the
actual wage paid be considered (from the budgeting point of view)
a "staff donation" to the operations of the center. It should be
noted, however, that few day-care operations would survive without the dedicated overtime of staff persons; our recommendation
that some overtime be considered "normal" does not mean it is in
any way insignificant.

For examples of single-center budgets, see the Amalgamated Day
Care Center and Greeley Parent Child Center budgets on pages
192-193 and 276-277.

Child-Care Systems and Costs

So far, we've been looking primarily at single day-care centers.
One of the alternatives to the single-center setting is the child-care
system, which is a group of individual centers or, in some cases,
day homes associated under one central administration. Systems
are a logical solution to the problems associated with providing
care for large numbers of children, particularly since substantial
funding is available. Funding for systems includes Title IVa of the
Social Security Act (matched by local and state funds), Model
Cities supplemental funds from the Department of Housing and
Urban Development, Office of Economic Opportunity grants, public school taxes, research foundation grants, United Fund money,
private endowments, and parent fees.

We have no evidence that child care in systems is of higher or
lower quality than care in single centers, but our evidence does suggest that special problems may arise when you try to provide good
care in *large* centers, particularly in the maintenance of favorable
staff/child ratios. Therefore, child-care systems tend to care for
kids in small, decentralized facilities. (A typical child-care center
in a system serves between 9 and 35 children.) Systems permit
centralized funding and a systematic response to demand, without
some of the time-consuming restraints found in single-center set-

tings. On the other hand, red tape and delays may be found in systems more often than in single centers. Two child-care systems are described in Part IV: the Family Day Care Career Program in New York City and the Rural Child Care Project in Kentucky.

Depending on the specific characteristics of the local community, the central administrations of systems may be very powerful or merely coordinating bodies. The overall director of a system is nearly always concerned primarily with the recruitment of resources and with major personnel and policy issues. Other administrative activities are shared in a variety of ways between the overall system director and the directors of individual centers within the system. The case studies in Part IV provide detailed descriptions of administrative activities in systems. All systems have an overall board of directors to which the system director is responsible. In addition, the director is typically supported by one or two advisory groups composed of parents and professionals who provide technical assistance.

The management level directly below the overall system director is typically composed of administrative office staff, early childhood education and curriculum supervisors, support service staff, and research staff, if any. The administrative office staff generally perform financial, clerical, and purchasing services for the system's subcenters unless the subcenters are very large (that is, more than 100 children). Research staff, educational specialists, and support service personnel, such as nurses and teacher trainers, may act as resource people for all of the centers in the system. Curriculum planning and parent relations are typically the responsibility of central office personnel. Thus, individual centers are usually staffed only with a center director, teachers and teaching aides, and a cook. Some larger centers also have a housekeeper, parent coordinator, and transportation aide.

In some systems, individual centers exchange staff to broaden staff experience, facilitate staff training, and cover absentees. Curriculum materials and light equipment may also be exchanged among centers. Some systems publish newsletters on a regular basis for distribution among their centers.

Child-care systems, particularly those with day homes, serve children of varying ages from infancy to adolescence. Infants are most frequently cared for in day homes. Handicapped children are more prevalent in child-care systems than in individual centers.

Systems are usually associated with umbrella community social service agencies and thus have access to a broad variety of supportive services, including homemaking, parent education and training, consumer education, housing assistance, legal services, family planning, career development, and bilingual education. As mentioned earlier, where center staff are extensively involved in providing supplemental services to parents and families, staff/child ratios may be negatively affected. Because of the apparent relationship between favorable staff/child ratios and the quality of child care, day-care planners should keep this consideration in mind. On the other hand, involving the whole family can mean more carry-over of the program's goals and methods into the home, more parent participation, and possibly more in-kind donations.

Two of the child-care systems we studied have been operating for many years. The Springfield, Massachusetts, system dates back to the 1800s, while the Berkeley, California, system began during the Depression. Indications are that system organization has a high potential for longevity, perhaps higher than that of single centers, which in our study were typically one to four years old.

A budget for the core program in a child-care system would be similar to the functional budget we described on pages 113-119 for a single center. Notable comparisons between single-center and system costs are as follows:

In systems with home care, *care and teaching* costs per child are somewhat lower because of the relatively low wages now being paid to home-care mothers.

Administrative costs per child, adjusted for the region of the country, are apparently somewhat higher in systems than in single centers; in some cases this is because there is in fact "more" administration—which may in turn be one reason some systems survive longer.

Costs associated with *supplemental services* are greater in systems. Such services aren't necessarily more expensive to provide in systems: rather, systems as affiliates of larger multiservice programs tend to spend more on such services.

Costs per child for the core program vary widely among systems, as widely as they do for single centers. No evidence as to economies of scale in systems emerged from our study.

Systems in our study were less dependent on donations than were single centers.

None of our systems offered extended health care, whereas eight of the twelve independent preschool centers were providing such a program. This does not mean that systems were neglecting the health needs of clients: such services were generally being provided by other affiliated agencies.

Table 9.2 gives a sample annual center care system budget for 1,500 children.

Home Care and Costs
Another alternative to the single-center setting, home care is child care for small groups of children in private homes under the supervision of a woman who frequently cares for her own children in addition to those she takes in. Home care in our study was provided only by systems. However, home care can also be provided by individuals not associated with a child-care system. Organized home-care systems offer warm, supervised, secure care, which is almost always very close to the children's own homes, and studies indicate that parents place high priority on this feature of child care. Home care is therefore particularly attractive, especially for isolated areas of the country.

Organized home care was found to be almost as expensive as center care, although care for infants, mildly sick children, children with special problems, and children in hard-to-reach areas is less expensive than similar care in centers. At the present time, home care also appears to be seriously underfunded. Provider mothers (those who take children in) are paid far less than federal minimum wages, and the educational programs offered tend to be very meager.

A provider mother may take in children for full or half days. The number of children in her home, including her own, if any,

Table 9.2
Center Care System Annual Budget[1] (1,500 children)

I. Care and Teaching		
188 Caretaker-teachers @ 4,500[2] (or $7,000)	$846,000	
Fringe benefits and payroll taxes @ 10%	84,600	
Educational consumables @ $30/child	45,000	
Other @ $35/child[3]	52,500	
Subtotal		$1,028,100
(cost per child)		(685)
II. Administration (assume 20 centers)		
System Director @ $20,000[4]	20,000	
Assistant System Director @ $16,000[4]	16,000	
2 System Secretaries @ $5,700	11,400	
1 System Bookkeeper @ $9,000[4]	9,000	
2 Subcenter Assistants @ $10,000	20,000	
20 Center Directors @ $9,400	188,000	
20 Center Secretary/Bookkeepers (1/2 time) @ $5,700	57,000	
Fringe benefits and payroll taxes @ 10%	32,100	
Other @ $74/child[5]	111,000	
Subtotal		464,500
(cost per child)		(310)
III. Feeding (assume 20 centers)		
20 Cooks @ $5,300	$106,000	
Fringe benefits and payroll taxes @ 10%	10,600	
Foodstuffs @ $132/child	198,000	
Other @ $9/child[6]	13,500	
Subtotal		328,100
(cost per child)		(219)

IV. Occupancy (assume 20 centers)

20 Custodians (1/2 time) @ $4,600	46,000	
Fringe benefits and payroll taxes @ 10%	4,600	
Rent @ $175/child	262,500	
Other @ $4/child[7]	60,000	
Subtotal		373,100
(cost per child)		(249)
Total	$2,193,800	
Cost per child (teachers paid an average $4,500)	$1,463	
Cost per child (teachers paid an average $7,000)	$1,807	

1. All figures based on averages from Abt Associates, *A Study in Child Care, 1970-71,* unless otherwise indicated.

2. Average of teacher salaries from Abt study ($5,700) and minimum wage for aides ($3,328), rounded. The $7,000 figure is included to show wages that may be considered preferable by child-care planners. Budget totals, however, refer to wages of $4,500.

3. Field trips, equipment depreciation, and miscellaneous.

4. Based on system of comparable size from the Abt study.

5. Equipment depreciation, office supplies, telephone, staff travel, liability insurance, and audit and legal fees.

6. Equipment depreciation, nonfood supplies.

7. Housekeeping supplies, utilities, taxes, and insurance.

ordinarily can't exceed six by state law. In the Family Day Care
Career Program in New York City, child placement in these private
homes is handled with the local office of the state's Department of
Public Welfare. If a regional office or subcenter is responsible for
day homes, the homes are generally supervised by counselors who
make regular rounds.

The office directly responsible for child-care homes generally has
a licensing or applications counselor who surveys neighborhoods
for demand and for suitable provider homes. Applications for both
placement and provider homes are processed centrally. Local
health and fire inspection of provider homes is usually handled by
the central office, and small grants (usually $100 to $300) are
made available for improvements and equipment needed to meet
local codes. In addition, prospective provider mothers and their
children must pass health examinations.

Central office placement counselors make a real effort to place
children in day homes near their own homes. In the Family Day
Care system, described in Part IV, the majority of children are
placed within three or four blocks of their homes, and many can
be placed within their own apartment buildings. Parents particularly liked this aspect of the system and remarked that they appreciated keeping the children in their own communities, "near home
where older brothers and sisters can come after school," as one
parent put it.

In addition to child placement and determination of provider
eligibility, the central administrative office usually employs a vocational counselor who coordinates vocational testing, training, and
placement for career mothers whose children are being cared for in
day homes. In some cases, vocational counselors are staff of the
child-care system. In other instances, such personnel may be on
loan from other agencies.

Women receiving Aid to Families with Dependent Children
(AFDC) and low-income families are the major users of organized
home care. In the Family Day Care system a woman may participate
either as a provider mother or career mother. Frequently, women initially entering the home care system as provider mothers decide to
further their careers through training. Career ladders within home-

care systems have enabled many women to advance within the system, a few of them advancing to top policy-making positions. Other women have advanced their careers by moving outside the system.

Training for provider mothers is conducted by central office staff or special consultants who schedule regular training sessions. In the largest system in our study, training consultants are paid by the local Board of Education to provide both preservice training and fifteen weekly or biweekly in-service training sessions for participating mothers. Mothers receive transportation and baby-sitting allowances to attend these sessions.

Supervisory personnel from the central office visit day homes regularly for quality control. In one system, visiting supervisors are responsible for ongoing training of provider mothers and field trips; they also frequently take care of children when provider mothers are ill. In addition, they keep records on participating families. These supervisors are the link between the day homes and the system administration, providing adult companionship for provider mothers as well as needed technical assistance.

In one large child-care system, the day homes are organized around local subcenters. Each subcenter may assume administrative responsibility for 20 to 200 individual homes. While child-care systems typically detail curricula and activities for children in day homes, funding is insufficient for adequate food, materials, equipment, and early childhood education training. However, observers of day homes found them to be exceptionally warm, and children appeared happy and secure.

One difficulty with home care noted by several participants is that of supporting the parent role. Career mothers who leave their children in a child-care home during the full working day have expressed an apprehension of losing the primary attachment of their children. Many children appear to become very dependent on their "foster mothers." The home-care programs in our study felt that this difficulty could be overcome if additional funds were available to work closely with parents.

Table 9.3 gives a home care system annual budget for 5,000 children, based on our current cost estimates.

Table 9.3
Home Care System Annual Budget[1] (5,000 children)

I. Care and Teaching		
1,000 Parent-caretakers @ $3,800[2]	$3,800,000	
Fringe benefits and payroll taxes @ 10%	380,000	
Educational consumables @ $30/child	150,000	
Other @ $35/child[3]	175,000	
Subtotal		$4,505,000
(cost per child)		(901)
II. Administration		
System Director @ $30,000[4]	30,000	
Assistant System Director @ $24,000[4]	24,000	
3 Subsystem Assistants @ $14,000[4]	42,000	
3 Clerk-typists @ $5,700[4]	17,100	
System Bookkeeper @ $12,000[4]	12,000	
40 Subsystem Directors @ $9,400	376,000	
40 Secretary/Bookkeepers @ $5,700	228,000	
80 Home Aides @ $4,500	360,000	
Fringe benefits and payroll taxes @ 10%	109,000	
Other @ $74/child[5]	370,000	
Subtotal		$1,568,100
(cost per child)		(314)
III. Feeding		
Foodstuffs @ $132/child	660,000	
Other @ $5/child[6]	25,000	
Subtotal		685,000
(cost per child)		(137)

IV. Occupancy

Home expenses @ $220/home/year	220,000	
Office space[7]	32,000	
Subtotal		252,000
(cost per child)		(50)
Total	$7,010,100	
Cost per child	$1,402	
Cost per child, all salaries raised 15%	$1,564	

1. All figures based on averages from Abt Associates, *A Study in Child Care, 1970-71,* unless otherwise indicated.

2. This average is roughly 15 percent above current minimum wage ($3,328/ year) but below poverty level ($4,000 for a family of four). Please note that this parent-caretaker receives in addition $900 per year for home and child expenses. It *may* also be assumed that of the five children, one or more might be own children. It is difficult to compare payment per hour (the Massachusetts Early Education Project's suggestion) with present payments per child in Massachusetts. (Under the present system the caretaker must pay child and home expenses out of her per-child earnings.) We believe, however, that these budgeted salaries are actually higher than modal earnings of most present parent-caretakers in family day care.

3. Field trips, equipment depreciation, miscellaneous expenses.

4. Based on systems of comparable size from the Abt study.

5. Equipment depreciation, office supplies, telephone, staff travel, liability insurance, and audit and legal fees.

6. Nonfood supplies.

7. An average of 75 square feet/person $\times$ 169 people requiring office space $\times$ $2.50/square foot rental.

Mixed Systems and Costs

Mixed systems are those like the Family Day Care Career Program, which includes both centers and day homes. Staff and parents we talked to who have had contact with or considered mixed systems expressed a clear preference for this kind of care. A mixed system obviously provides more options for parents than either center care or home care alone. Mixed systems seem to combine some of the best features of both home and center care: parents can keep children close to their homes, thus reducing transportation problems, while associated centers can provide curricula, materials and equipment, emergency service, and staff training for comprehensive child care.

At first glance home care appears to be less expensive than center care. For sick children, handicapped children, emergency care, for children from outlying areas, and especially for infants, this is indeed the case. But for preschoolers and school-age children, adequately funded home care is almost as costly as center care. Lower costs in some home-care systems occur only where systems pay provider mothers less than the federal minimum wage, as mentioned earlier. In the Northeast, mothers earn anywhere from $.25 to $2.00 an hour, with the average at $.95 an hour; in the South, hourly payments are considerably lower. Moreover, the educational programs offered are severely underfunded. If you're considering providing home care, don't count on saving money except with respect to special children, children from outlying areas, infants, staff training, and the like.

Developing a budget for a home-care system or mixed system presents some special problems. We could adequately analyze only the Family Day Care program, which has a central office and sub-centers to support its day homes and which is considered to be severely underfunded with respect to both provider-mother salaries and the educational program. Making allowance for the salary problem by imputing payment of federal minimum wages (see the Family Day Care Budget, pages 227-230), this type of system would allot about half the budget for child care and teaching, a fifth of total resources for administration, and another fifth for food and health costs.

Those who want to explore the possibility of a mixed system would likely want to make further changes by allowing for more adequate center space and educational programs. A possible budget for a center-home mixed system serving 5,000 children is presented in Table 9.4 on the following pages.

Table 9.4
Center-Home Mixed System Annual Budget[1] (5,000 children)

I. Care and Teaching

700 Parent-caretakers @ $3,800[2]	$2,660,000
188 Caretaker-teachers @ $4,500	846,000
Fringe benefits and payroll taxes @ 10%	350,600
Educational consumables @ $30/child	150,000
Other @ $35/child[3]	175,000
Subtotal	$4,181,600
(cost per child)	(836)

II. Administration

System Director @ $30,000	30,000
Assistant System Director @ $24,000	24,000
3 Subsystem Assistants @ $14,000	42,000
3 Clerk-typists @ $5,700	17,100
System Bookkeeper @ $12,000	12,000
20 Subsystem Center Directors @ $12,000	240,000
20 Subsystem Assistant Center Directors @ $7,000	140,000
20 Subsystem Center Secretaries @ $5,400	108,000
20 Subsystem Center Bookkeepers (1/2 time) @ $6,000	60,000
40 Home Aides @ $4,500	180,000
Fringe benefits and payroll taxes @ 10%	85,300
Other @ $74/child[4]	370,000
Subtotal	1,308,400
(cost per child)	(262)

III. Feeding

20 Cooks @ $5,300	106,000
Fringe benefits and payroll taxes @ 10%	10,600
Foodstuffs @ $132/child	660,000
Other @ $9/child[5]	45,000
Subtotal	821,600
(cost per child)	(164)

IV. Occupancy

20 Custodians (1/2 time) @ $4,600	46,000	
Fringe benefits and payroll taxes @ 10%	4,600	
Rent:		
$175/child for 1,500 children in centers	262,500	
$220/home/year for 700 homes	154,000	
Other @ $40/child for 1,500 children in centers[6]	60,000	
Subtotal		$527,100
(cost per child)		(105)
Total	$6,838,700	
Cost per child	$1,367	
Cost per child, all salaries raised 15%	$1,528	

1. All figures drawn from other system model budgets (Tables 9.2 and 9.3), unless otherwise indicated.

2. This average is roughly 15 percent above current minimum wage ($3,328/ year) but below poverty level ($4,000 for a family of four). Please note that this parent-caretaker receives in addition $900 per year for home and child expenses. It is difficult to compare payment per hour (the Massachusetts Early Education Project's suggestion) with present payments per child in Massachusetts. (Under the present system the caretaker must pay child and home expenses out of her per-child earnings.) We believe, however, that these budgeted salaries are actually higher than modal earnings of most present parent-caretakers in family day care.

3. Field trips, equipment depreciation, miscellaneous.

4. Equipment depreciation, office supplies, telephone, staff travel, liability insurance, and audit and legal fees.

5. Equipment depreciation and nonfood supplies.

6. Housekeeping supplies, utilities, taxes, and insurance.

If you know someone who wants to start a day care operation be sure they're prepared to give up sleep.

> Subcenter Director, Family Day
> Care Career Program
> New York, New York

Start-up Procedure
We've devoted most of this book to programs already in operation. The centers in our study were relatively new but past the start-up phase. The chief thing we learned, however, was that it takes a great deal of staff effort and resources to survive that first year. You can save yourself a lot of time and money by getting off the ground smoothly and efficiently. From the initial decision to start a child-care program to full-scale operation is a mighty leap. From our continued work and by reviewing the work of others in this area of child care, we've identified a number of steps almost every operator needs to know about. Some of them may not apply in your locality, or you may find extra steps we haven't mentioned as child care becomes more prevalent and new regulations come into effect. But generally speaking, here's the sequence most programs follow:

1. Initial planning

   Feasibility study

2. Implementation plan

   Detailed program design

3. Establishment of a facility

   Selection of a site (location and design)

   Negotiation of local zoning, health, and fire laws

   Financing

   Construction or renovation of facility

   Purchase and installation of equipment

   Utilities connection (electricity, gas, water, phone)

   Special tax assessments

4. Preoperational activities

   Application for state license

Legal organization

Insurance coverage

Fund raising

Staff recruitment and training

Initial advertising and public relations

Vendor/supplier negotiations

Initial program operation before operating capacity is reached.

Initial Planning Careful, intelligent, and informed planning maximizes your chances of success and minimizes start-up costs. Initial planning consists primarily of a feasibility study. Before you do anything, you must determine whether there's a need for day care in your community (or for *more* day care) *and whether you can meet that need at a tolerable cost.* This usually means making a demand survey and a survey of existing supply so you can estimate excess demand, if it exists. The nature of that excess demand—the kinds and amounts of services demanded and the prices potential users are willing to pay—will give you a basis for estimating total operating costs and whatever portion of those costs will have to be met by sources other than user fees. Again, there's no point in going a step further until you know that what you're offering can and will be paid for by either parents, organizational support, or government agencies. *Nearly all day-care planners overestimate the number of parents who need care and will pay for it the first year.*

Implementation Plan If you determine that a child-care program is feasible, you must next outline the major characteristics of the program you'll be offering and develop an overall plan to ensure the most efficient sequencing and scheduling of implementation tasks. One of the first major tasks in implementation is development of a detailed program design. A program design is important not only to show you where you're going in a broad sense but also to lay the groundwork for future considerations, such as building design and application for state licensing. Included in your program design should be:

Your plan for administration and staffing

Description of your proposed location

A possible floor plan of facility, showing indoor and outdoor
square footage for the number of children you'll have

List of furniture needed

List of indoor and outdoor equipment

Number and ages of children to be cared for

Proposed fees, if any

Daily program schedule

Menu plan

Budget of anticipated income and expenditures.

Establishment of a Facility Most of your nonpersonnel, amor-
tizable start-up costs are incurred in this area. Obviously, you need
a reasonable assurance that an acceptable facility is available before you can proceed with the rest of your plans. Location and
design of your site are determined by your feasibility study (to
find where heaviest demand is located), by the availability of acceptable land and/or existing structures, and by zoning laws. The
proposed facility must meet local zoning requirements, which can
present an obstacle if the location you want is in a residential area.
Proprietary child-care programs are considered "semicommercial"
operations, so be prepared to negotiate at some length if permission is required for residential location. Liaison with the local
health and fire safety authorities must also be developed to ensure
that all regulations are met. If liaison isn't close, you could find
yourself with unanticipated additional renovation or new construction costs. It's a good idea to develop working relationships
with local authorities from the very beginning of your project.
Although it may take more time, you're making their jobs easier
by keeping them informed instead of dropping your operation on
them as an accomplished fact. Usually they appreciate being
brought in early, and they can also make your job go more
smoothly.

Arrangements for funds to cover start-up costs must be made
early in the implementation phase. Although much of the personnel time required for start-up is often donated (requiring no cash
outlay), new construction or renovation, purchase of equipment,

staff training, and early program operation before capacity is
reached all require substantial cash outlays.

In some cases, government-subsidized programs can get planning
grants and grants for renovation. Government grants for new construction are at present rarely made. If you aren't in a position to
get grant money for start-up, you'll have to have equity or debt
financing or both. Equity financing is undertaken by private and
parent corporations organized to provide child-care services. In the
latter case, parents purchase shares in the program. Debt financing
for small programs must be obtained from a bank. For financing a
building, banks usually require that the structure be easily convert-
ible into office space. The Small Business Administration will
sometimes guarantee loans made by banks to child-care programs.

If you're going to construct a new building or are planning to
renovate an existing one, you'll need to find an architect, negotiate a contract with a builder, and make provision for periodic inspection of the work. These steps are usually the single most
costly element of the start-up phase.[1] Kitchen, office, play, and
maintenance equipment and child and adult furniture must then
be selected, purchased, and installed.[2] Next, arrangements must be
made for telephones, electricity, gas and water, and septic systems.
Typically, connection fees and deposits are required. In addition, a
new child-care facility may be subject to special tax assessment for
water and sidewalks.

Preoperational Activities In addition to establishing your facility,
there are a number of time-consuming and costly steps to be undertaken before your program can become fully operational.

You must apply for a state license. The application must usually
contain a comprehensive description of your proposed program
(using the kind of information drawn from the detailed program
design). Frequently, the proposed director must have a degree
and/or previous experience in the child-care field. State fire safety
codes must also be met, although these are generally less stringent
than local codes. In addition to state licensing, some of the larger
cities (Chicago and Oklahoma City, for example) have also established licensing requirements. Be prepared to spend a good deal of

time readying your applications and discussing special problems
with licensing officials.

The legal organization of your program is also crucial. Child-care
programs may be operated under public auspices (such as Head
Start), private nonprofit auspices (church-sponsored programs), or
private profit-making auspices. In the latter case, the business may
either be a corporation or a proprietorship. Unless a program is
operated by a public agency (such as a Community Action
Agency), arrangements must be made for establishing the program
as a legal entity, in which case the services of a lawyer will be
needed.

Arrangements must be made for adequate insurance coverage.
Liability insurance is essential, regardless of program design. Other
types of insurance typically required are fire insurance, workmen's
compensation insurance, auto insurance if you're providing transportation, business interruption insurance, and insurance against
vandalism and malicious mischief.

Unless all costs are to be covered by parent fees or a government
grant, funding from other sources must be solicited before the program can begin operating. Fund raising requires a great deal of
time and stamina. It may require educating the community about
child care through media campaigns and public speaking engage-
ments, and it may entail a lot of personal contact work with area
businesses, charitable groups, and organizations. A well-chosen
board of directors composed of influential community members
can often spread the fund-raising load and result in increased donations.

Key staff members must be recruited, interviewed, and hired before the program can begin operation. We've mentioned several
times how important a good staff can be: a good staff means the
difference between a good program and a mediocre one. In particular, much time and care should be taken to locate a good director: this person will greatly influence the subsequent development
of the program.

The need for staff training prior to program operation depends
to some extent on the amount of training and/or experience the
staff already has. In any event, a minimum of two weeks of orientation to your proposed program and procedures should be pro-

vided, together with special training by professionals who are experts in the age groups and backgrounds of children you'll be serving.

Parents must be informed about your program through advertising and a public relations campaign in your area's media. If you've estimated demand fairly accurately, a good campaign should do the job here. In time, word-of-mouth and low-key campaigns, plus your own waiting list, should keep you at or near capacity. It is important, however, to remember that most programs are not near capacity for the first 12 to 18 months. This is partly a matter of getting known, partly because it takes time to get the right mix of part-time and full-time children to reach capacity throughout the day. Staff needed for programs functioning at less than capacity are of course beyond the routine costs you expect.

If you'll be buying supplies on a controlled and regular basis, you'll want to arrange with suppliers or vendors for your materials and foodstuffs at this point. Some programs contract out their food programs to local boards of education or other agencies or firms, others contract transportation, laundry, and additional services.

Start-up Costs

All of the preliminary activities of starting up have associated costs. Some, such as the outlays for equipment, can be amortized over the useful life of the item and thus converted to an operating expense. Such costs may be expected to recur sometime in the future of the program and are not unique to the start-up phase. Other costs, such as the salaries of those involved only in establishing the center, are once-only costs unique to start-up operations.

The total of all start-up costs represents the initial capitalization of your program. This total and the distribution of the total between recurrent and nonrecurrent costs are important to the would-be operator of a child-care program.

Start-up costs for a particular program will depend on a number of factors, including:

Price differences: Construction costs and labor costs vary considerably from region to region. Even within a region, such costs will vary between urban and rural areas.

Program differences: Start-up costs for a center program differ from those for a home-care program in nature and perhaps in level (evidence is inconclusive). The comprehensiveness or scope of your program also affects start-up costs. For example, if transportation will be provided, you may have to purchase a vehicle.

Special circumstances: While it may be possible for some new programs to locate in facilities that need only modest renovation, you may have to build your center or use an existing building that requires extensive remodeling.

Other factors will affect your start-up costs. Efficient hiring and scheduling can save you money in the personnel category and minimize the interval of staff underutilization before you reach capacity enrollment. Finally, the way you use in-kind resources will affect your initial cash outlay. In-kind donations of labor have, in the past, served to conceal the true cost of start-up because only cash costs have been reported. These in-kind donations may or may not be as plentiful in the future, once your program is established.

Start-up costs for a child-care program can be classified as follows:

Capital costs of land, building, and equipment

Working capital

Professional and nonprofessional labor costs plus miscellaneous other expenses.

Capital Costs of Land, Building, and Equipment There is an incredible variation in the price of land, depending on location. Land in rural areas may cost only a few hundred dollars per acre, while comparable urban per-acre costs may be hundreds of thousands of dollars. An average cost for land in a middle-class suburb of a Midwestern metropolitan area has been estimated at $1 per square foot.[3] The total land area for a center serving 60 children has been estimated at 250 square feet per child, including building space, outdoor play areas, and areas for driveways and sidewalks.[4] Thus, a rough estimate of average land costs *per child* would be $250.

Construction costs for new child-care facilities have been estimated at $16 to $25 per square foot, based on the reported cost of various kinds of nonresidential buildings.[5] Assuming total indoor space requirements per child to range from 50 to 75 square feet (the legal minimum in most states is 35 square feet per child, but this is very restricted), the per-child cost of a new facility could range from $800 to $1,875. Capital outlays for facilities may be even higher than this. In a recent publication, the Women's Bureau reported the following:

Over the past few years various sources have been consulted and the consensus estimate for total capital outlay has been approximately $2,000 per child. In some areas costs are much higher.[6]

Renovation costs can vary from the few hundred dollars required to convert church space and private homes (in good condition) into child-care facilities to many thousands of dollars for new construction.[7]

Equipment costs for your center will depend on the demands of your program design and the willingness of your staff to make do with used and homemade equipment. High and low costs for a 60-child center have been estimated in a recent volume on the planning and operation of a day-care center and are given here in Table 10.1. Equipment costs for a 60-child center have been estimated by a day-care economist at approximately $20,000, or $333 per child,[8] so the range of costs given in Table 10.1 appears to be reasonable.

For day homes, there are usually no additional land costs, since the land on which the home is located is sufficient. The cost of renovation and equipment for home care may range from $50 to $300 per home.[9] Assuming an average of three children per home, the per-child costs here range from approximately $20 to $100.

If a facility is leased, the capital outlay for the land and building has been made by the owner and need not be provided for by the program operator. (The amortized value of these capital outlays will be reflected in the rental rates.)

Table 10.1
Equipment Costs

	Low	High
Educational	$1,705	$ 9,069
Caretaking and housekeeping	1,248	2,628
Office	440	1,890
Kitchen	6,000	8,000
Carpentry	217	—
Total	$9,610	$21,587
Cost per child	$160	$360

Source: E. Belle Evans, Beth Shub, and Marlene Weinstein, *Day Care: How to Plan, Develop, and Operate a Day Care Center* (Boston: Beacon Press, 1971), pp. 259, 263.

Working Capital Once your program begins operating, cash outlays (with the exception of underutilized staff, discussed next) are, by definition, for operating costs rather than start-up. These outlays must be made before income is received from user fees, government and/or private sources. If funding is from a government agency, you may experience a delay in payment of several months, so you'd be wise to provide for working capital to bridge the gap between initial operating cash outlays and receipt of your funds. The level of working capital required will vary from one week of operating expense (for centers whose only source of income is weekly user fees) to several months (for centers totally dependent on government funds). Assuming that the weekly cost per child will range from $10 to $40, the need for working capital per child could range from $10 (1 week × 10) to $480 (12 weeks × 40).

Professional and Nonprofessional Labor and Miscellaneous Costs Included in this category are all the labor required for planning and implementing your child-care program, the cost of underutilized staff during the first few months of operation, and the miscellaneous fees and tax assessments incurred during start-up.

One day-care economist has estimated that for a 60-child center, these costs could range from $10,000 to $40,000 with close cost control and could go as high as $60,000 with poor cost control.[10] Thus, the estimated per-child cost could range from $170 to

$1,000. Another economist has estimated such costs in the $500 to $1,000 per-child range.[11] One center with a capacity of 70 children, funded by the government, received a $60,000 planning grant to cover this category of start-up costs (that is, about $850 per child).[12] A range of $200 to $1,000 per child in this area seems reasonable. For a day-care home, start-up costs in this category (with equivalent provision for training and licensing) have been estimated to range from $230 to $650 per home.[13] Taken together, costs total as follows:

Capital cost of land, building, and equipment may range from $714 to $1,899 per child.

Working capital needed may range from $13 to $625 per child.

Labor and miscellaneous start-up costs may range from $250 to $1,167 per child.

Total start-up costs may thus range from $1,000 to $3,750 per child.

The most important conclusions suggested by this review are as follows. First, the range of estimated start-up costs is dramatic, even when the structure of demand is known. Second, the need to recruit money and other resources to cover start-up costs is critical to day-care success. Third, the level of start-up costs is very sensitive to the mix of homes and centers used for meeting needs. Because of the generally lower cost of facilities renovation, home care may require less "front-end" money. Finally, day-care planners at the local, state, and national level are beginning to realize that start-up costs, on an average basis, are higher than they first appear because many centers fail. The cost of these failures must also be taken into account.

Notes

1. For discussions of facility design considerations, see William W. Chase and Minnie Berson, "Planning Preschool Facilities," *American Education,* Vol. 3, Nos. 2-7 (December-January); and Deutsch, Martin, Nimnicht, and others, *Memorandum on Facilities For Early Childhood Education* (New York: Educational Facilities Laboratories, 1966).

2. For a discussion of considerations in selecting equipment, see U.S. Office of Economic Opportunity, *Equipment and Supplies: Guidelines for Administrators and Teachers in Child Development* (Washington, D.C.: U.S. Office of Economic Opportunity, 1965).

3. Joseph A. Lane, "Program Characteristics of the Standard (Mark IV) Day Care Center" (paper prepared for Abt Associates Inc., Cambridge, Mass., Sept. 15, 1970), p. 6.

4. Ibid.

5. Inner City Fund, *Potential Cost and Economic Benefit of Industrial Day Care,* A Report for the U.S. Department of Labor, Washington, D.C., May, 1971 (Washington, D.C.: Inner City Fund, 1971), p. 19. Construction costs of $15 to $23 per square foot were used in a recent study of day-care centers. See Contracting Corporation of America, *Day Care Center Feasibility Study: Preliminary Facts and Findings* (Chicago: Contracting Corporation of America, 1970), p. 30.

6. U.S. Department of Labor, Workplace Standards Administration, Women's Bureau, *Day Care Services: Industry's Involvement,* Bulletin No. 296 (Washington, D.C.: Government Printing Office, 1971), p. 22.

7. The KLH Child Development Center in Cambridge, Massachusetts, is located in a converted warehouse. Consisting of 12,000 square feet, it cost $75,500 to renovate (including architect's fees) or $6.30 per square foot. With a capacity of 70 children, the per-child cost of renovation was $1,080. See Joseph R. Curran and John W. Jordan, *The KLH Experience, An Evaluation Report of Day Care in Action at the KLH Child Development Center, Cambridge, Mass., 1970* (Cambridge, Mass.: KLH Child Development Center, Inc., 1970).

8. Lane, "Program Characteristics," p. 7.

9. Mary P. Rowe, "Start-up Costs for Child Care Homes" (paper prepared for Abt Associates Inc., Cambridge, Mass., Oct. 15, 1971), p. 1.

10. Joseph A. Lane, "Pre-opening and Start-up Costs" (paper prepared for Abt Associates Inc., Cambridge, Mass., Sept. 15, 1970), p. 2.

11. U.S. Senate Child Care Hearings for S. 2003, September 1971, p. 276.

12. Urban Research Corporation, *Proceedings of the Conference on Industry and Day Care* (Chicago: Urban Research Corporation, 1970), p. 22.

13. Rowe, "Start-up Costs."

To give you a clearer picture of what's involved in a typical day-care center, this chapter describes the program design, staffing, and functional budget for a typical center with an average daily attendance of 50 children. This basic program is common to all child-care operations regardless of size or scope and includes child care and teaching, administration, feeding, health, and occupancy. The model is a conglomerate picture of day care, incorporating many of the characteristics of the 20 centers we studied.

Center Layout
The floor plan of our typical center, shown in Figure 11.1, is based on the Central City Head Start Day Care Center. Located in a community building, the center consists of five classrooms with toilets and storage space in each (one classroom for each group and one multipurpose room), one adult bathroom, one kitchen, a small nurse's office/isolation room, an office area with desks for the director and administrative assistant, and a parent-teacher room. The multipurpose room is used for large-muscle activities, nap time, and meetings. All equipment and facilities are child-size or adapted for child use. The center is safe, warm, clean, and fun, painted in bright, cheerful colors. Equipment includes tables and chairs in the four classrooms and folding cots in the multipurpose room. Outside there's a fenced-in playground, which is a combination of grassy and paved areas. Typical equipment includes swings, a slide, climbing equipment, tricycles, playhouses, crawling tunnels, balls, and so on. The center has adequate square footage per child both indoors and outdoors to comply with local and funding agency licensing regulations. The indoor average is 80 square feet/child, and the outdoor average is 183.

Program Characteristics
The center is a nonprofit corporation in an urban setting and is funded by a public agency. It operates from 7:30 A.M. to 5:30 P.M. Monday to Friday, 52 weeks a year. The center serves preschoolers, ages three through five, of differing ethnic backgrounds. Admission policy is determined by the funding source, and no severely handicapped children are enrolled. The center is staffed to ensure an overall teacher/child ratio of 1:5 for its average daily

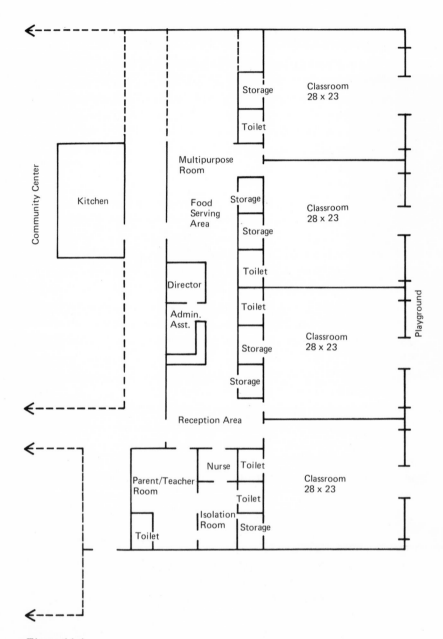

Figure 11.1
Floor plan of a typical day-care center

attendance (ADA) of 50 children. Children are grouped roughly by age, but allowances are made for individual child maturity and needs. There are two classes of 10 children and two of 15 children, with the younger kids in the smaller groups. Each class has one teacher and one assistant teacher, and there's a floating aide for every two classes. This center recruits its staff from the community to reflect the ethnic backgrounds of its children, and the roster includes several male staff. No volunteer labor is used.

Policy Making The board of directors is composed of parents of children in the program and community representatives from government, private, and public agencies. The board meets once a month to formulate long-range policy, approve the annual budget, determine admission policies (within the regulations of the sponsor), approve personnel decisions, and help with fund raising.

There is also a parent advisory committee composed only of parents and elected by all the center's parents. This committee advises on policy matters, helps mobilize resources from the parent community, channels advice and concerns to the board and center director, and, in general, serves as the voice of all center parents. The parent advisory committee also helps plan parent activities.

The director represents the center at board meetings and hires, fires, and determines salaries for staff with the approval of the board. He or she is thus involved in ongoing evaluation of both the staff and the center's overall program. In addition to drawing up the annual budget for submission to the board, the director is also responsible for short-range and day-to-day policy making and program planning.

Staffing Delineating absolute staff qualifications for this center is difficult, since individual personalities and situations vary. With all staff, reliability and punctuality are very important. As for formal educational qualifications, there are no hard and fast requirements, since formal education isn't necessarily a reliable indicator of staff quality. Relevant training and/or work experience is, of course, desirable. An undergraduate college degree may be desirable for the director. Education levels for teaching staff vary widely, from little formal education to a college, even graduate, degree. There seems to be a general trend for the higher-educated teachers to fill the higher teaching positions, but this center, like many, varies somewhat from that pattern.

In our interviews with teachers, one complaint has been voiced repeatedly. Teachers feel that time spent on noncare duties (housekeeping chores, fee collection, non-child-related paperwork) hinders their performance as teachers. In this center, teachers have been relieved of as many of these duties as possible. When such chores are unavoidable, they are distributed evenly among staff and aides. All full-time staff have at least a 45-minute break (again in response to teacher interviews): the pace of working with children is fast, and a break gives the teacher a rest so he or she can be more effective with the kids over the full day. Teachers do not have tasks to perform during this break.

There are 15 paid staff members and no volunteers. The staff is broken down as follows:

1 director, full-time
1 administrative assistant, full-time
1 head teacher, full-time
3 teachers, full-time
4 assistant teachers, full-time
2 aides, full-time
1 cook, part-time (27 1/2 hours/weekly)
1 custodian, part-time (15 hours/week)
1 nurse, part-time (8 hours/week).

Staff Training The staff training program isn't extensive, but it does offer an initial orientation and in-service training. Orientation consists of an explanation of program policies and practices, an introduction to the center and staff, and a period of working in the classroom, which is followed by a discussion session. In-service training involves working in the classroom with an experienced teacher who trains through suggestion and example. All teaching staff receive this training. In addition, there are weekly meetings of all center staff where specific classroom problems can be talked over. Sometimes an outside speaker or a staff member presents a talk or film on a child-development subject.

Staff Development The director works in the administrative office and outside the center. Her or his hours are at least 40 a week and often more. Absences are scheduled so that the administrative assistant, who works 40 hours a week, can cover for the director. The administrative assistant's hours might be 8 A.M. to 4 P.M. or 7:30 A.M. to 3:30 P.M. to allow contact with parents for fee collection. The nurse works two mornings a week, probably from 8 A.M. to noon. Reasonable hours for the cook would be 9:30 A.M. to 2:30 P.M. The custodian works 3 hours daily, probably from 5:30 to 8:30 P.M., or whatever best suits him and the center.

All 10 teaching staff are in the center eight hours a day and arrive and depart on staggered schedules. One teacher (including the head teacher) and one assistant are in charge of each classroom while the two aides divide their time among the four classes, although one aide may spend more time in the head teacher's class. In arranging staff schedules, it should be kept in mind that different teachers may be involved in early morning and later afternoon activities, so they'll need time to get set up and briefed on any events of the morning or previous afternoon. At least one teacher or assistant teacher should be with the kids at all times. This is especially important at the beginning and end of the day. An aide is likely to be young and/or inexperienced and new to the center. He or she might not be equipped to handle an emergency or an unusual situation alone.

The teaching staff are scheduled so the head teacher is available to supervise and help out at the beginning of the day, well in advance of structured activities. Teachers should also be in the center in time for structured periods or before they begin, if possible. The aides are scheduled so there is always at least one aide in the center at all times. We aren't saying this schedule is right for every center, but it would work for our typical program. It assumes a gradual arrival and staggered departure of the kids and is based on the assumption that the average number of hours each child spends in the center daily is about 8 1/2. This schedule, like those of most of the centers we studied, is flexible and subject to change if child attendance patterns call for it. For example, if most of the 50 children arrived by 8 A.M., more teachers would be needed on the early shift. Table 11.1 shows a possible staff schedule for this typical day-care center.

Core Program

Child Care and Teaching This center offers children thoughtful care in a safe, clean setting. While no detailed formal curriculum is followed, lesson plans are prepared in advance, based on various books and materials related to preschool care and teaching. Teachers keep informal, anecdotal notes on each child, which are used in progress conferences between teachers and parents. (These conferences are held several times a year or as requested by parents.) The children participate in field trips, informal play, individual and small-group activities. They can select from a wide variety of educational toys and materials, receive a good deal of one-to-one attention from the teaching staff, and, in general, are involved in a positive, supportive environment with emphasis on self-reliance, positive self-image, and so on.

Table 11.1
Staff Schedule

Time	Arrivals and Departures*
7:30	Teacher A and aide H arrive
8:00	Head teacher, administrative assistant, and nurse arrive
8:30	Teachers B and C and assistant teachers D and E arrive
9:00	Assistant teacher F arrives
9:30	Assistant teacher G, aide I, and cook arrive
12 noon	Nurse departs
2:30	Cook departs
3:00	Teacher A and aide H depart
4:00	Head teacher and administrative assistant depart
4:30	Teachers B and C and assistant teachers D and E depart
5:00	Assistant teacher F departs
5:30	Assistant teacher G and aide I depart Custodian arrives
8:30	Custodian departs

* The director works a minimum of eight hours per day. The time she or he is required to be in the center is flexible.

Health All children are required to have a medical and dental examination before admission and annually thereafter. Children must also have all inoculations and immunizations specified by program policy. The center checks to make sure these things have been done and arranges for the child to receive this care, if necessary. The center nurse instructs all staff in first aid and emergency procedures. Each child is checked daily for signs of illness. If a child becomes ill while at the center, his or her parents are notified, and the child is either taken for treatment or kept in an isolation room until the parents arrive. On admission, parents furnish a medical history for the child and sign an emergency permission form. Medical records are updated when serious illness occurs. Height and weight records are kept for each child to assess long-term growth and to help evaluate the center's nutrition program.

Nutrition The center serves a hot lunch and a morning and afternoon snack daily. Menus are planned in advance by a cook who confers with a local dietitian from time to time. (Dietitians are often employed by a local public school system, a university, public health agency, or other organization.) Meals are well-balanced and attractively served, and an effort is made to include a variety of foods. If a child has come to the center without breakfast, he is served a bowl of cereal. Teaching staff eat with the children to provide a warm and positive mealtime atmosphere.

Transportation No transportation is provided to and from the center. This responsibility rests with parents. However, the center does provide transportation for field trips and special events.

Table 11.2 shows a likely daily activity schedule for this center.

Staff Roles and Responsibilities
Figure 11.2 is an organization chart for our typical center for 50 children. This section lists the duties of staff members in detail.

Director The director coordinates the overall program and is the key person in charge of administration and all other areas. She or he

Table 11.2
Daily Activity Schedule

Time	Activity
7:30	Children begin to arrive — free play
9:00	Most kids present — classes separate, health check, structured activity
10:00	Snack, clean-up, toilet
10:30	Outdoor play or indoor active play
11:30	Quiet activities (music, stories) in preparation for lunch
12:00	Lunch, clean-up, toilet
12:30	Nap preparations and nap begins
2:30	During nap time, children who awaken early or do not sleep engage in quiet free play
3:00	Snack, clean-up, toilet
3:30	Outdoor play or group games, "Sesame Street," etc.
4:30	Free play until departure
5:30	All children have departed

Formulates both long-range and day-to-day policy, together with the policy-making structure

Is in charge of preadmission parent relations and oversees ongoing parent relations: shares parent relations with staff but is specifically responsible for admissions, group activities, and any contact that is not child-specific or related to particular classroom concerns

Heads up the health component in a management capacity, along with the nurse, who spends most of her time actually working with children and staff

Is in charge of purchasing according to the requests of teaching and support staff for supplies and equipment or according to her own perceptions of need; delegates actual ordering or purchasing to administrative assistant

Is in charge of overall staff matters: supervision, scheduling, hiring, evaluation, firing, and salaries

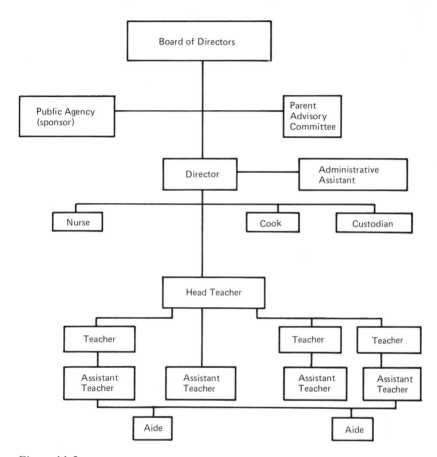

Figure 11.2
Organization chart for a typical center for 50 children

Handles all financial and budgetary matters (working under the overall budgetary control of the policy-making structure): prepares center budget for approval, keeps center books, pays staff, approves expenditures, and raises funds from the community and elsewhere (with help from the governing board)

Mobilizes resources (including donated money, equipment, and time and services from outside agencies or groups): develops linkages with community agencies to promote cooperation (for example, establishes a working relationship with a public health agency, which agrees to treat children)

Coordinates program planning for all aspects of the center

Works a minimum of 40 hours/week (most directors in our study worked 45-50 hours); attempts to be in the center at the beginning and end of the day as often as possible in order to be accessible to parents

Oversees orientation and in-service training for teaching staff.

Administrative Assistant The main duties here involve typing, filing, collecting fees and keeping fee records, coordinating all record keeping, assisting with purchasing, and so on. This person works under the direction of the director but is not involved in policy decisions or child care and teaching. In addition, the administrative assistant

Relieves director of other administrative duties, which often involve considerable responsibility

Is an office manager in charge of all purchasing under the director's guidance; maintains center's books

Acts as stand-in when director is out of the center but has more limited authority

Serves as an information and public relations source to visitors, potential clients, and parents.

Head Teacher The head teacher performs all the duties of a teacher, outlined in the next section. In addition, he or she

Relieves director of the majority of management for child care and teaching, which involves planning, organization, supervision, and day-to-day evaluation of the educational program in all classrooms, including his or her own: spends a quarter of the day (or two hours) on management activities

Is out of the classroom more often than a regular teacher: during these absences, an aide works in the classroom under the direction of the assistant teacher. Some absences will simply be interruptions as other teachers confer about plans or specific problems

Has to coordinate his or her time well so that work with other teachers does not take away from work with children.

Teachers These activities vary, but in general teachers

Have primary responsibility for lesson planning and implementing the educational program

Are in charge of management for their part of child care and teaching, supervising assistant teachers and aides

Check supplies and equipment and request needed items from the director

Handle ongoing parent relations, under the supervision of the director, and meet with individual parents periodically to report on child progress: teachers discuss concerns with parents and act on those concerns. They call homes to check on absent children

Maintain informal anecdotal records of child achievement and progress as well as problems

Maintain daily attendance records and daily sign-in sheets for parents

Are responsible for knowing the whereabouts of children at all times.

Assistant Teachers Assistant teachers do exactly what their title implies. In general, they

Help teachers perform all care and teaching activities in the classroom

Assist with parent relations

Take over in the classroom when teacher is absent

Contribute to the overall program through suggestions.

As mentioned earlier, the teaching staff is divided among four rooms, with one teacher and one assistant teacher per room. The two aides work wherever they're needed. The assistant teacher in the head teacher's classroom will have more responsibility because he or she will cover many absences. Teachers arrive and depart on a staggered basis with rotating shifts. Shifts are basically determined by need and staff preference where possible.

Aides Aides relieve teachers of some of the nonteaching duties that are a part of every day-care operation. They

Help out in the classrooms or on field trips as needed

Substitute for absent teachers or assistant teachers in times of sickness, vacation, or other absence

Perform duties that might otherwise take the teacher out of the classroom (stay with sick children in isolation room, for example)

Gather laundry once a week and get it ready for pick-up

Do light housekeeping—straighten up, mop up spills, etc., and help set up and put away special equipment but do not do things the kids are supposed to do themselves

Carry food between kitchen and classroom

Serve the afternoon snack after the cook goes home.

One of the aides will spend more time in the head teacher's classroom to help cover absences.

Cook The cook is largely responsible for the center's nutrition program. He or she

Works 27 1/2 hours a week, from 9:30 A.M. to 2:30 P.M. daily (this position might be suitable for a woman with school-age children); must be capable of planning an adequate, well-balanced nutrition program and carrying it out

Confers with dietitian from time to time to ensure good nutrition

Plans menus in advance

Keeps track of needs for equipment, supplies, and food (this includes paper meal service, if used) and requests additional items as needed

Prepares two snacks and one lunch daily

Cleans up after morning snack and lunch—does not do heavy cleaning.

Custodian The custodian is responsible for the maintenance and cleaning of the physical facility. In our typical center, he

Works 15 hours a week, three hours each evening after the center closes (hours are flexible)

Does all heavy cleaning and maintenance

Washes floors, bathrooms, kitchen, etc., every night

Repairs equipment and maintains facilities: does not do specialized work, such as plumbing and wiring

Is in charge of trash removal

Notifies director of any problems in his area.

Nurse The nurse is the focal point of the center's health program. She

Works two mornings a week (8 hours)

Checks to make sure all children have had their preadmission and annual medical and dental check-ups as well as necessary inoculations and immunizations: arranges for children to get this care if needed

Instructs staff in first aid and emergency procedures: gives emergency care when she's present

Gives children brief health checks for signs of illness

Answers parents' questions about child health

Weighs and measures all children periodically and keeps records of growth; keeps medical histories up to date

Confers with director on child health problems and helps the cook evaluate nutrition program.

Costs for Our Typical Center
The cost estimates we've developed for this center are based on averages taken across the 20 centers we studied: these costs are therefore representative of those programs. However, please keep in mind that personnel costs, rental costs, and, to a lesser extent, other costs may vary considerably from these estimates, depending on local market conditions.

Tables 11.3-11.6 show a model budget for a core program with an average daily attendance (ADA) of 50 children. Our average cost data are organized in functional categories (Table 11.4). The average cost of foodstuffs per child (ADA basis) was $150 per year, and this forms the basis for our estimate of foodstuffs and costs. Rental cost per child is calculated as the product of the average square feet of space per child (80) and the average annual rent per square foot ($2.50). We computed personnel costs by assigning salaries to each position based on salaries actually paid by centers. Fringe benefits and payroll taxes used represent the average rate among our centers (10.2 percent). For teachers, assistant teachers, the cook, nurse, and custodian, the full-time equivalent salary assigned was simply the average for such positions. Salary estimates for the other positions were derived as follows:

Director Our analysis shows a positive relationship between director's salary and center size (ADA). The relationship indicated a salary of $9,400 for a center serving 50 children. The average salary for directors of good programs, however, is somewhat higher ($9,700).

Administrative Assistant This position can be likened to that of a secretary with relatively heavy responsibilities, so the salary we've assigned is at the upper end for secretarial salaries. In our sample, salaries for this position ranged between those for an assistant teacher and for a full teacher. We're using here the average teacher salary of $6,000.

Head Teacher Salaries for head teachers with responsibilities similar to those we've outlined average about 12.5 percent above salaries for teachers, so this is what we've used.

Aide Average salary for aides is somewhat below the federal minimum wage. Because this probably reflects a lag in adjustment to minimum wage standards, we've used the minimum wage, or $3,450.

Once salaries, fringe benefits, and payroll taxes are computed, we estimate the total personnel component of the budget (Table 11.6). With per-child costs for the other components in each of the functional categories, the Functional Budget Detail (Table 11.5) can then be filled in. For example, foodstuffs cost per child is $150. The total cost of foodstuffs is simply $150/child × 50 children. Figures in Tables 11.3 and 11.4 are simply summary measures derived from Table 11.5.

Table 11.3
Summary of Operating Costs for Core Program of 50 Children (ADA)

Total estimated costs: $111,135
(74% personnel, 7% foodstuffs, 9% rent, 10% other)
Cost per child: $2,223 per year $1.06 per hour*

*Cost per child per hour based on estimate of child/hours as 8.4 hours/child/day x 250 days/year = 105,000 hours/year

Table 11.4
Functional Budget Summary for Core Program of 50 Children (ADA)

Category	Percentage of Total	Total Cost	Cost per Child
Care and teaching	56	$ 62,432	$1,249
Administration	19	21,171	423
Feeding	11	11,802	236
Health	1	1,650	33
Occupancy	13	14,080	282
Totals	100	$111,135	$2,223

Table 11.5
Functional Budget Detail for Core Program of 50 Children (ADA)

Category	Percentage of Category	Total Cost	Cost per Child
Care and teaching			
Personnel	94	$58,682	$1,174
Educational consumables	3	1,750	35
Other	3	2,000	40
Subtotal	100	$62,432	$1,249
Administration			
Personnel	80	16,971	339
Other	20	4,200	84
Subtotal	100	21,171	423
Feeding			
Personnel	32	3,802	76
Foodstuffs	64	7,500	150
Other	4	500	10
Subtotal	100	11,802	236
Health			
Personnel	79	1,300	26
Other	21	350	7
Subtotal	100	1,650	33
Occupancy			
Personnel	13	1,880	38
Rent	71	10,000	200
Other	16	2,200	44
Subtotal	100	14,080	282
Totals		$111,135	$2,223

Table 11.6
Personnel Component of Functional Budget for Core Program of 50 Children
(ADA)

Category		Salary Expenditure	
Care and Teaching			
1 Head teacher	@ 6,750	$ 6,750	
3 Teachers	@ 6,000	18,000	
4 Assistant teachers	@ 5,400	21,600	
2 Aides	@ 3,450	6,900	
Fringe benefits and payroll taxes	@ 10.2%	5,432	
Subtotal			$58,682
Administration			
1 Director	@ 9,400	9,400	
1 Administrative assistant	@ 6,000	6,000	
Fringe benefits and payroll taxes	@ 10.2%	1,571	
Subtotal			16,971
Feeding			
1 Cook, 2/3 time	@ 5,250	3,450	
Fringe benefits and payroll taxes	@ 10.2%	352	
Subtotal			3,802
Health			
1 Nurse, 1/5 time	@ 5,900	1,180	
Fringe benefits and payroll taxes	@ 10.2%	120	
Subtotal			1,300
Occupancy			
1 Custodian, 3/8 time	@ 4,550	1,706	
Fringe benefits and payroll taxes	@ 10.2%	174	
Subtotal			1,880
Total		$82,635	

The costs presented in these tables are essentially the same as those cited in Chapter 9 as representative of the 20 centers studied, with personnel costs accounting for three-fourths of the total budget.

Adjusting the Model Budget for Regions and Rising Costs

General Considerations The model budgets presented in Tables 11.3-11.6 are based on average 1970 costs in the centers studied. Some of the costs presented vary considerably over the United States and will vary further as costs rise over the years. Therefore, the operator must adjust the figures in the model budgets to fit his particular situation.

Salary Adjustment Table 11.7 is a list of factors for adjusting salaries for the state in which a center is located, based on 1970 figures. All one must do is to multiply the salaries presented in Table 11.6 by the factor presented in Table 11.7. Thus an operator in Mississippi desiring to operate a center of ADA 50 would multiply the personnel costs presented in the model budget for ADA 50 by .637 (the factor given for Mississippi). For instance, the teachers' salaries in the model budget are $6,000 per year. To adjust for Mississippi, we would multiply $6,000 × .637; the resultant figure of $3,822 represents the average for that state.

In addition, operators should review the employment market in their areas. Centers in urban areas tend to pay higher salaries than those in rural areas; experienced persons earn more than inexperienced; provision should be made for merit raises; and so on.

Costs have also been rising steadily. To adjust for rising costs, two rules of thumb may be used. The simplest is to multiply the 1970 estimates by some inflation factor, say 3 or 4 percent per year. An alternative would be to consider salaries as a percentage of the national average. Yearly, the National Education Association publishes a document entitled *Ranking of the States.* In that document are tables of estimated salaries in public schools. Included are average salaries of instructional staff in each state as a percent of national average. Since the day-care salaries presented in Table 11.6 are estimated to be 106 percent of their probable value in an "average" American center, the percentages for a state divided by 106 would give a factor to correct the model budget both for state and for year, provided, of course, that the most recent edition of *Ranking of the States* is used. Table 11.8 presents these percentages for 1969-1970. So, for example, for Mississippi in 1970 the percentage in Table 11.8 is 67.5; dividing by 106 gives .637, the factor for Mississippi in Table 11.7.

Other Costs Costs for the other parts of the model budget should also be adjusted. Unfortunately, we cannot present regional factors to apply to these other costs. The operator must therefore make his own judgment as to how much food, space, and equipment costs will vary from the model. The percentages in the functional budget summary (Table 11.4) will provide a rough check on these estimates.

Table 11.7
State Factors for Salary Adjustment*

State	Factor	State	Factor
Alaska	1.165	Tennessee	0.773
California	1.139	Louisiana	0.765
New York	1.081	Oklahoma	0.757
Michigan	1.074	Idaho	0.751
Illinois	1.055	South Carolina	0.742
Maryland	1.048	Alabama	0.737
Nevada	1.019	North Dakota	0.731
Hawaii	1.018	South Dakota	0.710
Indiana	1.015	Arkansas	0.683
New Jersey	1.007	Mississippi	0.637
Washington	1.007		
Connecticut	0.996		
Delaware	0.986		
Oregon	0.975		
Massachusetts	0.973		
Wisconsin	0.970		
Pennsylvania	0.954		
Arizona	0.951		
Rhode Island	0.943		
Iowa	0.940		
Minnesota	0.925		
Florida	0.911		
Ohio	0.911		
Wyoming	0.905		
Vermont	0.869		
Virginia	0.869		
New Mexico	0.861		
Missouri	0.858		
Maine	0.854		
New Hampshire	0.850		
Utah	0.844		
Montana	0.842		
Colorado	0.838		
Nebraska	0.832		
West Virginia	0.832		
Kansas	0.828		
North Carolina	0.821		
Texas	0.795		
Kentucky	0.790		
Georgia	0.781		

*The factors are derived from Table 11.8.

Table 11.8
Estimated Average Salaries of Instructional Staff as Percentage of National
Average, 1969-1970

State	Percentage	State	Percentage
Alaska	123.5	Kentucky	83.7
California	120.7	Georgia	82.8
New York	114.6	Tennessee	81.9
Michigan	113.8	Louisiana	81.1
Illinois	111.8	Oklahoma	80.2
Maryland	111.1	Idaho	79.6
Nevada	108.0	South Carolina	78.6
Hawaii	107.9	Alabama	78.1
Indiana	107.6	North Dakota	77.5
New Jersey	106.7	South Dakota	75.3
Washington	106.7	Arkansas	72.4
Connecticut	105.6	Mississippi	67.5
Delaware	104.5		
Oregon	103.4		
Massachusetts	103.1		
Wisconsin	102.8		
Pennsylvania	101.1		
Arizona	100.8		
Rhode Island	100.0		
Iowa	99.6		
Minnesota	98.0		
Florida	96.6		
Ohio	96.6		
Wyoming	95.9		
Vermont	92.4		
Virginia	92.1		
New Mexico	91.3		
Missouri	90.9		
Maine	90.5		
New Hampshire	90.1		
Utah	89.5		
Montana	89.3		
Colorado	88.8		
Nebraska	88.2		
West Virginia	88.2		
Kansas	87.8		
North Carolina	87.0		
Texas	84.3		

Source: National Education Association, *Rankings of the States, 1970* (Washington, D.C., Research Report, 1970-R1, 1970), p. 24, col. 43.

This section presents case studies of four of the twenty programs we studied: a small urban center (Amalgamated Day Care Center); a large urban home-care program (Family Day Care Career Program); a small program for migrant children (Greeley Parent Child Center); and a large rural child-care system (Rural Child Care Project). Each of these four programs received a two-year grant as Demonstration Programs for the Office of Economic Opportunity. An appendix at the end of each chapter includes forms and other material specific to the featured center.

These case studies were written after members of the Abt Associates field staff and selected day-care teachers and administrators visited these programs for one week in November of 1970. During the visits, our observers interviewed center personnel and parents and went into the classrooms to watch each center's program in action. Since that time, many of the centers have changed in terms of size and scope. Notes at the end of each chapter indicate recent changes we feel are significant.

Chapter 12

"A Rolls-Royce of Day Care"
Amalgamated Day Care Center
Chicago, Illinois

At a Glance
Single center
built for day care, owned by ACWA

Sponsored by
Amalgamated Social Benefits Association (private, nonprofit corporation), Amalgamated Clothing Workers of America (ACWA), AFL-CIO

Admission criteria
At least one parent a member of ACWA

Total children
60 enrolled; 54 average daily attendance (preschool)

Total paid staff
17 (11 full-time): 476 hours/week

Total in-kind staff
1 (0 full-time): 20 hours/week

Hours
M-F, 6:00 A.M.-6:00 P.M., 52 weeks

Space (sq ft/child)
Indoor: 68 Outdoor: 49

Center opened
March 1970

Staff positions
Administrative Assistant-ACWA (Union Liaison), Director, Psychiatric Social Worker, Pediatrician, Pedodontist, 4 Teachers, 4 Assistant Teachers, Secretary/Bookkeeper, Cook, 2 Custodians[1]

Ethnic distribution
Children: 42% black, 26% white, 19% Chicano, 4% Puerto Rican, 9% other Spanish-speaking
Staff: 27% black, 53% white, 13% Chicano, 7% Puerto Rican

Sex distribution
Children: 48% girls, 52% boys
Staff: 67% women, 33% men

Adult/child ratio
1 to 4.5

Adult/child contact hour ratio
1 to 4.9

Family status
85% complete, 15% mother only

Parent employment
100% employed

Costs to parents
None

Costs to center
$2,925 per child/year; $1.42 per child/hour

Estimated funding, 1970-1971
Amalgamated Social Benefits Association (ACWA) $154,100
                                    In-kind   3,900
                                               $158,000

Notable elements
Day care as union program: financing, educational program, health
care

Contact
Director, Amalgamated Day Care Center
323 S. Ashland
Chicago, Illinois
312-243-3147

Overview
The Amalgamated Day Care Center is located on Chicago's West
Side, in a re-emerging industrial area on the edge of a ghetto.
(Additional Amalgamated day-care centers will be located much
closer to the factories themselves, since there is no central residential area for them to serve, and transportation is a problem for
parents.) The center is a small, one-story structure immediately
adjacent to the five-story union building, which houses the Sidney
Hillman Health Center, Social Benefits Association, the ACWA

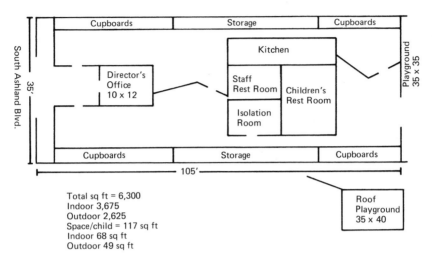

Figure 12.1
Floor plan of Amalgamated Day Care Center

retirees' center, and offices of the Chicago Joint Board. The buildings are just off the expressway, about ten minutes from down-
town Chicago.

The building was specifically designed for day-care use, although
not entirely successfully. The front and back walls are almost all
glass; glass doors and movable walls divide the classroom areas.
There is one small office for the director and the secretary in the
center-front of the building, and behind that, separated by a class
area, are the kitchen, rest rooms, and isolation room. Figure 12.1
shows the floor plan of the center.

When the center opened, the children, new to any kind of away-
from-home situation, lacked internal controls and were unaccustomed to limits and direction in working and playing with adults
and other children. The freedom of the building design intensified
this chaotic situation. The movable partitions were added as an
afterthought, in an attempt to alleviate the confusion. Despite
some current inconveniences for the staff, the building is bright,
colorful, warm, and fun for little children.

Each child has his own section of cupboard along the side walls
and his own small cot stacked underneath. The tables and chairs

are all child-size, as are the water fountains, sinks, and windows. The director's office is surrounded on two sides by glass so anyone can see in even when the door is shut. There is no room into which the children don't have either free access or a clear view to see what's going on. There is a playground in back of the building, and steps from it lead up to the roof of the building, which has also been made into a fenced-in play yard.

The atmosphere at Amalgamated is one of warm, relaxed fun, a bit hectic at times. Since there is no transportation system, the parents bring their children in on the way to work and pick them up on the way home. All day long there is a steady stream of parents, union officials, visitors, and children in and out of the building.

The center has been going for less than a year, and its staff have kept the operation open to a great deal of flexibility and change. In November the center was not yet up to its capacity of 60 children, and the addition of at least one more teacher was planned. The union considers the center a showplace for quality day care and uses it to encourage both companies and other unions to expand day-care capabilities.

The day-care staff, union officials, and union membership work well together, primarily because of the organizational and administrative efforts of two people: Muriel (Manni) Tuteur, center director; and Joyce Miller, administrative assistant to the manager of the Chicago Joint Board and vice-president of ACWA, Murray Finley. Teamwork between the two positions they fill would seem to be necessary in making any union day-care center work.

Manni Tuteur has been in the field of day care for almost 20 years, although this is her first experience working for a union. She was formerly with the Chicago Jewish Community Center. She admires what the union is doing and is determined to help make it work. She has a great deal of sensitivity to the children and their parents, as well as good rapport with her staff; she's friendly and easygoing, but she can be very tough and seems completely unflappable. There is a great deal of mutual respect between Manni and the staff. At the union headquarters she is the expert on day care, consulted and listened to on that basis.

While Manni Tuteur is the authority on day care, Joyce Miller is the expert on relations within the union. Joyce has been in the labor movement for several years and knows how to get things done. Once it was decided that day care was indeed a very important social program for the union to provide, she was given the go-ahead to make it work. Direct and to the point, she personifies the union's feeling of commitment to day care. With her help, the first center is now running smoothly, and she and Manni are looking at locations for the second one.

At first glance, one gets the impression that the entire Amalgamated program has been gone into almost casually, without a great deal of planning and forethought. Gradually, however, a picture and a plan emerge. In the next few years, quality day care will be available, free of charge, to every member of the Amalgamated Clothing Workers of America in the Chicago area.

Notable Elements

At Amalgamated Day Care Center union operation is in itself a notable element. The fact that the center is seen as a model for future expansion has resulted in the development of several other exemplary features, including financing, education, and health care. These features are a direct result of union sponsorship and can be duplicated only in the case of backing from an organization with similar commitment and resources.

Financing The Amalgamated Day Care Center is funded through the Amalgamated Social Benefits Association. This is an independent trust, established through a collective bargaining agreement between the ACWA and the employers of the garment industry. The employers supply a certain amount of money equal to a percentage of the monthly payroll, the amount therefore varying from factory to factory. The union is free to use this money to provide services for members. Union trustees decided in 1969 to use a portion of this money to establish day-care centers.

Building plans for the first center were initiated with the express idea that this could become a model quality day-care center upon which additional centers could be based. A new building was

erected for the center. In the first year of operation the director
was given freedom to spend whatever she felt was necessary to
efficiently establish and operate a day-care center that would more
than adequately meet the educational, emotional, recreational,
social, and nutrition and health needs of the union members'
children.

This financial arrangement has enabled the director to devote
the majority of her time to working with the staff and the children,
developing a total child development program for their specific
needs. None of her time is required for fund-raising activities.
Administrative work is kept at a minimum, and most of the
accounting and public relations functions are handled by the appropriate union offices.

After the first year of operation, a careful evaluation of this pilot
project will produce reasonable budgets and guidelines to plan and
operate additional centers as efficiently and economically as possible. Under later, more limited budgets, however, directors will still
not have to be concerned with fund raising and many other administrative functions that take up a great deal of most center directors' time. Amalgamated will remain—albeit at a relatively higher
cost—the "model" center, or, as one of the union people put it,
"a Rolls-Royce of day care."

Educational Program Early education is a special need for children
whose environment limits the amount of intellectual stimulation
they get in their preschool years. In consultation with the psychologist who visits the center periodically, the staff has assessed
its client children as experientially deprived and has planned a complete educational program for them on that basis. Although all
aspects of the program are interrelated, primary emphasis is placed
on intellectual development, particularly on general language development. Many of the children do not speak English or speak and
understand it poorly; parents have expressed particular concern
about this, wanting to be sure the children are prepared to enter
the public schools.

Because the center is relatively new, the curriculum is still extremely flexible. The aim is a program oriented to the total child,
so that the child is always surrounded by, and constantly made

aware of, colors, shapes, textures, consistencies, counting, measuring, and tactile experience through work and play with the materials around him. The process is not random, however; there is a basic structure to the day with constant, ongoing evaluation.

The staff meets once a week with the director to discuss and plan the program. At each meeting, six or seven "things that need to happen with the child" are brought up; then new program ideas are worked out to make them happen. Progress since the previous meeting is also evaluated.

A guiding principle in the center program is the attempt to understand the child's behavior in the light of his background and family situation. Work with the parents is just beginning, but parents are gradually realizing that the people at the center are truly concerned not only with the children but also with the overall improvement of the family's life. No attempt is made by the center, however, to gain information about individual family incomes. The sole criterion for admission is union membership, and only information related to the child's development is requested.

Children are encouraged to develop a strong sense of self-reliance: they take off and put on their own clothing, have their own tables, chairs, sinks, toilets, and water fountains. They have their own locker and storage space, at child height. They have open snack times and are encouraged to help with serving and fixing food and to clean up after themselves.

There is also emphasis on developing a strong self-image in the children. Activities are designed to encourage positive, successful experiences, avoiding competitive situations that the child's experience has not prepared him for. The staff praises and encourages achievements in language, reading development, cooperative peer relations, and self-reliance. At the beginning of the year, the children are rewarded with M&M candies—a controversial feature of the program with some parents—but gradually, verbal praise is substituted for the candy rewards.

One of the main areas of concern is the development of inner controls, which most of the children lack upon enrolling in the program. The child is encouraged to accept limits, controls, and directions from adults and to work with other children. There is no corporal punishment for misconduct, which often creates conflict with parents who are accustomed to responding to misconduct or conflict with physical punishment.

Strong emphasis is also placed on ethnic backgrounds. Staff selection criteria included mixed ethnic backgrounds and both male and female sexes, with considerable attention given to finding strong male-image black staff. The present staff is a successful mixture of black, white, Chicano, and Puerto Rican men and women. There are also appropriate ethnic materials for the children to use, including records, books, puzzles, and dolls. Different ethnic foods are served for lunches.

Cooperative work and play among the children, and between teacher and children, is encouraged. A rocking boat that holds four children, lotto games, large hollow blocks for building structures for dramatic play, doll houses and furniture, and helping in the kitchen are all provided as regular activities to stimulate cooperation.

In answer to strong parental concern about language development, the Peabody Language Kit is used as a starting point, as part of the daily routine. The Peabody Kit is considered helpful only if followed up with a great deal of staff reinforcement and expansion. This is complemented by use of some of the techniques found in the *New Nursery Book* and individual work with the children. Prereading skills are developed by reading to the children, listening to them, and giving them opportunities to tell stories both to the group and to the teacher separately, as well as by the graphics on the walls and cupboards.

Science experiments, unit blocks, and graduated cylinders are aimed at logical conceptual development, while a wide range of puzzles, games, toys, books, and so on, are used for sensorimotor, perceptual, and numerical concept development. Television sets are available so that "Sesame Street" is also used, but the program is not a regularly scheduled part of the day's activities.

Special time is set aside for art, crafts, and music. Record players, paints, clay, crayons, books, easels, chalk, scissors, etc., are all supplied for use on specific projects, as well as for free play activities, especially in bad weather. One particularly successful project was painting the four-foot-high doll house. Each child was draped in protective plastic and allowed to use hands or brushes to help with the painting. All of the center activities and experiences are supplemented by field trips. Children are taken to museums, zoos, and parks, usually in small groups so that each child can derive a fuller experience.

In short, Amalgamated's educational program is a day-care rarity: the director and staff have the opportunity to make full use of existing materials and to seek out new ones, to construct the fullest possible development program without any substantial budgetary constraints. As a cautionary note, it has been found that children and staff may fail to take appropriate care of the materials and equipment available in an aura of unlimited funding. Teachers are also now being encouraged to develop some of their own materials, not because of financial restrictions, but as a training and involvement technique.

Health Care Amalgamated Clothing Workers of America sponsors its own health clinic, available to union members and members of their families 13 years of age and older. This complete medical, dental, and pharmaceutical clinic offers free medical service and prescription drugs as well as physiotherapy, and so on. The center has a staff of 36 doctors, located on two floors of the Social Benefits building next door to the day-care center.

With the initiation of the day-care center, the union has now extended the comprehensive health program to include preschool children enrolled in the center, as well as the day-care center staff who become members of ACWA. Each child is given an examination and inoculations, and a medical record is begun. A pediatrician has been retained, who visits the center three times a week. Any serious problems are discussed with the parents and then referred to the health clinic for immediate attention. Dental work is referred to a private pedodontist but financed by the union. Drugs, eyeglasses, and any corrective measures such as braces or orthopedic shoes are also taken care of.

The nutrition program supplements the health program by providing two well-balanced meals, breakfast and a hot lunch (plus snacks), adjusted where necessary to compensate for previously deficient diets. As a further supplement to the health program, a psychiatric social worker spends one day per week at the center,

and in instances of severe emotional disturbance children have
been referred to other institutions, with union financing.

Background Information

History Research by the Amalgamated Clothing Workers of
America indicates that one in every three workers is a woman.
The economy of the United States is today dependent on the
women who have entered the work force. While the garment
industry itself at one time employed 80 males for every 20 females,
now the opposite is true. Women have been encouraged to join the
labor force, but little has been done to solve the problem of caring
for their children.

The women in the garment industry by and large have to work,
and in the absence of quality day-care facilities they are forced to
leave their children without proper supervision. The ACWA has,
therefore, recognized day care as something to which working
parents are fully entitled, and consequently as a responsibility of
both labor and management.

Thus in 1969 the Baltimore Joint Board of the ACWA negotiated
a collective bargaining agreement with the garment industry in
that area, which included establishing a special trust fund to provide day-care centers for members' children. Members enrolling
their children were asked to pay $5 per week. By November 1969,
the first center was in operation with 80 children; now the Baltimore Joint Board has 4 centers and eventually hopes to serve more
than 2,000 children. The union is primarily responsible for day-to-
day operations of the centers, with both management and labor
represented on the Policy Board.

In 1969 the Chicago Joint Board of ACWA began to look into
the possibility of providing day care for their members. In Chicago,
however, it was decided to provide day-care services out of the
money already supplied by management through the Social Benefits Association, at no direct cost to the members. The Baltimore
operation and European day-care systems were studied, and plans
were started to build a center on land belonging to the Chicago
Joint Board. In January of 1970 the director was hired, and on
March 28, 1970, the center opened its doors.

Community For Amalgamated, the community is the union membership throughout the Chicago area. It is composed of a wide ethnic mix, including blacks, Chicanos, Puerto Ricans, and first- and second-generation European immigrants. At least one parent in each member-family is working, but a recent slowdown in the industry has resulted in many layoffs and shorter work weeks. The factories shut down completely last summer for a two-week vacation, so the day-care center was also closed.

Information about the center has been spread primarily by shop stewards and by the union newspaper. The membership is already familiar with other social benefits provided by the union, such as the health clinic, the retirees' program, and the guaranteed financial support for college educations for children of union members, as well as insurance, pension benefits, and low-income housing. The general feeling among union management is that if the centers are there, the children will come. Plans are already underway for a second center, as the original one approaches its capacity of 60 children.

It is not known exactly how many children of union members are in need of day care, but it is presumed to be a considerable number, since membership in the union is now more than 70 percent women. In the Chicago area there are more than 38,000 children of preschool age who could use day-care centers; only 4,000 spaces for children in day-care centers now exist. Many of these are privately operated and cost $20-$35 per week, far out of the range of possibility for average- and low-income working mothers. Facilities are needed throughout the entire metropolitan area for infants, preschoolers, and school-age children.

Parents Parents of most center children—both mothers and fathers—are average- to low-income blue-collar workers. Incomes range from $4,000 to $12,000 annually, and the average wage is $3.40 per hour. Most of the families are complete, with one or two children. Day-care centers will only be accepted by these parents gradually; most of the parents and grandparents come from old and proud traditions and are opposed to receiving any kind of charity or welfare. It is more generally acceptable to them to leave children in the care of relatives or neighbors than in a school with strangers.

There is great interest, however, in seeing the children develop, both mentally and physically, and because of this, the confidence of the parents is gradually being gained. Because the parents work, they are not free to come into the center during the day to investigate its benefits; after work they are tired, with little interest in coming to evening parent meetings. Therefore, education of the parents with regard to center capabilities is a slow process. There has been only one parent meeting held, on a Sunday. Attendance was 50 percent. The parents do bring the children in the morning and pick them up at night, so there is a brief opportunity to see what the children are doing and to visit with the staff.[2]

Parents so far regard as most important the breakfast, hot lunches, health care, and preparation for public school. Many of the parents speak little or no English and are very happy that their children are learning to read and write, as well as speak English. The director hopes to develop Parent Advisory Committees for the center and to hold regularly scheduled parent meetings to involve the parents more fully in the center and ensure that what is learned in the center is reinforced in the home.

Basic Program

Education The children are divided into four "classroom" areas on the basis of age and ability: three-year-olds, three- and four-year-olds, four-year-olds, and four- and five-year-olds. One teacher and one assistant teacher serve each group of from 8 to 15 children. The classroom areas are all similarly equipped (since the classroom area was originally designed to be one large room). Movable walls and swinging glass doors about six feet high are the only dividers. There is a good deal of interchange among classrooms and groups in order to use some of the larger equipment (such as the rocking-boat stairs), the rest rooms, and the kitchen.

The entire building has wall-to-wall carpeting, and all of the cupboard space is built into the walls. Cupboards for the child's personal property and play equipment start a short distance above the floor and reach almost to the ceiling; the child-size cots are stacked underneath. The cupboards have sliding doors, easily workable by the children, which are covered with large, brightly colored numbers and letters. The children pull out their own cots and set them up for nap time. Each area also has its own child-size table and chairs to work on and for eating meals and snacks. Chalkboards, easels, record players, books, puzzles, and blocks are readily available.

There are two outdoor play areas, one immediately at the back of the building and the other on the roof, with stairs going up from the first level. Both play areas are well equipped with large-muscle exercise toys, including sandbox, sliding board, jungle gym, and UFO play structure. The two areas provide enough space so that all of the children may go out at one time, if necessary.

The teacher and assistant teacher work with their group on an individual basis, in small subgroups, and as a class. Since the center is open from 6:00 A.M. to 6:00 P.M., the teacher hours are staggered. The director works individually with the teachers and children, sometimes in the company of a psychiatric social worker who comes once a week. Arrangements have also been made for a psychologist to come periodically to test the children.

The basic schedule for the day begins with breakfast at 8:00 A.M., followed by clean-up, structured activity, free play, music of some kind, outdoor play, wash-up and story, snack, shape and concept learning, free play, Peabody Kit, wash-up and prepare for lunch, lunch, nap, then individual work or free play as the children begin to leave. The methodological approach to education has been covered in the "Notable Elements" section. A complete daily schedule is included in the appendix to this chapter.

Food The center provides breakfast, morning snack, hot lunch, and an afternoon snack every day. There is a fully equipped kitchen in the building and a full-time cook. Food is ordered in bulk from local wholesale houses, and menus are planned by the secretary in consultation with the director. Meals are planned within the guidelines of the Chicago Board of Health. A sample weekly menu is included in the appendix to this chapter. Different ethnic foods and holiday specialties are served throughout the year, and a birthday cake is provided for each child.

The food is brought from the kitchen into the rooms on two-tier trays. The children help set the little tables in each room and also

clean up. Teachers eat their meals with the kids, encouraging them
to try everything and not to take more than they can finish. There
is no pressure for kids to clean their plates. The children are allowed
to leave the table when they are finished. Meals and snack times
are considered an integral part of the total learning experience and
are generally a very pleasant part of the day.

Transportation The center does not provide transportation for the
children. The director estimates that about two-thirds of the children are brought to the center by the parents in their own cars,
and approximately one-third are dependent on public transportation. This presents some problems for parents who must cope with
public bus schedules, transfers, and fares while attempting to
deliver small children and get to work on time. It should be noted
that pay rates in the garment industry are based on piecework, so
that every minute taken away from scheduled work hours results
in direct loss of pay.

   The center hopes to alleviate this problem in two ways. The first
is to establish more centers close to the garment factories, a plan
already being followed in the establishment of the second center in
a renovated building right next to a factory. The second possibility
is establishment of a center in the moderate-income housing project
the union is currently building. An additional solution might be
union-provided transportation on a joint basis for day-care children and retirees, since both groups face the same transportation
problems in getting to facilities next door to each other.

Social Services The day-care center in and of itself is a social service
resource to the union. It is also proving to be a very useful means
of approach to other areas of social need for union members, on an
almost happenstance basis. For example, one woman sought help
from the center in filling out her unemployment compensation
forms. She did not want to accept "charity" and could not read
English well enough to fill out the form. One of the Spanish-speaking teachers at the center explained the form and helped her fill it
out; then a phone call was made to the appropriate office to ensure
there would be no difficulty when she picked up her check. When a
child in the center was found to be severely emotionally disturbed

to a degree that made his continued attendance deleterious to center programs, he was referred by the director to a preschool clinic for emotionally disturbed children, one that accepts children only if the parents agree to counseling at the same time.

Because of this kind of experience, the center is now exploring the possibility of a more active role in social services. The exploration is tentative, because the client population tends to shy away from any hint of social welfare in the usual terms. Present thinking is in terms of an additional staff member to handle these situations full-time, to follow up on them, acting as liaison when necessary between the union member and any outside agency. The service is needed, and there are indications that the union will agree to supply it.

Parent Education There is very little formal contact with parents at the ACWA center, encounters being limited almost entirely to pick-up and delivery of children to the center. Additional parent contact through day care and social services is at present in the developmental stages.

Organization

Figure 12.2 shows the organization of Amalgamated Day Care Center.

Policy Making Policy for the day-care center is set by the Amalgamated Social Benefits Association, an entity of the Chicago Joint Board of the Amalgamated Clothing Workers of America. The board consists of eight union officials. The Amalgamated Social Benefits Association is a separate trust established through collective bargaining, based on a percentage of payroll, to operate the union's health and welfare programs. Decisions are based on what is best for the union membership.

The manager of the Joint Board, Murray Finley, who is also an elected vice-president of ACWA, has been the primary driving force behind establishment and operation of the center. His administrative assistant is the liaison between the Joint Board, the Social Benefits Association, and the center director. Policy decisions are transmitted through the administrative assistant;

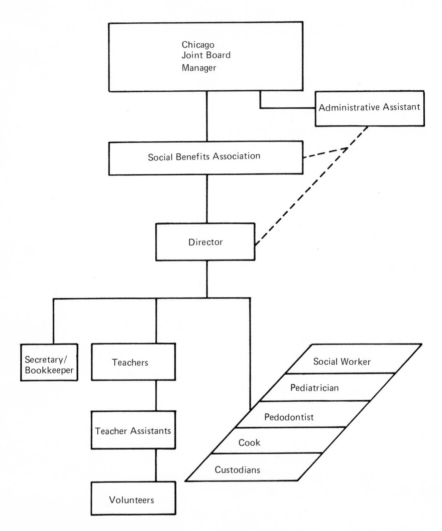

Figure 12.2
Organization chart of Amalgamated Day Care Center

center needs affecting policy are transmitted back to the board by the same route. Final approval on policy matters, however, rests with the Social Benefits trustees.

Since the program is new, most of the planning is done by the Joint Board Manager, his assistant, and the center director. The director is the authority on substantive decisions regarding day care, while the others are concerned with strategy for union participation and approval and employer relations, particularly in the present expansion plans. As other centers are established and Parent Advisory Committees are formed, other program-planning arrangements are likely. During this first year, no definite budget was set. The center is considered a model from which the others will be fashioned. A set budget is anticipated for the future, however, and will probably be developed by the director and the administrative assistant, with approval of the trustees of the Social Benefits Association. All personnel matters are handled by the director in consultation with the administrative assistant. Basic program structure and curriculum were developed by the director and are now subject to continual evaluation and change by the director and the teaching staff, in joint and individual meetings.

Staff Organization The director administers the day-to-day operations of the center and is responsible to the Joint Board of ACWA. She has daily classroom contact with the children and the teachers. It is anticipated that when the second center is opened, she will continue in the present center full-time but will supervise both centers. Figures 12.3 and 12.4 are a breakdown of the director's activities at present.

The secretary/bookkeeper handles administrative detail work, including record keeping, ordering supplies, and secretarial duties. She also plans the menus and orders all food. She comes in at 10:00 A.M. and stays until 6:00 P.M. or until the last child has been picked up. She also substitutes in the classroom when teaching staff are absent for short periods of time.

The pediatrician attends to health problems either directly or by referral to the clinic, the pedodontist is responsible for all dental care, and a psychiatric social worker and psychologist consult regularly with the director, teachers, and parents.

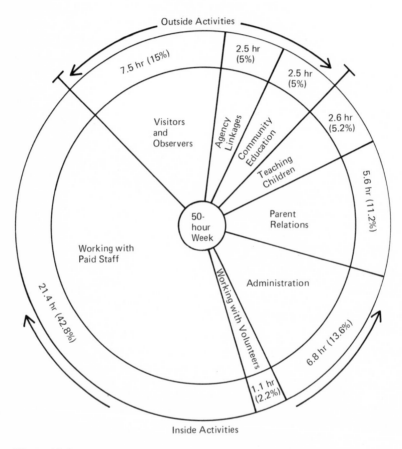

Figure 12.3
Breakdown of administrative duties of Amalgamated Day Care Center
director

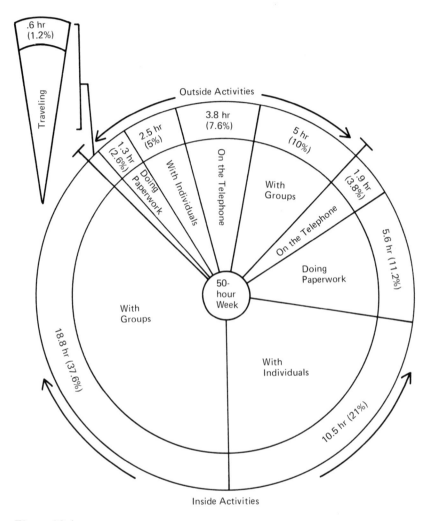

Figure 12.4
How the Amalgamated Day Care Center director spends her time in the performance of her administrative duties

The teachers are in charge of daily activities in their own classrooms; they also plan curriculum within the basic structure, subject to review by the director and the other staff. There is a teacher and an assistant teacher in each class area; both are responsible
for carrying out general child education, social-emotional development activities, and physical-recreational activities. Only one regular volunteer is currently available to the center: more are hoped
for in the future. Table 12.1 lists the paid and unpaid staff positions with their average hours per week spent in the center.

Staff Meetings and Records The entire staff meets regularly once a
week to discuss children's problems, curriculum, and program
plans and approaches. The director meets at least once a week
with each teacher separately and individually throughout the week
as needed. Each teacher keeps daily notes on each child and prepares detailed reports twice a year. A copy of the report form is
included in the appendix to this chapter.

Table 12.1
Average Work Week of Staff by Position

Staff Position	Hours/Week	Child Contact Hours/Week
Paid staff (17: 11.9 full-time equiv.)	476	435
Administrative assistant	8	—
Director	50	25
Psychiatric social worker	8	8
Teachers (4)	160 (40)	144 (36)
Assistant teachers (4)	160 (40)	144 (36)
Pediatrician	2 - 4	2 - 4
Pedodontist	2	2
Secretary/bookkeeper	40	20
Cook	40	20
Janitor	5	—
Assistant janitor	5	—
In-kind staff (1: .5 full-time equiv.)	20	20
Volunteer aide (1)	20	20
Total staff (18: 12.4 full-time equiv.)	496	455

Staff Selection and Training Recruitment and hiring of staff is centered around training, experience, and the ability to relate to and respect young children of different cultures, rather than strict professional paper qualifications. The only policy guideline on staff selection was to seek an ethnic as well as a male-female mix. The results: of the three men teachers, two are white, one black; of the five women, two are white, two black, one Puerto Rican.

The staff development program is designed to acquaint staff members with educational psychology, music, programming, arts and crafts, child literature, cognitive development, racial and ethnic awareness, and a knowledge of working-class families. All staff members receive two weeks of formal training and at least two hours a week of in-service training. This includes lectures on child development by day-care specialists and visiting professionals, as well as working with a psychiatric social worker, a pediatrician, and a (part-time) child psychologist. The union also provides resources for any staff member wishing to continue his formal education. This program has enabled the director to hire three people who would otherwise have been disqualified for lack of experience and/or formal education. It has also allowed salary increases for staff. Table 12.2 presents a profile of paid staff in terms of education, sex, and ethnicity.

How Resources Are Used

Tables 12.3 and 12.4 show the functional breakdown, in summary and in detail, of the way 1970-1971 income (shown in "At a Glance") will be used. The "In-Kind" column may include one or more of the following types of donations: materials, facilities, underpaid labor, volunteer labor, and labor paid for by another agency.

For the sake of clarity, expenditures are divided into four categories—standard core, varying core, occupancy, and supplemental services (these categories have been described in detail in Chapter 9). Together, the first three make up basic child-care costs.

Conclusion

The observation team felt that the Amalgamated Day Care Center provided quality child care and educational development. In some

Table 12.2
Overall Paid Staff Profile

Education	
M.D.	1
D.D.S.	1
M.S.W.	1
Graduate work	1
B.A.	4
Teacher certificate	1
College experience	3
High school	5

Sex	
Male	7
Female	10

Ethnicity	
White	11
Black	3
Chicano	2
Puerto Rican	1

Parents of project children	0

Table 12.3
Summary of Amalgamated Estimated Dollar and In-Kind Expenditures
1970-1971*

	Percentage of Total	Total Cost	Cost/Child/ Year	Cost/Child/ Hour
Standard core	80	$126,600	$2,344	$1.14
Varying core	4	6,700	124	.06
Occupancy	16	24,700	457	.22
Totals	100	$158,000	$2,925	$1.42

*Costs rounded to nearest $100; percentages to nearest 1%.

Table 12.4
Detail of Amalgamated Estimated Dollar and In-Kind Expenditures 1970-1971*

		Percentage of Total	Total	Dollar Cost	In-Kind Dollar Value
Basic Care	**Standard core costs**				
	Child care and teaching	56	$ 88,200	$ 84,300	$3,900
	Administration	14	21,500	21,500	0
	Feeding	10	16,900	16,900	0
	Varying core costs				
	Health	4	6,700	6,700	0
	Transportation	0	0	0	0
	Occupancy costs	16	24,700	24,700	0
	Overall personnel costs	81	127,180	123,280(80%)	3,900 (100%)
	Totals	100	$158,000	$154,100 (98%)	$3,900 (2%)

*Costs rounded to nearest $100; percentages to nearest 1%.

areas, notably parent involvement and social services, the center could be doing more and undoubtedly will as it matures and expands. In other areas, excellence already exists. At the basic care level, all elements are being provided in exemplary fashion: protection, nutrition, health, tender loving care, and general stimulation of mind and body. In addition the center, as a part of a larger comprehensive social benefits program, has a rich mixture of program elements that meet many of the developmental needs of children, staff, parents, employers, and union. Some of these elements are:

For children:
planned skill teaching in self-reliance; self-image enrichment; peer cooperation; health and nutrition; cross-cultural appreciation

For staff:
advancement through training; in-service support; adequate pay; exceptional fringe benefits

For parents:
lessened financial strain; knowledge of adequate care for child; less absenteeism; health care and social service assistance otherwise not available

For employers:
increased productivity and efficiency; less absenteeism; more stable work force; less turnover; decreased tension in the factory during working hours

For union:
greater unity of organization; opportunity for meaningful service to union members who are parents of children three to five years old.

The Amalgamated Day Care Center is an excellent example of quality service, directly responsive to community need, provided by the union for the benefit of its members with funds negotiated from the employers. Comments by parents and teachers as well as observers, attesting to the success of the program on a personal level, are included in the appendix to this chapter.

Notes

1. Since November 1970 there have been some changes in staff positions. One of the four original teachers now serves the dual role of assistant director/ teacher. Staff additions include one volunteer, one graduate student, one high school student studying child care; and Amalgamated has initiated an intern program at the center for nursing students from two local schools of nursing.

2. Since this case study information was collected, more emphasis has been placed on parental involvement. In addition to regular bimonthly parent meetings, staff also hold meetings now for small groups of parents after children have been enrolled in the program for a few months to tell parents how their kids are getting along and to discuss parent expectations for the children and the program as a whole. Individual parent-teacher conferences are also held on a regular basis now. A Parent Advisory Committee, which will advise the center staff and the Amalgamated Social Benefits Association, is in the process of being formed.

Appendix to Chapter 12

Daily Schedule
Sample Menu
Child Progress Report Forms
Parent, Staff, and Observer Comments

Amalgamated Day Care Center Daily Schedule

6:00 - 8:00 Teachers arrive* and supervise activities while
              greeting the new arrivals
8:00 - 8:30 Supervise breakfast and clean up
8:30 - 8:50 Structured activities
8:50 - 9:15 Free play
9:15 - 9:35 Music
9:35 - 10:00 Outdoor play or indoor activity depending upon
              the weather
10:00 - 10:15 Wash-up and story
10:15 - 10:30 Snack
10:30 - 10:45 Shape concept training
10:45 - 11:00 Free play
11:00 - 11:30 Peabody Language Kit
11:30 - 11:45 Wash-up and prepare for lunch
11:45 - 12:15 Lunch
12:15 - 2:30 Nap (During this time the teacher meets with the
              director or plans her program.)
2:30 - 6:00 Individual activity or free play as children leave

*The teacher who comes in at 6:00 A.M. leaves at 2:00 P.M.

SAMPLE MENU

CHICAGO BOARD OF HEALTH-NUTRITION SECTION
CIVIC CENTER

Day Care Center Menu Planning Form

Name: Amalgamated Child Day
Care and Health Center   Director's Name: Muriel Tuteur

Address: 323 S. Ashland   Zone: 60607   No. of Children: _____

Telephone: 243-3147   Date: November 2-6, 1970

MONDAY   WEDNESDAY
Baked chicken with dressing   Hard-cooked eggs
Buttered green peas   Broiled bacon
Celery sticks   Cheese sticks
Enriched white bread/butter   Hash brown potatoes or rice
Gelatin   Green peas
Milk   Enriched white bread/butter
                                   Fruit-flavored gelatin
                                   Milk

TUESDAY   THURSDAY
Spanish rice with ground beef   Hot dog with bun
Carrot sticks   Mustard or catsup
Buttered spinach   Mashed potatoes
Applesauce   Cabbage and carrot salad
Whole wheat squares/butter   Fresh fruit
Milk   Milk

FRIDAY
Baked fish sticks with tomato sauce
Brown rice
Tossed fresh vegetable salad
Buttered spinach
Orange slices
Milk

SNACKS: Midmorning   Midafternoon

Noon Meal Guide   Morning Snack Guide

Meat, poultry, fish, cheese,   4 oz. orange or grapefruit
or egg dish   juice or 8 oz. tomato juice
Potato
Dark green or yellow vegetable   Afternoon Snack Guide
Bread w/butter
6 oz. milk   6 oz. milk
Simple dessert—pudding or fruit   Plain cookie or cracker

AMALGAMATED CHILD DAY CARE AND HEALTH CENTER
323 S. Ashland Blvd.   243-3147

P R O G R E S S   R E P O R T

CHILD'S NAME _____

SEX _____   BIRTHDATE _____

ADDRESS _____   PHONE _____

FATHER'S NAME
_____

MOTHER'S NAME
_____

            DATE OF REPORT
                            _____

            SUBMITTED BY _____

FORM TO BE FOLLOWED ON PROGRESS REPORT

THE FOLLOWING AREAS SHOULD BE COVERED IN THE
REPORT: (Please indicate changes, growth, or regression)

1. DESCRIPTION OF THE CHILD

    a. Physical appearance
    b. Muscular development
    c. Health and attendance
    d. Speech
    e. Self image
    f. Interests
    g. Intellectual characteristics
    h. Fears
    i. Thumbsucking, masturbation, if any, in what situation?
    j. Unusual behavior
    k. Attitude toward family

2. CHILD'S ARRIVAL AT THE DAY-CARE CENTER

3. CHILD'S DEPARTURE FROM THE CENTER

4. RELATIONSHIP WITH TEACHER

5. RELATIONSHIP WITH OTHER ADULTS

6. RELATIONSHIP WITH OTHER CHILDREN

7. RESPONSE IN ROUTINES

    a. Bathroom
    b. Mealtime
    c. Rest time
    d. Dressing
    e. Clean-up

8. RESPONSE TO MATERIALS AND ACTIVITIES

9. TEACHER'S RECOMMENDATIONS

Comments

Parents:

"It's a second home for my child. She's eager to go back every day." "I like it that it's integrated. The union helps all nationalities. They want to help people be people." "His mind is made up. Now we say grace before meals or we don't eat." "It's brought the family closer together. We have a common thing to talk about— the center." "Now she lets you know when she doesn't want something or when she has had enough. She didn't do that before." "No, they don't punish him for misbehavior. I wish they would." "It's helped me be more patient, and given me a better understanding of my own child." "Now when I go to work there's no need to worry. I trust the staff." "Now I notice him more closely. I can see that he catches on easily and can express himself more." "I think it's giving him a good base to build on. He's learned to get along with other children, to use materials and equipment constructively, and learned numbers and the alphabet."

Teachers:

"The most important need for a preschooler is a responsive environment. We try to give him one that allows for his individual needs while impressing on him the group's needs. The classroom needs to be both stable and exciting." "What makes a good teacher? (1) patience, (2) a good reaction to children, (3) a realistic perception of children, (4) a real liking for children, (5) some theoretical training." "In cases of misbehavior, I try to undercut the situation in a way that cools the violence. I take the child outside the situation so he can get a picture of it." "The best thing about this place is Manni Tuteur's willingness to listen to anything. The worst thing is the building. It's chaotic." "Good behavior is generally responded to with a smile or a pat on the head, with a few words of praise, with a hug." "The director is nondirective and nonauthoritative. It's difficult for her to make a firm decision." "If he persists in bad behavior, he's put in the think chair to think over what he's been doing. The teacher then explains to him what the trouble is. He usually decides to come back to the group."

Observers:

"I ate two meals with them and didn't see any great amount of concern for who was eating what. No one tried to force them to clean their plates and that routine." "The attitude toward the day-care center from the union is really wild. 'Build the center,' they said. 'The kids will come.' " "Many of those who do bring their kids are very concerned with the traditional learning skills. One mother was very concerned that her child learn to read. It later turned out that she herself could not." "It struck me that the more you have, the more you expect. Staff know that the finances are in pretty good shape, and they can in fact go out and buy minor things. The depreciation rate on equipment has been extremely high." "The children come first at Amalgamated with the director and staff."

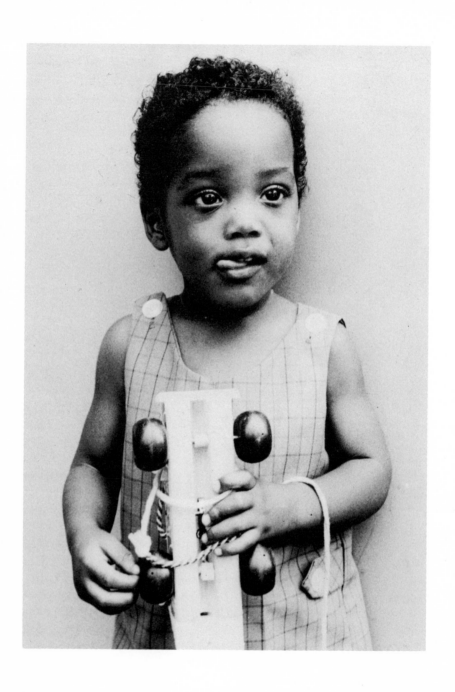

Chapter 13

"I'm a New Woman Now"
Family Day Care Career Program
New York, New York

At a Glance
System of
21 subcenters, most administering 40-60 day-care homes

Sponsored by
The City of New York (local government)

Admission criteria
Public assistance or low-income parents (not to exceed $6,200 per year for a family of four); parents must either work or be in training or school

Total children
3,570 average daily attendance (30% half-day; 20% infants, 51% preschool, 29% school age). Typical center has 180 ADA.[1]

Total paid staff
1,364 (976 teacher mothers, 378 subcenter staff, 10 central administrators/full-time): 62,720 hours/week[2]

Total in-kind staff
None

Children per day home
Maximum 6

Hours
M-F, 8:00 A.M.-6:00 P.M., 52 weeks

Space/home
Each home licensed by city for certain number of children

System started
July 1967

Typical subcenter staff positions
Director, Day-Care Counselor, 2 Day-Care Aides, 10 Educational Aides, Secretary, Bookkeeper, Custodian, Applications Counselor, Vocational Counselor, Educational Consultant, 49 Teacher Mothers

Ethnic distribution
Children: 63% black, 31% Spanish-speaking, 4% white, 2% other (mostly Italian)
Staff: Principally black and Spanish-speaking

Sex distribution
Children: 50% girls, 50% boys
Staff: 97% women, 3% men

Adult/child ratio
1 to 2.1

Adult/child contact hour ratio
1 to 2.6

Family status
25% complete, 75% mother only

Parent employment
100% employed or in training

Costs to parents
None

Costs to system
$2,287 per child/year; $0.92 per child/hour

Estimated funding, 1970-1971
New York Department of Social Services	$5,600,000
New York State	800,000
HUD-Model Cities	150,800
In-Kind	1,612,200
	$8,163,000

Notable elements
Human returns, making do, ease of transportation, responsive and
stable growth, career development

Contact
Director, Family Day Care Career Program
220 Church Street
New York, New York 10013
212-433-4525

Overview
The Family Day Care Career Program, commonly known as FDC,
is a system of organized home care with 21 subcenters located in

New York City communities, each administering 40 to 60 homes
in the neighborhoods they serve. The subcenters are coordinated
by a central office, which provides technical support to the centers. The central administration consists of an overall director, her
assistant, four technical assistants, and four clerks. At each subcenter level, a director, day-care counselors and aides, educational
aides, and specialized consultants support the work of teacher
mothers, who take children into their own homes, and career
mothers, who are working and need day care.

The average subcenter is in a slum area. It's in a storefront,
church, or any other space that's usable. Subcenter buildings range
from cramped, tiny corridors with a Xerox machine crowded onto
a coat-rack to an enormous barn of a church. In many cases only
basic office equipment is provided—electric typewriters and secretarial desks. The centers operate on a shoestring budget, but the
people who work there make them work. Center staffs seem to
have a very special feeling for the people they serve. They understand the kinds of problems parents encounter because they have
experienced the same problems firsthand.

Basic child care is accomplished in day homes licensed for space
and sanitary facilities by the city and state. Enrollment is limited
to six children in a home, including those of the teacher mother.
There is often a mixture of ages and ethnic backgrounds. Teacher
mothers provide hot lunches and two snacks daily on an inadequate budget of $15 per child per month. Children and all mem-
bers of their immediate families are required to have physical examinations before entering the program; centers help with such
arrangements. Parents are also responsible for taking children to
and from the day homes (usually located close to the parent home).

The educational program is severely limited by underfunding.
There are few materials available, although teacher mothers are
assisted eight hours each week by subcenter educational aides and
are provided with lists of activities for children. There are also excursions and activities arranged by the subcenters, which involve
all the children in the program.

At the start of the program, there were serious problems of allocation of responsibility for the children. Before the day-care
staff began dropping in unannounced, teacher mothers occasion-

ally left children with a baby-sitter or older child so they too could
get out to work or shop. Some teacher mothers were just too tired
to do much for the children, and others were baffled by mothers
who dumped their children and left, not to return until late at
night.

Many career mothers work at dull, low-paying jobs hours from
home, returning tired and discouraged at the end of the day, unable to relate happily with their children and too tired to try. The
Family Day Care system doesn't have the resources or staff to
combat the erosion of the parental role that often occurs. Work with
teacher mothers must be tactful, explicit, and continuous to
ensure that these warm and wonderful foster homes do not under-
mine the real parents, partly because many day-care homes offer
love and stability to children who have neither in their own
homes. Although there are activities at the centers with center
staff, much more work with center staff would be necessary to
balance the strong teacher mother/child ties and build support for
career parents.

Children clearly benefit from entering a system likely to expose
or remedy their special medical and nutritional needs, but probably none of them receive the intellectual stimulation desirable;
and since there are no adequate programs for older children in
sports, tutoring, drug or vocational education, younger children
are really better off than school-age children. The children in this
system also need many more men in their lives. Most provider
homes either lack a permanent male figure, or the male adults are
essentially uninvolved with the child-care activities of the teacher
mother.

For the time being, career mothers are least involved in the
system, perhaps because the system requires too little of them.
Women staff members, in their sympathy for the career mother's
fatigue and discouragement, require far more of themselves than
of career mothers. The teacher mother is usually emotionally
hooked on the system and involved with the children; she grows
ever more responsible and independent. The career mother is
structurally dependent on the free day care and on the teacher
mother, often increasingly so. There is no obvious source of pride
in parenthood and child nurturance built into the system for

career mothers, and until funding becomes more stable and more realistic, the center programs that might foster career mother involvement and interest cannot occur.

Family Day Care responds to non-day-care community needs on a serendipitous basis. Referrals to legal, family planning, and housing services occur daily. In general, though, day care and related needs already more than absorb the paid and unpaid time of the staff.

So the visitor sees, in the gaps in the program, the terrible problems of alienation and poverty that the system addresses. It is enormously to the credit of this program and everyone connected with it that these bitter problems are held at bay while children go daily, unquestioningly, to the homes of women who yesterday were strangers in a jungle.

Notable Elements

Human Returns

It has given me a new personality. I never went anywhere. I was ashamed to have anyone come into my house. When my children needed shoes or a coat, I had to go to the nearest bargain basement and pick up the leftovers that were shoddy and didn't wear. When I looked at my children, I cried. Now if my children need shoes, I get them out of the money I've earned [as a teacher mother], and I get them what I want them to have. I had no social life. I had no contact with adults; just baby talk with the kids. The program is not only a job, it's a new way of life. I am now on an adult level. I like to have people come to my house and go to meetings of the Parent Advisory Committee.

> Teacher mother, Family Day
> Care Career Program
> New York, New York

Let's not forget what it has done for the children. When I sat at home with my five kids, I was so frustrated and fed up I didn't care what happened. I knew I wasn't teaching them what they needed to know, but I was too exhausted to do any of the things I knew I should do. Now I am a new woman and you should see my little ones. They're eating properly, they can count, they know colors and letters, they sing lovely songs, I have to set the table

just right for meals because they know the way it should be, and
we're proud of each other.

> Career mother, Family Day
> Care Career Program
> New York, New York

These stories are from the minutes of a Family Day Care City-
Wide Policy Advisory Board meeting (included in the appendix to
this chapter). They are not unusual for Family Day Care: there
are literally hundreds of them, and they are one of the most striking aspects of this system. The letters and internal correspondence
of the program make clear the enormous human returns for both
career and teacher mothers, the users and providers of this system.
Family Day Care exploits women—provider mothers clear between
$1.50 and $3.40 a day—but chiefly for each other, and the difference it has made for them, the difference between loneliness
and vegetation on the one hand and purposeful employment with
cash returns on the other, is immeasurable.

The system has helped a great many women fulfill themselves
and contribute more to society, not only in the face of poverty
and the apathy it breeds but also despite severe social criticism.
Dozens of women who are now participating have been beaten by
their men for lifting their heads to consider working outside their
homes. Some of these happily provide care for the children of
career mothers—for the present, it's the only work that they or
their men are willing to accept. Others have persisted in their efforts to be independent and have gone on to training and jobs outside the home. Most of the career mothers who have been freed to
work have been happy to get out of the welfare system and all it
implies.

Family Day Care provides focused contact with adults in many
ways. A mother who inquires about the system (most people come
to FDC through word of mouth) has a choice of providing or using
child care. She is thus at once pulled into the adult working world
of planning and decisions. Her choice is sympathetically discussed
and supported. The abler day-care staff give mothers the same
emotional support found in AA or a very successful community
project, while at the same time helping them upgrade their job per-

formance in or out of their homes. The staff, and particularly the subcenter directors, are on call all the time for emergencies, and emergencies are many. They, in turn, call freely on the central office technical assistants, who may often be found following up for days on one mother's problems. This setup provides for inner-city mothers a "frontier community" organization like those of women in the early West, with comparable security and pride for participants. Each center is linked into a larger network of job and social service resources, and these are used as much as possible to help those who have decided to be career mothers find their way.

Prospective teacher mothers are carefully interviewed about their interest in child care. Their homes are checked, and observers also note their relations with their own children. They receive early childhood training at city-wide and local center sessions before they begin taking children into their homes. The centers do a sensitive job of placing children in homes. The staff tries to find a teacher mother whose home is close to the child's. An effort is made to mix the ethnic backgrounds of children, and in most centers, the children are not grouped by age. One mother may have two infants, a toddler, a preschooler, and two school-age children. In this way, children can help each other, and the teacher mother is able to direct her attention to those who need special assistance. Good matching of teacher mothers and children is a delicate art and one the staff tries to achieve in every case.

Center personnel support teacher mothers in many ways. Educational aides visit the homes to help with activities and discuss problems. Day-care aides check on the care given and also offer support. Centers baby-sit for the children when the teacher mother has medical appointments or must be out of the house for some other reason. The system provides suggested activities and some materials, although the educational component of the program is badly underfunded.

Making Do One of the most remarkable things about Family Day Care is the fact that it keeps going at all. Its greatest accomplishment, aside from the differences it has made in the lives of its participants, is that its people continue to give the best of themselves,

day in and day out, for long hours and grossly inadequate pay. But
that's the kind of "frontier" operation it is.

A very inefficient financial system is made worse by a total
lack—indeed deficit—of working capital. Teacher mothers are
seriously underpaid. The educational component of the program is
so underfunded that it scarcely exists. Red tape and the lack of
funds mean that participants in the system don't know if they will
be reimbursed for a purchase (all administrative expenditures are
on a cash-reimbursable basis instead of a spend-your-budget system), much less when and how much. Financial difficulties occur
from the top down: the City of New York approves the yearly
budgets months late; central office financing is absurdly low and
insecure; teacher mothers still get their stipends late despite major
protests; subcenter directors have an approved budget but may or
may not receive the authorized monies.

Responsiveness to needs is warm but poverty-stricken. The day-
care staff work overtime: directors and the central office technical
assistants, especially, work 12- and 16-hour days. Staff members
constantly spend from their own salaries for Family Day Care. At
the top, the visitor finds that unpaid overtime work and many
public relations expenses are borne by the staff; at subcenters one
finds staff contributing heavily to emergency needs with both time
and money. Teacher mothers receive $90 per child per month:
$75 salary and $15 for the child's food (two snacks and a hot
lunch for 75¢ daily). In practice, teacher mothers often spend
about $20-25 per child per month for food and from $5-80 per
child per month on other expenses—transportation, raises in rent
due to improvements, cleaning materials, laundry, and so on.

A low-income mother with one FDC child who really spent only
$15 a month for the child's food would be earning $3.40 per day
($75 divided by 22 days) for a day that should not exceed 10
hours but sometimes lasts for 12. The mother on public assistance
gets about $.85 an hour. Although it would be possible—in the-
ory—to earn as much as $2.00 an hour if five children stayed only
ten hours and were actually fed on $15 per month each, mothers
often have their own children in the home (three to four on the
average), for whom they are not compensated, and can take only
as many FDC children as they are licensed for—no more than six

children in total. Add to this dismal picture the fact that the welfare payments of the teacher mother are cut because she has earned a salary.

Why do they keep on? Why is the system growing so fast and steadily? One answer must be that this system, inadequate as it is, has provided immeasurable gains for everyone involved. For staff, it is satisfaction in helping others. For career mothers, it is a chance to improve their lives through employment or training, a chance to get on in the world. For children, the foster homes are warm, loving places where they are fed, cared for, and cared about—for many children, being visibly loved is in itself a wonderful novelty. For teacher mothers, many of whom are lonely, destitute, with no contacts outside their homes, it is a chance to care for children, to become less dependent on welfare, to join the real world in a respectable, purposeful way. It is a satisfying job for many who haven't the confidence, the skills, the opportunity, or the health to cope with the business world. In a trade-off between expansion and heavy improvement, most people in the system opt for expansion simply because having no care means such a terribly bleak existence for so many parents and their children.

Ease of Transportation The career mothers in Family Day Care (like all parents interviewed in major child-care demand surveys) place high priority on having their children close to home. Parents continually note both the convenience of not having to transport children and infants and the psychological benefit of having their children stay in the neighborhood. FDC mothers with children placed in the same apartment building are particularly grateful for not having to dress toddlers against the cold or take them on subways and buses. Others have spoken of being glad to have their children "in the same community," "near home when older children return from school," "near friends."

Transportation to and from child-care centers is often assumed to be a necessity in providing day care in America. This is unfortunate in light of the fact that parents of every income class consistently ask for child care close to home. Areas of high population density can succeed in establishing centers to which all children walk. The Family Day Care system suggests that home care can deliver close-to-home service in a much wider range of residential areas.

Responsive and Stable Growth There are typically severe growth problems in large organizations that double in size each year. Family Day Care is growing at a remarkably steady rate. Demand for child care and supply of potential teacher mothers still far exceed the capacity of the system, but the system is responding steadily. It is a particular tribute to the staff of FDC that their warmth and involvement have been so consistent. This is not to say there have been no problems. Day care is now being transferred in the Human Resources Administration to a new Agency for Children department. This transfer has meant uncertainties and dislocations. The role of mothers in policy making is becoming an ever more important question. The financial setup of FDC has resulted in innumerable problems, uncertainties, and wasted time. Creating good relations with other agencies as the system grows takes continual time and care. Nevertheless, one remarkable feature of FDC is its steady, swift responsiveness to the needs of mothers and children wishing to join the system.

Career Development Family Day Care has two career development paths: one internal to the program, one outside the system for career mothers. All mothers who enter the program may become either provider or career mothers; many provider mothers later become career mothers. The vocational counselor (who works for the Manpower Development Agency but is housed at the subcenter) works with each career mother to see that she receives testing, training, and job placement as appropriate as possible to her interests and abilities. Since the program began, 4,623 FDC career mothers have been in training and/or found paid jobs. Some women have finished high school, a few junior college and specialized training. The system abounds with stories of the woman with seven children who is a top lab technician, the woman who became a Wall Street office manager, the woman whose whole extended family went back to school after she set an example.

The system also has an internal career development program, which funnels staff upward. At one of the centers we observed, there had been five promotions in the past year: a day-care counselor became the director; the director became an outstanding technical assistant in the central office; a bookkeeper became a day-care counselor; and two educational aides became day-care aides—all, of course, with corresponding increases in pay and responsibility. Dozens of staff have been promoted this way. A center director we met had started as an educational aide, become a day-care counselor, then director. At her center during the past year, there had been two other promotions: an educational aide became a day-care aide, and a day-care aide moved up to a day-care counselor. Another center recorded seven promotions—and so on. The system is committed to hiring from within, giving its own people, with their specialized knowledge of their communities, a chance for more responsibility and better pay.

Background Information

History The original proposal for Family Day Care was written by a New York City Department of Social Services employee. The program was designed to provide employment for welfare recipients and to provide child-care services for welfare mothers who wanted employment or training.

In June 1967 the city-wide Head Start Committee was asked to approve and help launch this project, for which $3,500,000 in OEO funds was to be made available. Major start-up operations included obtaining administrative and home facilities, licenses, and recruiting clients, teachers, and career mothers. The support and cooperation of crucial agencies in New York—Community Development Agency of the Human Resources Administration and the Board of Education—were secured during this time. Absolute priority was to be given to welfare mothers who wanted jobs or training, and where feasible, they were to be given preference in employment as day-care aides and educational aides.

The program began in July 1967 and got off to a slow start. The Interim Committee, which worked through the summer of 1967 screening and selecting the first 10 centers, worked with central staff to get a modification of the priority for welfare mothers that had been written into the original proposal. This was in order to

expand services to hundreds of very low-income families who have
a comparable need for help but who haven't applied for welfare.
The Human Resources Administration agreed that low-income
mothers might participate. This group is, therefore, not penalized
for *not* being on welfare.

Since the program's inception, eleven more centers have been
added, and in November 1970, Family Day Care served more than
3,600 children in a thousand homes.

Community Family Day Care subcenters are located all over the
New York metropolitan area: on a Harlem hill, near East Harlem
public housing, near the Brooklyn waterfront in the area made
famous by the Mafia and Marlon Brando. A list of the 21 subcenters appears in the appendix to this chapter.

Basic Program

Education There can be up to six children in each home, including
the teacher mother's own children. Also, there can be no more
than two children under two years of age in one home. Children
are usually assigned to a home near them, after interviews have
disclosed that teacher mothers, career mothers, and children are
compatible. The system's children are reported to be "normal"
both mentally and physically. The centers are not equipped to
handle disturbed children but may refer families needing help to
appropriate agencies.

In the past, the system provided mothers with a daily schedule
to be followed, but this was not workable, and teacher mothers
now schedule their activities in the way most convenient for themselves. Children have a great deal of free time, and spontaneous
activities are encouraged. The system issues guidelines on dangerous toys and also gives lists and descriptions of activities for the
children. Samples of such documents are included in the appendix
to this chapter.

The child curriculum is organized around the areas of social
studies, mathematics, science, art, and music. Within these areas,
specific materials are developed for different age groups. The
quantity of materials available in each home is limited by lack of

funds. Teacher mothers can occasionally obtain materials by re-
questing them from the center. The teacher mother is the only real
staff person in the home. She is assisted by an educational aide for
a maximum of eight hours a week and occasionally receives support from the center's educational consultant.

Space available for indoor child activities varies with each home;
the greatest number of rooms in any one home is six. Equipment
consists of regular home furnishings—radios, television sets ("Sesame Street" is a favorite program), books, occasional blocks,
puzzles, toys, games, magazines, housekeeping apparatus (children
often help with meals, housework, or with younger children), and
so on. Each home is near a playground, and there is generally
space for outdoor play. In addition, children sometimes join other
day-home children at the subcenter for planned excursions and
special events.

The atmosphere in the homes visited was friendly and cheerful.
Contact between teacher mother and children was affectionate
and initiated equally by both. Younger children seem to form
close attachments with older children in their groups. Group
games, toys for two, and sharing activities promote cooperation.

An optimum day's schedule includes toileting and washing periods; meal and naps; group games with a toy or flash cards; art periods with drawing and painting; music activity with songs, finger
plays, and rhythms; sometimes math study with number cards,
counting games, calendars; language study with storytelling, nursery rhymes, and puppets; discussion periods covering science and
social studies topics; and outside play with group games—dodge
ball, tag, and so on. In practice, the television set is ubiquitous,
and many days are just spent quietly.

Food The nutrition program is maintenance oriented. As already
mentioned, children get two snacks and a hot lunch (meat, potato,
a vegetable, dessert) daily. The funding of $15 per child per month
is inadequate, and teacher mothers spend their own money to give
the children additional food.

The teacher mother determines the feeding schedule for all children. While children are to eat at scheduled times (continuity in
chronically disrupted lives is seen as important), irregular eating

habits will be accommodated. Usually, the mother serves the children, although in some cases older children may help with preparation or clean-up. Center personnel visit the homes to check on the overall program, including meals.

Health Care There are no direct health services provided by the subcenters. Each child in the system must have a general physical examination—including dental, hearing, and optical examination—each year. Centers often help arrange for these check-ups with local physicians and hospitals. Problems are diagnosed, and families are referred to appropriate agencies. If a child becomes ill while in the day-care home, the teacher mother calls the center, which in turn contacts the child's mother. Parents are responsible for caring for their children if they are ill.

Transportation Career mothers are responsible for taking children to and from the day home. Most homes are near parent homes, either in the same housing project or within two or three blocks. Teacher mothers are responsible for the school-age children in their care, escorting them to school, back home at lunch time and after school, and on field trips.

Social Services The most common social problems among center families are lack of self-confidence, limited employment skills, and low incomes. The centers provide emotional support for mothers and job counseling to all parents in the program, but no other direct services are available for lack of funding. Centers do a good deal of referral work. Social services in the area include health services, family planning, nutrition, a food stamp program, welfare and employment, and limited legal, housing, and social services. Most commonly used are the general health clinics, job training programs, and social services. Follow-up is done by the centers because many agencies to which parents have been referred provide little help and poor follow-up.

Parent Education and Involvement The centers have no funds for formal parent education programs other than the Board of Education training of teacher mothers as staff. Each center has a Parent

Advisory Committee composed of elected community members
and parents, who make suggestions but do not control. The
policy-making bodies are described under "Organization."

Organization
Family Day Care operates on both a city-wide and a local level.
Figure 13.1 shows the city-wide organization of the system, and
Figure 13.2, the local operation.

Policy Making Family Day Care is formally sponsored by the City
of New York, under the Human Resources Administration, Community Development Agency. At the local level, each of the 21
subcenters is run by a "sponsor," which has a board of directors
composed of 10 to 21 residents. The local boards are in charge of
implementing activities, but in practice sponsors have spent very
little time on day-care problems.

There are both city-wide and local policy advisory committees.
The city-wide policy advisory board is composed of 35 percent
teacher mothers, 35 percent career mothers, and 30 percent representatives from professional, civic, and social welfare organizations.

Parent advisory committees at the local level work with the
sponsoring agency (centers are sponsored by local groups, churches, community organizations) to elect representatives to the city-
wide PAC. Local PACs are composed of community residents,
teacher mothers, and career mothers, who address center and
family problems arising in the center's operation. Of the 21 centers, about 15 have really active PACs, with regular monthly meetings and continuous projects. Each center sends two representatives to the city-wide PAC, which meets monthly.

Both local and city-wide boards of directors are involved in planning the overall program; in practice these boards serve chiefly as
communication links in the system. Most planning occurs in the
FDC central office. The total project budget is developed by the
central office director of Family Day Care, in conjunction with
local program directors and CDA personnel. The sponsoring
agency is responsible for hiring, firing, and promoting staff, based
on recommendations from the local program directors. Curriculum

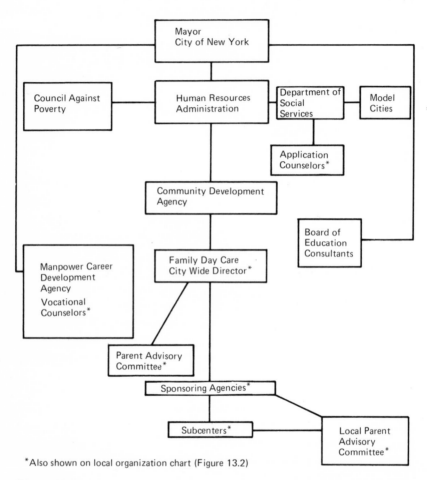

*Also shown on local organization chart (Figure 13.2)

Figure 13.1
City-wide organization chart of Family Day Care Career Program

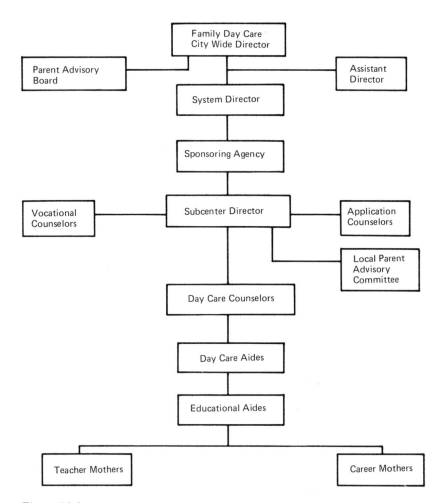

Figure 13.2
Local organization chart of Family Day Care Career Program

is determined by the local center director in conjunction with Board of Education consultants and the advice of parents. A day-care counselor serves as advisor to the teacher mother, who suggests and implements daily program activities.

There appears to be relatively little conflict in the policy-making process. Staff responsibilities and the chain of command are well defined, and the total process is well coordinated and relatively efficient. Parents do not hold decision-making powers, but they are definitely involved in the process. For example, parents have had a strong influence on the content of the Board of Education training programs.

Staff Organization At the central office, the director, with the aid of her assistant, is in charge of overall administration, funding, staffing, and anything else that affects the system as a whole. Four technical assistants work directly with the subcenters as staff advisors. They handle problems local staff cannot solve including endless liaison and lobbying with city agencies. They offer support for day-care counselors and teacher mothers. The central office also has four clerks who handle routine work for the staff. These people spend much more time than they are paid for and are a major reason this program works as smoothly as it does.

A local center staff is organized as follows: The *director* is responsible for the administration and supervision of the Family Day Care program. He or she writes proposals and reports, acts as liaison between the community and the program, and coordinates with other governmental agencies. Directors always work overtime, coping with emergencies and helping with the hundreds of problems of people related to the center. Figure 13.3 shows how a local program director spends his or her time in a typical subcenter.

The *teacher mother* provides full-time, social-emotional and educational care and nutrition for the children in her home.

The *educational aide* provides support to day-care homes, relieves teacher mothers when necessary, recruits participants for the program, writes progress reports, and makes home visits.

The *day-care aide* receives initial applications and presents the program to prospective families, makes potential client referrals to

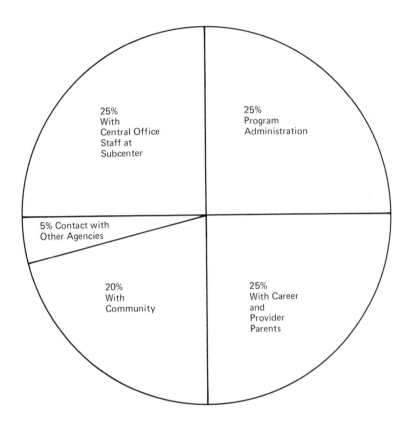

25%
With
Central Office
Staff at
Subcenter

25%
Program
Administration

5% Contact with
Other Agencies

20%
With
Community

25%
With Career
and
Provider
Parents

Figure 13.3
How a local program director spends her time in a typical Family Day Care
subcenter

appropriate staff members, performs clerical duties, gives support to day homes in emergencies, directly supervises educational aides, and makes medical appointments for applicants.

The *day-care counselor* is responsible for the total program in every day home. The counselor directly supervises day-care aides and makes use of the community's resources to help center families.

The *application counselor* is assigned to each program by the Department of Social Services. Duties include approving and licensing day-care homes, consulting with career and provider mothers for placement purposes, and serving as liaison with local centers and the Department of Social Services.

The *vocational counselor* serves as liaison between the day-care program and the Manpower Training Agency of the Department of Social Services. Duties include counseling, testing, and placement of career mothers in job or training situations.

Volunteers are used in this program on an extensive *ad hoc* basis at the subcenter level. Volunteers include, for instance, medical and social work professionals working with mothers. Table 13.1 gives the average work week of staff by position.

Staff Meetings and Records At the city level, there is a monthly directors' meeting, involving the 21 local directors and the city-wide director, to discuss policy, budget, and administrative problems. Also at the city level are bimonthly meetings for fiscal matters involving the 21 local directors.

At the local center level, the director meets weekly with the staff to discuss center business and any difficulties involving homes or children. There is also a weekly or biweekly training session, run by the educational consultant, for teacher mothers. Staff members meet individually with directors as needed. Administrative decisions affecting the overall program are usually conveyed through meetings and memos to each local director and by direct contact with technical assistants.

The subcenter director evaluates her staff in writing; the subcenter staff keep careful notes on their work. These notes often include review of the progress and activities of the homes. Em-

Table 13.1
Average Work Week of Staff by Position*

Staff Position	Hours/Week	Child Contact Hours/Week
Central office (10: 11.9 full-time equiv.)	475	N.A.
Director	65	
Assistant director	50	
Technical assistants (4)	200 (50)	
Stenographers (2)	80 (40)	
Typists (2)	80 (40)	
Subcenters (378: 336.1 full-time equiv.)	13,445	2,150
Directors (21)	1,365 (65)	
Secretaries (21)	840 (40)	
Bookkeepers (21)	420 (20)	
Custodians (21)	420 (20)	
Day-care counselors (21)	840 (40)	
Day-care aides (24)	960 (40)	
Educational aides (215)	8,600 (40)	2,150 (10)
Teacher mothers (976: 1,220 full-time equiv.)	48,800 (50)	48,800 (50)
Total paid staff (1,364: 1,568 full-time equiv.)	62,720	50,950

*In-kind staff are not included in this table for reasons of space. They include Board of Education teachers, local hospital personnel, application and vocational counselors from manpower and social services agencies, private attorneys, and many others.

ployee Evaluation and Child Progress forms are included in the appendix to this chapter.

Staff Development and Training The teacher mother receives special training before and during the time children are placed in her home. This training is done by early childhood specialists from the Board of Education. They have training sessions three times a year, four days each session, seven hours a day. There are also weekly sessions held at the local centers. Certificates are given every six months to those who have attended thirteen sessions or more during that period. All teacher mothers must attend training at the local level. Training consists of early childhood development (more practice than theory), discipline, separation of child from mother, safety, health, and other topics. For city-wide training sessions, centers provide teacher mothers with transportation, lunch money, and baby-sitting.

Educational aides assist the educational consultant in training teacher mothers, although observers noted that in some cases they seemed to have minimal child development training themselves. Our observers felt that both teacher mothers and educational aides could benefit from more and better training.

How Resources Are Used

Two estimated expenditure budgets for 1970-1971 for the Family Day Care Career Program are presented in Tables 13.2-13.5. Tables 13.2 and 13.3 show the estimated costs for the system, in summary and in detail, without a consideration of whether teacher mothers are being underpaid for their time and the use of their homes. From a strictly economic point of view this is an accurate representation. There is a large waiting list of mothers who are willing to work under these economic arrangements; hence no dollar value can reasonably be attached to these "donations."

However, there are three good reasons to present a second budget (Tables 13.4 and 13.5), which does give a dollar value to these two important in-kind contributions: (1) The most compelling reason is that a woman's willingness to work as a teacher mother on an average of $.96 per hour should be questioned on other grounds. A supply of cheap labor that is in some measure inexhaustible is not sufficient grounds for using that labor at what the market will bear. This was one of the arguments against slavery. (2) From the standpoint of replication it is not absolutely clear that the supply of women willing to work under such conditions is universal. Therefore, if organized home care is seen as a viable option, then it should be costed at what an operator would have to pay if he were unwilling to pay less than the minimum federal wage or were obliged to compensate on that basis, and it should also reflect what he might reasonably pay for the use of mothers' homes. (3) The second budget more fairly represents costs that are comparable to the other 19 centers in the study.

In developing the value of underpayment and facilities in-kind costs for the second budget, $1.65/hour was taken as the realistic hourly wage for teacher mothers and $50 per month for use of the home facility ($13.50 per child per month). To derive the costs of a typical subcenter of 170-180 children, divide the system budget by 20.

It should be clear that these considerations are not meant to reflect a negative view of the FDC management. It has no choice and is doing a great deal with very little.

Table 13.2
Summary of Family Day Care Estimated Dollar and In-Kind Expenditures 1970-1971 (excluding in-kind estimate of teacher mother time and facilities underpayment)*

	Percentage of Total	Total Cost	Cost/Child/ Year	Cost/Child/ Hour
Standard core	89	$7,270,800	$2,037	$.82
Varying core	3	218,200	61	.02
Occupancy	3	238,000	67	.03
Supplemental services	5	436,300	122	.05
Totals	100	$8,163,300	$2,287	$.92

*Costs rounded to nearest $100; percentages to nearest 1%.

Table 13.3
Detail of Family Day Care Estimated Dollar and In-Kind Expenditures 1970-1971 (excluding in-kind estimate of teacher mother time and facilities underpayment)*

		Percentage of Total	Total	Dollar Cost	In-Kind Dollar Value
Basic Care	**Standard core costs**				
	Child care and teaching	39	$3,176,400	$2,511,400	$ 665,000
	Administration	27	2,190,100	1,812,000	378,000
	Feeding	23	1,906,300	1,606,500	299,900
	Varying core costs				
	Health	3	218,200	168,600	49,600
	Transportation	—	—	—	—
	Occupancy costs	3	238,400	217,000	21,400
	Supplemental service costs				
	Career development	5	433,600	235,300	198,300
	Overall personnel costs	75	6,122,300	5,371,700 (82%)	741,600 (46%)
	Totals	100	$8,163,000	$6,550,800 (80%)	$1,612,200 (20%)

*Costs rounded to nearest $100; percentages to nearest 1%.

Conclusion

It was the judgment of the observation team that visited Family
Day Care in November of 1970 that children were being cared for
in warm, family atmospheres, and while the educational component was minimal due to lack of funding and equipment, teacher
mothers were providing plenty of love and attention. In addition,
the program represents a real step up for both career mothers and
teacher mothers in allowing them to do purposeful work and earn
a salary. What the system offers to its clients are the following:

For children:
protection, nutrition, tender loving care, a home setting; medical
referrals; skill teaching in self-reliance; communication; peer cooperation; community awareness; cross-cultural appreciation;
some self-image enrichment; some bilingual education

For career mothers:
chance to work; awareness of adequate care for children; job counseling; referral to social service agencies; parent advisory role;
parent-community social events

For teacher mothers:
chance to work at a minimal salary; companionship; very positive
contact with adults and community; child-care training and in-

Table 13.4
Summary of Family Day Care Estimated Dollar and In-Kind Expenditures
1970-1971 (including in-kind estimate of teacher mother time and facilities
underpayment)*

	Percentage of Total	Total Cost	Cost/Child/ Year	Cost/Child/ Hour
Standard core	86	$ 8,914,900	$2,497	$1.00
Varying core	2	218,200	61	.02
Occupancy	8	824,000	280	.11
Supplemental services	4	433,600	122	.05
Totals	100	$10,390,700	$2,960	$1.18

*Costs rounded to nearest $100; percentages to nearest 1%.

Table 13.5
Detail of Family Day Care Estimated Dollar and In-Kind Expenditures 1970-1971 (including in-kind estimate of teacher mother time and facilities underpayment)*

		Percentage of Total	Total	Dollar Cost	In-Kind Dollar Value
Basic Care	Standard core costs				
	Child care and teaching	47	$ 4,818,500	$2,511,400	$2,307,100
	Administration	21	2,190,100	1,812,000	378,000
	Feeding	18	1,906,300	1,606,500	299,900
	Varying core costs				
	Health	2	218,200	168,600	49,600
	Transportation	—	—	—	—
	Occupancy costs	8	824,000	217,000	607,000
	Supplemental service costs				
	Career development	4	433,600	235,300	198,300
	Overall personnel costs	75	7,793,000	5,371,700 (82%)	2,380,700 (62%)
	Totals	100	$10,390,700	$6,550,800 (63%)	$3,839,900 (37%)

*Costs rounded to nearest $100; percentages to nearest 1%.

service support; some advice and support on improving their homes.

Due to severe underfunding, the Family Day Care Career Program of New York does not approach the perfect home-care system: supervisory staff and teachers are paid very little on a per-hour basis; there is not enough money for adequate educational programs or even a minimum supply of educational materials. The FDC system has, however, somehow surmounted these difficulties in its creation of a warm, swiftly growing, cohesive, and very creative "frontier" community. Its internal personnel communications are generally a model of responsible, honest human contacts at every level. The shortcomings of the system must be seen in the light of the enormous step forward FDC represents for participants: close-to-home, reliable child care and a chance to join the world of working adults. Comments by career mothers, teacher mothers, and center directors appear in the appendix to this chapter.

Notes

1. In June 1972 the system was serving 4,017 children.

2. In June 1972 the system was employing 1,454 staff (1,067 teacher mothers, 378 subcenter staff, and 9 central administrators).

Appendix to Chapter 13

List of Participating Centers

Minutes of a City-Wide Policy Advisory Board Meeting

"The Ministry of Family Day Care": Letter from a Teacher Mother

Toys on the Federal "Danger List" (in English and Spanish)

Educational Aides Guide

Biweekly Activity Plan

Employee Evaluation Form

Weekly Recording Form for Home Visits

Child Progress Form

Parent and Staff Comments

List of Participating Centers

Hunts Point Family Day Care
Bronx, New York

East Side House
Bronx, New York

Concerned Parents
Bronx, New York

Bronx Action Committee
Bronx, New York

Youth Village, Inc.
Bronx, New York

Haryou-Act Family Day Care
New York, New York

Community Life
New York, New York

East Harlem Tenants Council
New York, New York

University Settlement
New York, New York

Clinton Child Care
New York, New York

Church on the Hill
New York, New York

Community Development, Inc.
New York, New York

East New York Family Day Care
Brooklyn, New York

Brownsville Community Council
Brooklyn, New York

Bedford-Stuyvesant Family
Day Care
Brooklyn, New York

Willoughby House
Brooklyn, New York

Red Hook Family Day Care
Brooklyn, New York

Park Slope Family Day Care
Brooklyn, New York

Martin De Porres Center
Long Island, New York

Jamaica Day Nursery
Jamaica, New York

Silver Lake Lodge
Staten Island, New York

Minutes of a City-Wide Policy Advisory Board Meeting

Later in the meeting we were joined by several Council Against
Poverty members who had been attending another meeting in the
building. They expressed strong support for the program, and all
agreed that a concerted effort must be made to pull together the
facts and the experience of the Provider and User Mothers to
demonstrate what it is that we are all concerned with protecting.
The following are a few examples of the kinds of things we heard
last night from the 30 Board members present [70 percent of the
Board members and all the officers are Provider and User
Mothers]:

A User Mother from Ft. Greene, who was one of the prime
movers in the establishment of the restaurant that was recently
opened to serve Afro-American food, told us how the group
worked to obtain funds with which to get started and to demonstrate the level of responsibility, which brought about the loan
from Chase Manhattan. Plays were written and acted by the mothers, there were fashion shows, and food prepared and sold in the
neighborhood—apparently they prepared meals that were either
picked up by the purchasers or delivered by them in shopping
carts. The restaurant was opened on October 31st. The mothers
are still working without pay but on December 1st a staff of 13,
including these mothers, will be on salary.

A User Mother from Astoria reported that she is now completing
a liberal arts program and will begin practical nurse's training in
February. She mentioned three other User Mothers. One, a woman
who had been on welfare for years, was found in the course of a
door-to-door canvas. She was so discouraged and without hope
that she seldom left the house. The Vocational Counselor referred
her to NCDA for testing and apparently she tested so high that she
wound up being trained and is now working as a tester and counselor. Another has been accepted at the Bellevue Hospital Hema-
tology Department, where she is being trained as a technician, and
still another is being trained in data processing.

Claudia Hawkins, a Provider Mother from Bedford-Stuyvesant,
who has been on the Board from the beginning, stressed the psy-

chological value of the program. "It has given me a new personality. I never went anywhere. I was ashamed to have anyone come into my house. When my children needed shoes or a coat, I had to go to the nearest bargain basement and pick up the leftovers that were shoddy and didn't wear. When I looked at my children, I cried. Now if my children need shoes, I get them out of the money I've earned and I get them what I want them to have. I had no social life. I had no contact with adults; just baby talk with the kids. The program is not only a job, it's a new way of life. I am now on an adult level. I like to have people come to my house and go to meetings of the Parent Advisory Committee." She then invited everybody to attend a fashion show that the PAC is giving Thursday night, November 21st. All the clothes were made by the mothers on the PAC, and they will do the modeling. They also have a pianist and vocalist who have agreed to perform and they hired a piano for the occasion.

At the conclusion of this discussion of what the program has meant to Provider and User Mothers, the User Mother who is going to nursing school said: "Let's not forget what it has done for the children. When I sat at home with my five kids, I was so frustrated and fed up I didn't care what happened. I knew I wasn't teaching them what they needed to know, but I was too exhausted to do any of the things I knew I should do. Now I am a new woman and you should see my little ones. They're eating properly, they can count, they know colors and letters, they sing lovely songs, I have to set the table just right for meals because they know the way it should be, and we're proud of each other."

One Provider Mother from Brownsville who has eight children of her own said that she is only sorry that her five older ones, who are now out of the home, never had what the three younger ones are enjoying because she is a Provider Mother, getting help from the Education Aide and counseling for the day care children, and her own children benefit by it too.

A Provider Mother from Ft. Greene, a very attractive, well-groomed woman in her 30s, said that she had been on welfare for 10 years trying to scrape out a living for her kids and occasionally doing a day's work as a domestic when they needed clothes so desperately and she couldn't get it from welfare. Her house was a wreck, she never went anywhere because she had no decent clothes and the things she could buy for the house were so cheap that they didn't last at all. Now she's off welfare, her house is a place she is proud to have people come to visit, her children are out from under "the welfare" and she's her own boss.

"The Ministry of Family Day Care": Letter from a Teacher Mother

They teach me we are our brother's keeper in spite of the fact that we are to suppress our beliefs and pretend this is a hard cold Government City-wide program.

Family Day Care has one the strangest relationships between families than any other organization I've ever witnessed outside of the missionaries set up by churches.

Family Day Care in Red Hook is a Masterpiece of a great work begun for the families to feel and know each other's needs regardless of race, creed or color.

It has brought happiness and filled the empty gaps in many women's lives who are alone. It has helped them to fight off the inner warfare that they alone know. It has caused peace of mind— peace for those who once thought they'd never know. Family Day Care is a way of life for those who want to be honest and face facts, that there are young working wives who have gained dignity by being able to support their family. Yes, the women are women indeed and our Nora Newby is a woman among women. She has touched the lives of so many families as well as her staff and coworkers. Her behavior is the work of faith, the labor of love and the patience of hope. I have learned much from her inasmuch as I was supposed to have been a Christian, but like a tea bag, you never know what kind you are until you are in hot water.

As for myself, I've humbled myself and learned mountain top experience which are only to make one strong. The work is down in the valley touching lives. It is easier to follow the leader than it is to lead the followers. I've learned much from Family Day Care. I thought God never puts his children through the fire until He first makes them fireproof. I've been through both fires; the facts are Family Day Care has been a blessing to me. I can work and receive a salary in my home taking care of lovely children and I thank God because I have never been able to work in a public place or on a job in years because of health. I am happy and have gotten certain household articles and furniture. Since I have been working as a Teacher-Mother along with my welfare check and all that I have gained and all I have seen teaches me to trust the Creator for all I have seen. I was taught my Father was rich and I being His child am to share some of these riches while living on the planet earth. I'm sorry I can't write like others, but this is what Family Day Care has done for me. Made my prayers and dreams come true. My trips to places where I have never been before—to Canada—I count it a blessing.

I hope I have been some good to the Family Day Care Program. The Lord Bless All of You—

Humbly submitted,

Angelina Scott

FAMILY DAY CARE PROGRAM
COMMUNITY DEVELOPMENT, INCORPORATED
58 West 89 Street
New York, N.Y. 10024

Toys on the Federal "Danger List"

1. ETCH-A-SKETCH: Magic slate is made of glass, not plastic.
   Danger of being broken accidentally by child with resulting cuts
   and lacerations.

2. JARTS: (Dart Game) with metal tip that is capable of punctur-
   ing tin cans. Many children have suffered damage to eyes and
   face.

3. PARTY FAVORS: Blow out with whistle inside that dislodges
   easily. One child died when whistle stuck in his throat.

4. PLAY OVENS: That heat to 650 degrees! Children have been
   severely burned. Your oven at home heats to between 550 and
   600 degrees.

These toys, if purchased, should be used only under adult supervision and with very strict safety rules.

FAMILY DAY CARE PROGRAM
COMMUNITY DEVELOPMENT, INCORPORATED
58 West 89 Street
New York, N.Y. 10024

Toys on the Federal "Danger List"

1. ETCH-A-SKETCH: Pizarra mágica confeccionada con cristal, no con plástico. Peligrosa si el niño la rompe accidentalmente ya que, los fragmentos pueden herirlo.

2. JARTS: (dardos o flechas) con puntas de metal capaz de agujerear una lata. Muchos niños han sufrido series daños en los ojos y la cara cuando han jugado con ellos.

3. PARTY FAVORS: (Pitos y cornetas) con silbato interior capaz de desprenderse con suma facilidad. Un niño murió cuando el silbato se le alojó en la garganta.

4. PLAY OVENS: (hornos de juguete) que se calientan a temperaturas hasta de 650 grados F ! Algunos niños han recibido intensas quemaduras al usarlos. Considere que el horno de su casa sólo se calienta entre los 550 y 600 F.

NOTA Si estos juguetes son adquiridos, deben usarse solo bajo la vigilancia de los adultos y dentro de las más estrictas medidas de seguridad.

COMMUNITY LIFE CENTER, INC.
FAMILY DAY CARE - CAREER
15 Mt. Morris Park West
New York, New York 10027
Tel. 427-6313 -4-5

BOBBIE R. MARBURY
Director

EDUCATIONAL AIDES GUIDE

MONDAY	TUESDAY	WEDNESDAY
AIM: To teach colors and free expression	AIM: To recognize numbers	AIM: To practice good safety and health habits
ACTIVITY: Painting Visit to paint store	ACTIVITY: Matching numbers Make cards that can be used to match numbers	ACTIVITY: Learn health and safety rules Science Visit new Medical Center
------	------	------
MATERIALS NEEDED:	MATERIALS NEEDED:	MATERIALS NEEDED:
------	------	------
EVALUATION: (1) Good response (2) Did not wish to participate (3) Would be better for a rainy day	EVALUATION: (1) Good response (2) Did not wish to participate (3) Would be better for a rainy day	EVALUATION: (1) Good response (2) Did not wish to participate (3) Would be better for a rainy day

THURSDAY	FRIDAY	RAINY DAYS
AIM: Music appreciation — to give children knowledge of music other than rock and roll Story telling	AIM: Literary arts appreciation ACTIVITY: Dramatic play Poems — nursery rhymes Introduce children to simple poetry and rhymes — let them make up plays	1. Music — records — free play 2. Story hour 3. Play-acting 4. Sing a song — let child pick out a record and act it out singing or dancing — just what they feel like doing (self expression) 5. Girls — sewing class Boys — can work on making simple card games
MATERIALS NEEDED:	MATERIALS NEEDED:	MATERIALS NEEDED:
EVALUATION:	EVALUATION:	EVALUATION:

ACTIVITIES TO BE INCLUDED WEEKLY: Music, area trips, arts and crafts, language arts, mathematical concepts, and social living. Also Science — exploring world around us (with nature study included).

COMMUNITY LIFE CENTER INC.
FAMILY DAY CARE CAREER
15 MT. MORRIS PARK WEST
NEW YORK, NEW YORK 10027

Bobbie Marbury   Christine Sheppard
Director   Day Care Counselor

BIWEEKLY ACTIVITY PLAN

DATE: _____

NAME: _____

FOCUS OF INTEREST:
New York City
Statue of Liberty

LANGUAGE ARTS:	MATERIALS NEEDED
To explain and read about the statue and its purpose	*Books from the library*

ARTS AND CRAFTS:	MATERIALS NEEDED
To draw pictures of statue	*Paper, pencils, crayons*

MUSIC AND MOVEMENT:	MATERIALS NEEDED
To watch how it stands in the water	

SCIENCE:	MATERIALS NEEDED
To visit inside of statue and see how it is made and put together	

TRIPS:	MATERIALS NEEDED
To take boat ride to Statue of Liberty	*Fare + lunch*

CONCEPTS:	MATERIALS NEEDED
To know and understand what the statue represents	

OTHER INTERESTS:	MATERIALS NEEDED

FAMILY DAY CARE CAREER PROGRAM
Employee Evaluation Form

Name _____

Job Title _____

Length of Service _____

Evaluation for period from _____ to _____

Last Grade Completed _____

Directions:
1. Use the code listed below, and place on the line the number that
best indicates rating.

Code:

  1   Unsatisfactory

  2   Fair

  3   Satisfactory

  4   Very Good

  5   Excellent

2. If more space is required when writing comments, additional
sheets may be stapled to this form.

WORK QUALITY:

_____   Accuracy of written reports

_____   Neatness

_____   Knowledge of work

_____   Learning speed

_____   Application of instruction to work

_____   Attitude toward directions or instructions

_____   Participation in community activities

_____   Recognition of community-based problems

_____ Judgment

_____ Ability to work under pressure

_____ Amount of supervision and follow-up required

For Supervisors only (Day Care Counselor, Day Care Aides):

_____ Skill in planning work

_____ Skill in guiding and directing

_____ Skill in judging and rating subordinates

_____ Organizational ability

_____ Proficiency in training and leadership

WORK QUANTITY:

_____ Amount of work produced in terms of the particular job

_____ Effect of the employee on the general flow of work

_____ Skill in handling special assignments

For Supervisors only:

_____ Skill in getting work out

WORK ATTITUDES:

_____ Cooperation

_____ Relationship to other employees including Day Care
      mothers and children

_____ Dependability and loyalty

_____ Adaptability and alertness

_____ Initiative and enthusiasm

For Supervisors only:

_____   General handling of subordinate staff

_____   Skill in development of employee morale

_____   Skill in preventing and/or handling employee problems

WORK HABITS:

_____   Regular attendance

_____   Punctuality

_____   Use and application of time

_____   Care of property

_____   Effect of habits on the work of others

_____   General appearance

COMMENTS:

Work Quality _____

_____

_____

Work Quantity _____

_____

_____

Work Habits _____

_____

_____

Overall Job Performance and/or General Comments: _____

_____

_____

_____

_____

_____

Attendance and Punctuality

Month	Late	Sick
January		
February		
March		
April		
May		
June		
July		
August		
September		
October		
November		
December		

* * * * * * *

Length of Service on Date of Rating: years _____ months _____

Has employee been up-graded during employment? _____

If so, what position was held formerly? _____

What position is held now? _____

Certification by Rater:

_____ Place a check (✓) on the line provided

    I hereby certify that this report constitutes my best judgment of the service value of this employee and is based on my personal observation and knowledge of his/her work.

                                  _____

                                  (Signature of Director)

                                  _____

                                  (Date)

Certification by Employee:

_____ I hereby acknowledge that I have personally reviewed this
report.

_____

(Signature of Employee)

_____

(Date)

_____ I would like to discuss this report with the Technical Assistant
of Central Family Day Care Career Program or with the Divisional
Supervisor of this sponsoring agency. I will submit an auxiliary report of the subject to be discussed.

_____

(Signature of Employee)

_____

(Date)

FAMILY DAY CARE

WEEKLY RECORDING FORM FOR HOME VISITS

NAME _____

DATE _____

NAME _____

TIME ARRIVED _____

Who was in the home when you arrived?

(name)   (age)

_____   _____

_____   _____

_____   _____

_____   _____

Describe condition of home.

Describe condition of children (appearance, health, dress).

State problem Day Care Mother initiated (questions she asked you).

Comments about mealtimes.

Comments about nap time.

Activities (What you did with the children?).

General Comments.

CHILD PROGRESS FORM

Monthly Evaluation

- 1 -

NAME OF PERSON FILLING OUT FORM _____

POSITION (e. g., home helper, day care mother) _____

CENTER _____

(Fill out the following form for EACH child in the home)

NAME _____ Date _____ Age ____

Does the child do any of the following:

Yes   No   Sometimes

Yes	No	Sometimes	
			1. Likes to be held
			2. Is comfortable with adults
			3. Needs reassurance (encouragement)
			4. Wants to be alone
			5. Needs a favorite toy
			6. Sucks thumb or fingers
			7. Rocks or swings
			8. Cries
			9. Cries when angry
			10. Cries when sad
			11. Has a good appetite
			12. Has good eating habits
			13. Rests easily or sleeps
			14. Hits
			15. Kicks
			16. Bites
			17. Spits
			18. Scratches
			19. Throws things
			20. Breaks things

- 2 -

Yes	No	Sometimes		
			21.	Pulls hair
			22.	Sulks or pouts
			23.	Daydreams
			24.	Likes to talk
			25.	Adjusts to various situations
			26.	Lets off steam
			27.	Listens
			28.	Enjoys trying a new game
			29.	Stands up for his rights
			30.	Waits his turn
			31.	Plays well by himself
			32.	Shares toys
			33.	Finishes an activity
			34.	Seems to enjoy himself—is happy
			35.	Is a healthy child
			36.	Enjoys books
			37.	Enjoys records
			38.	Watches TV

OTHER HABITS: _____
_____
_____
_____
_____
_____

- 3 -

(Social Development)

Yes	No		
			1. Knows official first and last name
			2. Knows home address
			3. Knows age in years
			4. Knows names of adults in home
			5. Knows and uses names of adults and children in day care home
			6. Identifies self as boy or girl
			7. Attends day care home regularly
			8. Makes friends in day care home
			9. Uses forms of polite usage, e.g., please, thank you
			10. Follows daily routines
			11. Speaks freely to other children and familiar adults in home

(Intellectual Development)

			1. Recognizes and names objects in day care home
			2. Names and groups things that go together (foods, clothing, etc.)
			3. Sees likenesses and differences in shapes, sizes, and colors
			4. Has developed certain concepts, e.g., up-down
			5. Identifies sounds (clapping, voices)
			6. Listens and responds to music
			7. Enjoys stories, picture books, games
			8. Consistently holds picture book right side up
			9. Uses equipment and materials well
			10. Likes to draw, paint, paste

- 4 -

Yes	No		
			11. Speaks in sentences
			12. Relates ideas in logical sequence, retells stories
			13. Shows ability to pay attention
			14. Tells own experiences
			15. Memorizes and sings simple songs, can describe objects
			16. Speaks clearly
			17. Asks questions
			18. Builds things

(Physical Development)

			1. Is toilet trained
			2. Handles materials with ease, e.g., scissors, manipulative toys
			3. Uses two feet alternately in going up and down stairs
			4. Ties shoes and fastens clothes
			5. Feeds self
			6. Has good posture

(Health and Safety Habits)

			1. Knows correct way to cross streets
			2. Knows what to do if lost
			3. Recognizes community helpers, e.g., policeman, fireman
			4. Tries new foods

How many days a month is the child

home ill _____ ?

Comments

What career mothers like for their children:

"[Their teacher] has made a positive impression on our kids."
"The staff comes into the home care mother's home and teaches
the children. The kids are more aware of things and want to learn
more." "The kids are always provided for—good meals, under
supervision at all times, in a home with a family atmosphere."
"The educational aide works with them till lunch, then they nap
and play." "I like the family atmosphere. The children have gained
independence, they can communicate, they have learned Spanish,
they get along better." "At the end of the day, I'm glad to see
them." "She has patience with the children. The children are
trained, and the home care mother is kind." "[My child] listens
more, seems more at ease. She is more willing to eat and feed herself." "They play games, eat lunch, learn the alphabet, numbers,
counting, they watch "Sesame Street," take a nap, go outside to
play. . . . my oldest child helps the mother with her chores." "She
gives discipline, and the kids enjoy going there." "It's dependable
care, and they're very thorough in their special placement. The
kids must be checked over." "My kids are more disciplined, they
have more patience. They like to do things together more." "He
eats better, is neater, has better table manners."

What career mothers like for themselves:

"It's convenient, educationally and financially. You're sure of
who you're getting because they're interviewed themselves. Also,
they take young babies." "It was recommended by a friend. I got
a job through the center." "It has helped me go to school and get
a job." "I'm in school all day. If there was no free home care, this
wouldn't be possible." "It gives me plenty of time before work."
"My income has increased 100%." "No payment is necessary, and
a good baby-sitter is hard to find." "It lets me go to school." "It
takes my guilt feelings away about having to leave them. Now I
can be involved in school and community things."

What career mothers don't like or would like to see in addition:

"Parents haven't made enough decisions about the program, but it's their own fault because they haven't participated. Reasons for this are no baby-sitter, or the meetings are on a bad day." "I have a hard time getting her to eat dinner because she's fed so heavily during the day." "Parents are involved a little, but meetings are hard to attend because of no baby-sitters. Parents could make more difference, but few attend." "The center's hours are inflexible."

What teacher mothers have to say:

"I have three girls and a boy at the moment, from 8:15 A.M. to 5:00 P.M. An educational aide comes in to help me—to work with the children and go on trips to the park and so on." "We have activities, outdoor play, naps, arts and crafts. I could do more if I had more space, more time, and more help." "The center takes care of the children if I have to go to the doctor. They help with educational aides, day-care aides and supplies." "I'm a home care mother because I wanted to be home with my own children. I was working in a factory." "We take trips with the children. I'd have to have more money to do more for them." "I go to school two days a week. An aide comes while I go. If I'm sick, someone comes. The center will help any time I need it." "My children have grown up and I was very lonely before I became a home care mother. I love children. I don't like to be alone. I have the time to care for them, and I learn from the children." "I never refuse to accept a child. I treat children like they are my own." "I teach them to speak Spanish as well as the regular activities. I'd like to do more, but I need more money and more equipment." "If an accident happened, I have the center to turn to." "The center helps me with educational aides and day-care aides and equipment, which we can now request." "I'm a home care mother because I felt I had to work, but I'm slightly incapacitated. I love children." "We go on walks and neighborhood excursions. Working in a system like this means a steady income, and it gives me a feeling for this community. Also, it's good to have your work commented on by the center people."

What center directors have to say:

"We try to support our teacher mothers through educational aides, baby-sitting help, and social service help on any problems—housing, legal, etc. When examining a new day-care home, we look at the health of the mother and all in the household; we determine her ability to relate to children; the Bureau of Child Welfare has licensing requirements—a fire escape, etc. Teacher mothers are trained in early childhood, nutrition, and the rules and regulations of the program. All new mothers must attend city-wide training for five days. They are given baby-sitting money and lunch money while in training." "Teacher mothers now have Blue Cross and Blue Shield, same as the center staff; this will have to be altered because of cost. We evaluate the day-care home by staff visits—the day-care aides and counselors observe lunches, snacks, the treatment of children—how relaxed a child is, etc. The educational aide must fill out a form. Also, career mothers report informally from time to time; if we have not seen them for a couple of months, we write them a letter asking them to come in at a certain time." "Placement of children is the work of the applications counselor, the vocational counselor, and the director; it's based on geographical location and the day-care counselor's perception of the personalities involved. In a day home, we look for cleanliness as opposed to neatness; we see the mother in relation to her own children, and we discuss her basic personal philosophy on child raising; we look at the mother's appearance and her interest in day care—is it money or a feeling for children? She must also be able to be licensed relative to apartment size and number of children." "Most of our day-care homes are in public housing projects, so they meet safety requirements. Teacher mothers are trained in early childhood education for 32 hours a month and also General Equivalency Degree training. We have had little turnover in teacher mothers—most have stayed from the time they began. Someone from the center goes into the homes twice a week, more often if necessary. Teacher mothers often do more than regular activities; it depends on human need. We have constant, ongoing evaluation of the programs in our homes."

Chapter 14

"Like Being at Home"
Greeley Parent Child Center
Greeley, Colorado

At a Glance
Single center
in converted church[1]

Sponsored by
Greeley Parent Child Center (private, nonprofit corporation)

Admission criteria
OEO poverty level guidelines for migrant children

Total children
47 enrolled/38 average daily attendance (preschool)[2]

Total paid staff
6 (4 full-time): 216 hours/week[3]

Total in-kind staff
12 (2 full-time): 160 hours/week[4]

Hours
M-F, 8:00 A.M.-4:00 P.M., 52 weeks

Space (sq ft/child)
Indoor: 70 Outdoor:100

Center opened
April 1969

Staff positions
Director, Head Teacher, 2 Teacher Aides[5]

Ethnic distribution
Children: 96% Chicano, 4% Anglo
Staff: 67% Chicano, 23% Anglo

Sex distribution
Children: 49% girls, 51% boys
Staff: 83% women, 17% men

Adult/child ratio
1 to 3.3

Adult/child contact hour ratio
1 to 5.5

Family status
51% complete, 49% mother only

Parent employment
Mothers: 36% employed, 9% in school or training, 30% not seeking
work, 25% unemployed

Costs to parents
Sliding scale (see appendix to this chapter)

Costs to center
$1,445 per child per year; $0.89 per child per hour

Estimated funding, 1970-1971
Welfare	$10,300
University of Northern Colorado	500
United Fund	2,500
State Food (DOA)	5,100
Colorado Migrant Council	7,100
Monfort Meat Packing Company	1,200
In-kind (including $6,000 of director's	
salary paid by the Colorado Migrant Council)	28,000
	$54,900

Notable elements
Parent control, community involvement

Contact
Director
Greeley Parent Child Center
925 B Street
Greeley, Colorado
303-353-1639

Overview
The Greeley Parent Child Center is a day-care program for migrant
seasonal and rural poor children and their families living in and
around Greeley, Colorado. It is operated by the parents, with
advice and assistance from the local community, a college, and a
university. It is an effective example of parent control and com-

munity involvement functioning smoothly in a new cooperative
effort between Chicano migrant, rural, and Anglo communities.

The center sees itself as far more than a baby-sitting service. The
center believes that it ". . . provides an atmosphere conducive to
the teaching of educational and social readiness for an optimum of
forty children." The educational program is carried out by the
director, the head teacher, and two teacher aides. Health care is
provided by a core of professional volunteers, and food service is
contracted for with the public schools. Outdoor and indoor space
is adequate (the building has just been remodeled by center parents), as are materials and equipment.

As you enter the Greeley Parent Child Center, housed in a converted church, in the small foyer you discover a series of hooks for
the children's coats. Over each hook is a color Polaroid picture of
the child with his name written under it. This had just been inaugurated when the observation team arrived in November 1970.
The children had not yet gotten over the excitement of seeing
themselves and finding their names when they arrived.

Immediately after going through the second set of swinging
doors, you enter a large, open room, which was the sanctuary.
Steel pipes cross from side to side to keep the roof from sagging.
Eventually, movable canvas curtains will be hung from these steel
rods so that the large space can be divided up. Staff hope that this
will slow down some of the more active children who treat the
main hall as a carpeted gymnasium. To the left of the door, many
toys and games are neatly stacked around the outside of the room.
At the far end there is a raised dais with round tables and book-
shelves for quieter activities. From the platform a door leads
out to the fenced-in playground, which now has grass, thanks to a
donation from the University of Northern Colorado (UNC). The
children go there for playtime in the afternoon, usually accom-
panied by two tall and lanky Chicano Neighborhood Youth Corps
boys assigned to work at the center.

The stairs to the basement lead down to the right from the main
entryway past the girls' washroom, counterpart of the boys' room
on the other side, and back of a desk. At the foot of the stairs to
the left is the kitchen area and beyond it is the storeroom, which

has been converted into an office. Directly in front of the stairs
are small tables for eating and off to the right, past the furnace
room on one side and a storage room on the other, is the space
used for children's naps and for the younger children's playtime.
Figures 14.1 and 14.2 show the layout of the main floor and basement, respectively.

The director of the center is Ann Heiman. For the past three
years Ann has responded to the enormous need created by the
flood of migrant workers who harvest Colorado's summer crops. At
the focal point of that need stands the migrant child. If he is old
enough, say, seven or eight, he will join his parents in the fields
from sunup to sunset. Piecework wages and a short earning season
make long days a necessity. If he is too young to work in the field,
the child will be taken care of by a grandmother, a pregnant
neighbor, an older sister who will do the best job she can, or he
will remain by the side of the road or field where his parents are
working. Ann reported that two years ago while working in one of
the Head Start summer programs for migrant children, she found
nine children under the age of seven being cared for by a twelve-
year-old girl. There was a six-month-old baby among them who
was starving. It had stopped crying. Within two months the baby
had almost doubled its weight and had come alive again as a tiny
human, thanks to the program's efforts.

It wasn't easy for Ann to make her way into the trusted inner
circles of service provided by the almost all-Chicano agency called
the Colorado Migrant Council (CMC). In particular, she had problems with Dr. Leonard Mestas, the bright, quick, competent coordinator of Migrant Head Start and day care for the CMC, who
originated the idea of four year-round model child-care centers for
migrant children. The years 1967 and 1968 were militant times,
but Ann stuck it out teaching in a variety of Head Start programs.
She was particularly struck by the need for day care for "settled
out" Chicanos who had stopped traveling the migrant trail to take
jobs in Greeley—many of them working at Monfort Meat Packing
Company, second-largest meat packing company in the United
States. Out of Ann's perseverance and the support of Leonard
Mestas and a number of other people, the Greeley Parent Child
Center was born. "Miss Ann" now has the warm respect of

Leonard Mestas: he considers her one of his most able resources
for the seasonal Head Start migrant program.

Despite a very successful fund-raising dinner in November 1970,
attended by several leading figures from the community and the
university, the center still needs more money. The need for additional staff is also great, and finding qualified Chicano teachers is
difficult. There is a full-time VISTA worker who is dedicated to
the center and has considered staying on when her time is up. The
director still does not draw her full salary. The director's daughter,
Cheryl, works over 40 hours a week as a volunteer in the center,
and her sons drive the VW microbus to pick up and take home
kids at the end of the day, as well as volunteering for everything
from teaching to cooking. Although one senses that Ann's hus-
band watches the whole operation with some bemusement, he is
invariably drawn into assisting with laying carpet or substituting
on the bus run. So it can be said that the whole Heiman family is
involved in the Greeley Parent Child Center, and happily.

Notable Elements

Parent Control The significance of parent control at Greeley is
great. Most of the parents indicated that they had never been involved in an organization before in which they themselves held
key positions. They have formed their own corporation and are in
a position to make decisions about what happens to their children
and to themselves. The sense of ownership that devolves from
actually constituting the governing board, being involved in negotiations for mortgages and the purchase of the property on a mort-
gage basis, and control of hiring and other policy issues has re-
portedly had a large impact on the parent group. Both mothers
and fathers show enormous pride in their involvement with the
center. Statements recorded by the observers in the appendix to
this chapter confirm strong, favorable parent feelings.

The center sees itself as providing more than a comprehensive
child-care program for the children. It also serves as an educational
facility during the evenings for programs pertaining to child
growth and development, consumer education, and a wide variety
of other subjects of interest to the parents, thus further involving

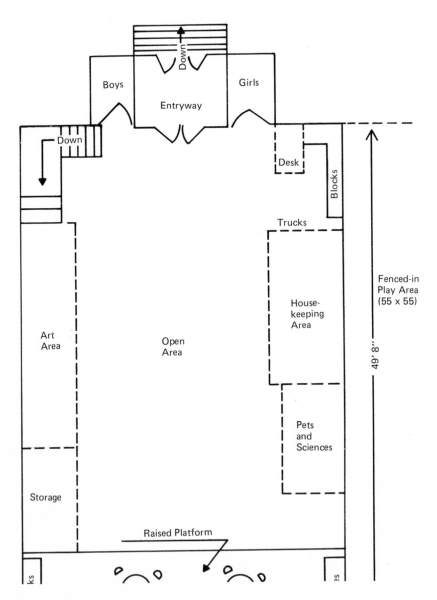

Figure 14.1
Main floor plan of Greeley Parent Child Center

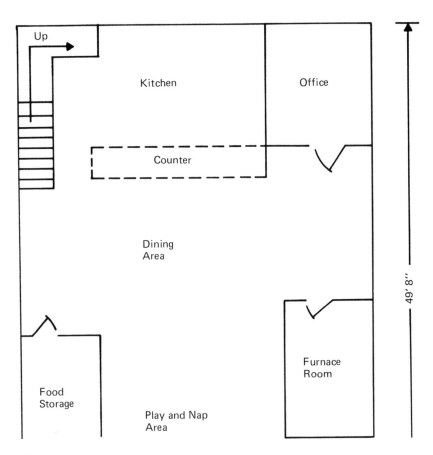

Figure 14.2
Basement floor plan of Greeley Parent Child Center

the parents in their own educational program as well as their children's. Aims Community College has participated in providing these educational programs. Under its guidelines, when six or more community residents want a course, Aims will find and pay someone to teach it.

Community Involvement Greeley lies just north of Denver and, like many towns in that area, is dependent on migrant labor for picking crops from April through October. Relations between the migrants—especially those who have decided to stay in the area— and the Anglo community have traditionally been very poor. The Greeley Center has done a great deal to improve these relations.

The involvement of key Anglo community members on the advisory board and in other supportive roles is one of the secrets of the Greeley Center's ability to stay alive. Control rests in the hands of the parents, while support and technical assistance rests with the larger community. Across this bridge, there is clearly a great deal of value flowing in both directions. The administration, faculty, and students of two universities, as well as leading bankers, major industrial leaders, members of the school board, ministers, and city officials, have all been involved in the center. The center receives donations, both cash and in-kind, to support the development of an adequate supply of educational materials, toys, and equipment. The center has consistently received favorable attention in the local media and is protected from serious attack because of the powerful group of people associated with it.

In November 1970 the street in front of the center was being paved. This street also houses many poverty-level Chicanos who have settled out. The paving was instigated by the parent board and supported by the advisory board: the results will benefit not only the center but also the entire neighborhood. This tangible accomplishment will give credence to the center's programs and some hope for the continued development of a meaningful relationship with the community as a whole.

Background Information

History The Greeley Parent Child Center was originally funded by the Colorado Migrant Council (CMC) with Head Start money.

Leonard Mestas began the center as a model to be duplicated in each of the migrant areas. It was hoped the center would have an umbrella effect. With a year-round care staff serving migrant seasonal and rural poor families, the center would act as a handle, expanding to cover migrant needs in the summer. This plan would eliminate the need to hire new staff and open temporary centers for the migrant season each year, while maintaining a competent child-care staff for the next season.

A church was found and renovated by CMC to meet state licensing requirements, and the center opened in April 1969. But the center had to look elsewhere for support in the fall of 1969, when the council's money was cut back. At this point, the Weld County Opportunity Agency, the University of Northern Colorado, and Monfort Meat Packing Company of Colorado stepped in and enabled the center to continue through January of 1970. Next, the University of Northern Colorado Foundation cosigned with the Greeley National Bank Foundation to purchase the church building in which the center was located on a rental basis. The funds were provided by the Weld County Bank at a very favorable interest rate. Since that time, Monfort Meat Packing Company has paid the $100-a-month mortgage payment as a donation to the center.

In January 1970 the parents of the children attending the center formed a nonprofit corporation. The center applied for and was granted a license by the Colorado Department of Social Services. Funding is primarily through the University of Northern Colorado and in-kind donations. (See the "At a Glance" section at the beginning of this chapter for a further breakdown of funding.)

Community Greeley is a town of about 35,000 people in northern Colorado. The primary crop here is sugar beets, with other vegetables requiring some seasonal labor. During the peak season some 12,000 farm workers are employed. Other major crops in the state include onions, broom corn, and fruits. As jobs in the packing plants have opened for unskilled and semiskilled labor, the number of migrants choosing to put down roots and "settle out" has increased at a steady pace all over the state. The Colorado Migrant Council serves these people. In establishing a day-care center in

Greeley (the first community in the state to have a year-round center for migrant children), the council demonstrated the kind of stable and long-term support needed to serve the migrant community.

The council began in the spring of 1966 as a nonprofit corporation. Its purpose was "to initiate and operate programs to assist migratory and other seasonally employed agricultural workers and their families." The following December, a grant by OEO provided funds for (1) infant education programs, (2) itinerant tutor programs, (3) evening adult education, and (4) day adult education. Additional funds six months later allowed CMC to expand its services to farm workers and their families, including summer Head Start and VISTA programs. The council focuses on local seasonal laborers who reside in Colorado and travel to work daily as well as migrants who come into the state from Texas, New Mexico, Arkansas, and elsewhere to work the crops. The four areas in which the council operates are the southeastern region (Arkansas Valley), the San Luis Valley in south-central Colorado, northern Colorado, and the western slopes region. Governance of the Colorado Migrant Council is through regional councils and subcouncils, establishing a pattern of local community involvement and control, which is reflected strongly in the Greeley Parent Child Center.

During the summer of 1969, CMC served 1,600 children—about 700 in the infant age range (from birth to three years) and about 900 preschoolers (three to five years old). That number has recently been reduced to 1,400 because of funding cuts. The full-day Head Start program operates in 25 centers (usually school buildings) for the summer. The problem with school buildings is that care can't be provided until school is out, and it must end in August, whereas the growing season is several months longer.

Parents The center serves primarily Chicano families, although at present there are two Anglo children enrolled along with the 46 Chicano preschoolers. General admission policies respond to the needs of the children and their families. Income levels of families of children enrolled in November 1970 are shown in Table 14.1

Center families tend to be large, partly as a result of the Catholic background of the parents. One mother in the center is twenty-

Table 14.1
Income Levels of Families of Children Enrolled at Greeley Parent Child Center
in November 1970

Yearly Income	Percentage of Families
Below $2,000	23.4
$2,000 - 4,000	51.1
$4,000 - 10,000	25.5

five and has nine children. Many center families, therefore, need
infant and after-school care, but at the moment neither the center
nor the CMC can adequately provide these services.

Basic Program

Education The center would like to be doing a good deal more
with its education program than it is now. It is understaffed, and
there are some days when simply getting through from morning to
evening is the major task. Nonetheless, there are structured
activities in art, storytelling, singing, numbers, names, and letters.

The Peabody Language Kit is available for use principally by volunteers, and an exciting stimulation kit was devised at the
Kennedy Development Center in Denver with Ann Heiman's help.
This stimulation kit contains a series of soft cloth bags with things
inside to play with, feel, put together, puzzle over, and otherwise
enjoy. The bags are packed in a brightly colored suitcase, and it is
an enormously useful device for introducing a new volunteer to
the children. It allows instant use of any people who show up
without time-consuming instructions. These kits are described in
detail in the appendix to this chapter. Other materials include
records, a record player, a filmstrip projector, a television set,
balls, crayons, swimming pools, and a piano. Homemade materials
include a rocking boat, steering wheels, blocks, a paper carton
playhouse, bean sacks, noisemakers, and so on.

There are approximately 22 or 23 older children in the large
main room at any one time, with 16 or 17 younger ones down-
stairs. About 14 children come in the morning from 8:00 A.M.
to 11:00 A.M. and then go off to a Head Start program. One

teacher aide works with each group, and the head teacher divides her time. The director fills in where she can, and volunteers are incorporated as they arrive. There is an effort to plan activities that will enhance school readiness. Occasionally, small groups of children are taken on field trips.

Food The center works to maintain a well-balanced diet for the children, providing a hot breakfast in the morning, a hot lunch, and an afternoon snack of fruit or vegetables. The food program is contracted through the local school district. One of the problems with the contract food service is that seconds are rarely available.

Health Care The center has organized the services of several volunteers to provide health care for the children. The nurse in the local public health office sees the children regularly for about three hours a week. A local dentist is paid by a community services agency to provide ten hours a year of free dental care. A local pediatrician spends an average of half an hour a week dealing with center children.

While the observers were at the center a five-year-old boy, going at a very high rate of speed, was pushed into the wall; the impact raised a very large bump on his forehead. The pediatrician was called, and he advised that the child be brought over to see him immediately. The doctor saw him within a half hour. Within another half hour the child was back in the center, fully recovered.

Transportation Families who live within walking distance or who have their own transportation see that their own children get to the center. The center director's son drives the family microbus on a regular route, picking up the other children and taking them home at the end of the day.

Organization
Figure 14.3 shows the organization of the Greeley Parent Child Center.

Policy Making Center policy is determined by parents through the

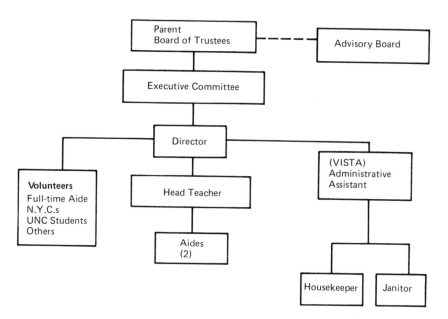

Figure 14.3
Organization chart of Greeley Parent Child Center

Greeley Parent Child Center board. All center parents are members
of the board, and they vote at board meetings. In practice, only
the more interested ones attend regularly to get the work done.
The 19-member advisory board, made up of some of the leading
figures in the town and of UNC, is available to the center board
for advice and help on a wide range of matters.

The parent board, interested members of the advisory board, the
director, and teachers all have voices in planning the overall center
program. The director makes the final decisions using policy established and approved by the board. The budget is developed by the
director in consultation with both the advisory and parent boards.
The parent board makes decisions on staff. The director seeks
prospective staff members, interviews them, and makes recommendations to the board. The evaluation of the staff is informal and is
done by the director when needed. In general, there is a high degree of cooperation among quite different elements in the center
structure—the parents, the staff, and the advisory board.

Staff Organization The director is in charge of, and administers, the entire program. The center director does a good deal of general family counseling as well as specific counseling about individual children. Formal teacher-parent conferences are scheduled at regular intervals and as necessary. Figures 14.4 and 14.5 break down the director's duties and the time and techniques involved in performing them. The VISTA aide handles administrative detail work, including record keeping, ordering supplies, and interviewing prospective clients. The head teacher, in practice, is in charge of daily activities and supervises the aides. All staff carry out general child education, physical recreational activities, and other care of children to the best of their abilities.

The housekeeper sets up and cleans up for snacks and lunch, after the meal is delivered by the local school district. The custodian works half-time to maintain the building.

In addition to the volunteers already mentioned, the following people contribute time and professional skills to the center's operations. A psychiatrist from the Greeley School District provides 50 hours of consulting time each year. Two child development specialists from the Kennedy Center in Denver each provide 80 hours a year of their time in both individual case counseling and general support. A professional nutritionist donates 20 hours per year of work. Some parents call on the Colorado Rural Legal Services.

Table 14.2 is a staff roster for the center, including the number of hours per week each staff member spends in the center.

Staff Meetings and Records Staff meetings are on an *ad hoc* basis. The director confers frequently with the head teacher about program matters. There is a constant flow of communication about individual children and program problems. The director meets with the staff individually as needed. General records are kept on each child by the VISTA volunteer. Copies of the major health and family record card forms will be found in the appendix to this chapter.

Staff Training Lack of money has made formal staff training impossible. However, there is an informal self-teaching and each-one-teach-one atmosphere that promotes growth. About one-third of

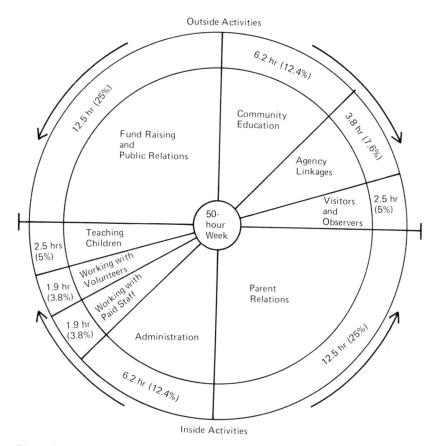

Figure 14.4
Breakdown of administrative duties of Greeley Parent Child Center director

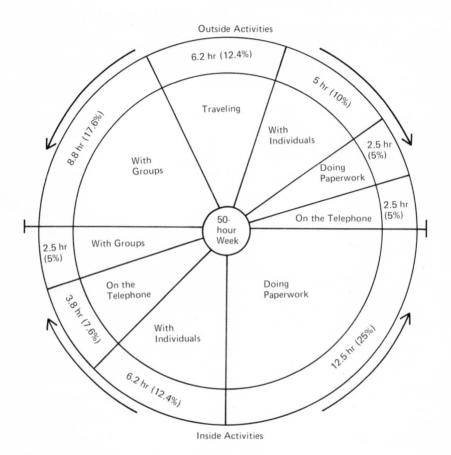

Figure 14.5
How the Greeley Parent Child Center director spends her time in the performance of her administrative duties

the staff have some college training, and half attend courses offered by Aims College, which are also available to the parents.

How Resources Are Used
Tables 14.3 and 14.4 show the functional breakdown, in summary and in detail, of the way 1970-1971 income (shown in "At a Glance") will be used.

Conclusion
The observation team that visited the Greeley Parent Child Center in November 1970 was impressed with the day-care program provided for the center's children. At the basic care level every element was present: protection, nutrition, general stimulation of mind and body, health care, and genuine affection. Moreover, the center has a rich mixture of services designed to meet the needs of the children, parents, staff, and community at large:

For children:
self-image enrichment; self-reliance and determination; communication; peer cooperation; health and nutrition; cross-cultural appreciation

For staff:
in-service support; opportunity to work with particularly needy children; classroom freedom; strong community support; effective parent-teacher relations

For parents:
chance to work; awareness of adequate care for child; community control of program; maintenance of parent role; social service referrals and other assistance; further education; parent-community social events

For community:
improved migrant worker-community relations; good flow of information about center activities through the local media; better living conditions for the migrant community; volunteer opportunities; social service information and liaison.

The Greeley Parent Child Center is an excellent example of what parents and a community can do to improve the lives of their chil-

Table 14.2
Average Work Week of Staff by Position

Staff Position	Hours/Week	Child Contact Hours/Week
Paid staff (6: 4 full-time equiv.)	216	125
Director	50	5
Head teacher	45	36
Aides (2)	86 (43)	72 (36)
Housekeeper	15	7
Custodian	20	5
In-kind and volunteers (12: 4 full-time equiv.)	160	98
Volunteer aide	50	36
VISTA aide	50	5
N.Y.C. (2)	30 (15)	30 (15)
University of Northern Colorado aides	20	20
Bookkeeper	2	—
Nurse (Public Health)	3	3
Others	5	4
Total staff (18: 8 full-time equiv.)	376	223

Table 14.3
Summary of Greeley Estimated Dollar and In-Kind Expenditures 1970-1971*

	Percentage of Total	Total Cost	Cost/Child/ Year	Cost/Child/ Hour
Standard core	73	$40,500	$1,066	$.66
Varying core	14	7,400	195	.12
Occupancy	12	6,400	168	.10
Supplemental services	1	600	16	.01
Totals	100	$54,900	$1,445	$.89

*Costs rounded to nearest $100; percentages to nearest 1%.

Table 14.4
Detail of Greeley Estimated Dollar and In-Kind Expenditures 1970-1971*

		Percentage of Total	Total	Dollar Cost	In-Kind Dollar Value
Basic Care	**Standard core costs**				
	Child care and teaching	35	$19,200	$12,600	$ 6,600
	Administration	27	14,900	1,400	13,500
	Feeding	11	6,400	6,300	100
	Varying core costs				
	Health	9	4,800	–	4,800
	Transportation	5	2,600	1,800	800
	Occupancy costs	12	6,400	4,600	1,800
	Supplemental service costs				
	Social services	1	600	–	600
	Overall personnel costs	81	44,500	16,800 (63%)	27,700 (98%)
	Totals	100	$54,900	$26,700 (49%)	$28,200 (51%)

*Costs rounded to nearest $100; percentages to nearest 1%.

dren and their families while bringing the Chicano migrant and Anglo communities together effectively. The center is serving as more than a place to care for children; it is in fact a place for parents, children, and community and could well be called the Greeley Family and Community Center.

Notes

1. The program now uses two buildings for child care, one facility housing 20 toddlers and the church building handling approximately 40 preschoolers.

2. The average daily attendance is now 60 children.

3. Paid staff now totals 23.

4. Volunteers include two bus drivers and one person who does all the program's laundry.

5. Present staff includes the director, an administrative aide, an educational director, 3 head teachers, 7 teacher aides, 2 teacher aide trainees, a parent coordinator, a nurse, a secretary, 2 cooks, 2 custodians, and a part-time accountant.

Stimulation Kits

Weekly Fee Form

Record Cards (originals on 5-1/2 × 8-1/2 stock)
Family Record
Parental Consent Form
Physician's Report
Immunization Record

Parent and Staff Comments

Stimulation Kits

The purpose of the stimulation kits described here is to provide simple, mostly homemade toys for children up to three years of age whose parents are migrant workers and who will be cared for this summer in migrant day-care facilities. The original kit was put together at the John F. Kennedy Center for Child Development, at an estimated cost of about $15 to $20. For one person working alone, it should take approximately 10 to 12 hours to make.

The Bags

There are cloth bags of three different colors in the kit corresponding to the three age groups from birth to three years. The pink bags are for babies from birth to one year, yellow bags for children one to two years, and blue bags for children two to three years. They should be made out of fairly sturdy material, each bag made from a piece of cloth 15 inches long and 12 inches wide. Each kit needs 8 pink, 8 yellow, and 11 to 12 blue bags.

Directions for Making the Cloth Bags

1. Fold sides in 1/2 inch and stitch down.

2. Fold top down 5/8 inch and stitch down (stitch about 1/2 inch from the top—leave enough room for the drawstring).

3. Fold bag in half and stitch according to diagram, leaving a space at the top for the drawstring.

4. Turn bag inside out and put drawstring in.

5. Label each bag with the appropriate age group, the name of the toy inside, and directions on how to use the toy. Use a black felt tip pen that won't run.

Things to Put in the Bags

0-1 year

1. Noisemakers

Old Keys
Plastic (or rubber) squeeze toy
Empty plastic prescription
bottle

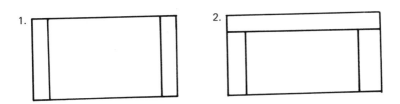

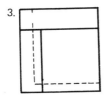

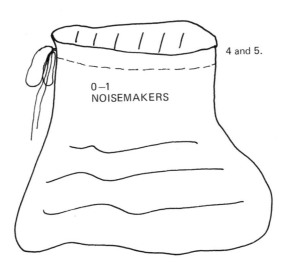

0–1
NOISEMAKERS

4 and 5.

2. Dangling spool man

4-5 brightly painted wooden spools (unpainted spools can be purchased at Larimer Square) and a string. Paint a face on the top spool.

3. Mobile

One long (about 1-yard) piece of 1/2-inch elastic. Three smaller (10-inch) pieces of 1/2-inch elastic with bright objects attached (pictures pasted on cardboard, red sock, plastic spoon, etc.). The long piece of elastic is stretched across the crib (tied to the sides) with the smaller pieces hanging from it.

4. Cuddly toys

Use soft materials, such as terry cloth.

5. Covered doll

Small doll can be found at any toy store or Woolworth's, etc. Enclose a kleenex to use as a wrapping.

6. Coffee can
   (Fill 'n' Dump)

Use standard 1-pound coffee can, paint it, and cut a slit in the plastic top. Fill it with different shaped and sized items that baby cannot swallow— plastic spoons, plastic juice can lids, big buttons, painted spools, etc.

7. Book

Any very elementary book— cloth or soft plastic, with only one or two items per page (Target, Woolworth's, etc.).

8. Hidden object

Use any small toy that a baby is likely to be interested in—small truck, doll, brightly colored block, etc. These can be purchased at any toy or variety store.

9. Pick up small object

The object should be edible—raisins or red-hots. Use small, clean plastic prescription bottle.

1-2 Years

1. Ball

2-3-inch diameter ball from any toy or variety store.

2. Cubes

1-inch colored cubes or small blocks from any toy store. Milk carton bottoms, cut and fit together.

3. Coffee can

Same as for 0-1 year.

4. Book

Same as for 0-1 year.

5. Hidden doll

Small doll from any toy store. Three painted orange juice cans (different colors).

6. Wrapped toy

Small toy (truck, doll, ball, etc.) from any toy store, kleenex for wrapping.

7. Noise toy

Painted orange juice can filled with bottle caps and sealed shut.

8. Puppets

Fingers of old gloves with faces drawn on them, Crazy Foam tops, tongue blades with faces drawn on.

2-3 years
Same as for 1-2 years.

GREELEY PARENT CHILD CENTER

Pre-School

Weekly Fee

Yearly Income

Family Size	$3500	$4000	$4500	$5000	$5500	$6000	Over
1	3.00	3.50	4.00	4.50	5.00		
2	4.00	4.50	5.00	5.50	6.00		
3	5.00	5.50	6.00	6.50	7.00		

You may make your own allocation. You do not have to place your income. Just remit the charge you feel suits your family size and income level. If your income falls between the figures, you choose the one closest to the lowest figure.

If you feel you are not able to pay the preceding fee, please contact the director and arrangements can be made.

NAME _____

ADDRESS _____ PHONE _____

AMOUNT ALLOCATED PER WEEK _____

GREELEY PARENT CHILD CENTER   (front)
FAMILY RECORD

Child's Name   address   phone   birthdate

Parent or Guardian

Work or School emergency address & phone number

Marital Status: Married   Single   Other _____

Yearly income: _____   Source: _____

Language other than English spoken in the home _____

Own home _____ Renting _____ Living with relatives _____

How long have you been in this community? _____

                                                    (back)

	NAME	SEX	AGE	BIRTHDAY	EDUCATION
FATHER:					
MOTHER:					
CHILDREN:					

GREELEY PARENT CHILD CENTER   (front)
PARENTAL CONSENT FORM

I give my consent that whatever examinations, emergency treat-
ments, and immunizations are necessary for protecting the health
of _____
                          Child's name
may be performed by the doctor, dentist, nurse, and dental hygienist designated by the Greeley Parent Child Center.

Reports and records of whatever services are rendered will be kept
strictly confidential and released only to other official agencies and
school authorities who have need for them in providing future services or care. I also give my permission for my child to go on trips
away from the premises of the school whether by foot or vehicle.

_____
            (Parent or Guardian)

_____   _____
        (Witness)   (Address, town, state)

_____   _____
        (Date)   (Date)

                                                     (back)
_____
Child's Doctor's Name   Address   Phone

Special health conditions, allergies, or reactions to medication:

_____

_____

Circle any of the following that your child has had:

10-day measles   chicken pox   whooping cough   pneumonia

3-day measles   broken bones   serious accidents   mumps

Has your child had any other diseases? _____

Operations? _____

GREELEY PARENT CHILD CENTER   (front)
PHYSICIAN'S REPORT

Date _____ Age _____ Years _____ Months _____

Wt ____ # ____ % Ht ____ in ____ % Head Cir ____ cm _____ %

Check left-hand column if area unremarkable. Elaborate abnormali-
ties of each area in right-hand column.

Nutrition _____   _____

HEENT _____   _____

Chest _____   _____

Heart _____   _____

ABD _____   _____

Genitalia _____   _____

Ext _____   _____

Neuro _____   _____

Skin _____   _____

Other _____   _____

(back)

GREELEY PARENT CHILD CENTER

_____
      Child's Name   Age   Birthdate

TESTING RESULTS:

1. Hb _____ gms   Hct _____ %

2. U.A.   Date _____ Alb ____ Sugar ____ Acetone ____ SpGr ____

3. T.B. Skin Test   Date _____ Type _____ Result _____

4. Hearing   Date _____ Results: R: _____ L: _____

5. Vision   Date _____ Results: R: _____ L: _____

6. Dental   Date _____ Results: R: _____ L: _____

GREELEY PARENT CHILD CENTER
IMMUNIZATION RECORD

Name _____ Birthdate _____

D.P.T. #1 _____ #2 _____ #3 _____ B _____

Oral Polio #1 _____ #2 _____ #3 _____ B _____

Trivalent
Measles _____ With G.G. _____

Rubella (3-day measles) _____

Smallpox _____ Primary Reading _____

Tine _____ Reaction _____

Adult D.T. #1 _____ #2 _____ B _____

Comments

What parents like for their children:

"The center seemed to suit me the best, and the children were happy. All the staff were real friendly." "He always says good things about the teacher." "Gives her a chance to be around kids her own age. She learns about school things." "She gets along better with children at home." "I feel the program does really well even though there isn't much money." "Before the center director makes a major decision she brings the matter to the board for their consideration." "My girls talk about the volunteer that comes in." "I want my child to respect her parents and other adults, to do well in school and to keep loving. She must mind adults." "They give her praise, praise and more praise." "I like the things my child is learning—basic facts, as well as good discipline. I know she's well cared for." "The community is not as aware of the existence of this center as it should be, but the cooperation of the University has been outstanding." "This center seemed to have more love and individual attention than any other nursery I'd ever seen." "My child arrives at 8:00. He is greeted happily, then he has free play. They have some group activities in the morning. At 11:15 my boy gets on the bus for Head Start. That's the end of his day here. This is more like being at home." "I'm very happy with the staff and their discipline rules." "They give him verbal praise, let him be the helper." "The teachers are friendly and happy with the children." "I like all the things that my child learns and the good feelings he gets about himself. There is nothing unsatisfactory." "He obeys me readily now." "It has made us a closer family." "His eating habits have improved." "I admire the staff because they have done so much here. Our director never gives up no matter how many problems." "The children learn their colors, numbers, names, etc., watch films, go on field trips. They have books, stories, educational and manipulative toys to use." "He is there for the learning and social experience." "She will be a well-adjusted child, more advanced than others her age." "The teachers are good because my child is learning many things, developing good language habits and increasing her vocabulary. "It's easier for me to talk to my child now." "She has become more considerate and understanding of other family members and other children as well." "I'm very impressed with all that the children are learning." "Children with deep problems are given special attention or referred to the proper person for help." "My child is shy, needed to learn to get along with other children, so thought this would be the best place for her." "They reward her with praise and love." "There is a happy atmosphere in the center any time you come in." "She is more mindful of me, follows through with my requests and no back talk." "My child likes it very much." "I have learned to listen to him." "They helped my little boy learn to talk."

What parents like for themselves:

"All parents are involved. They have really helped in the improvement program." "I think parent involvement is very good." "I am now able to work at another school." "I'm able to go to different meetings at the public school." "The center has lots of parent involvement. I see cars parked over there all the time. We are fixing things up or going to meetings." "The general appearance of the building has improved so much because of parent and board actions, especially parent labor." "It's allowed me to get a job." "Our family income has increased 20%." "I became involved as a board member. I also work with public health people. I attend night class at college." "I'm now attending night school." "It was nice to be given a chance to get involved." "Increased parent interest spurs the business community to help and provide more needed funds and donations." "I'm able to go to sewing class and give more help to the school and community." "I only come to the social meetings." "I think parent involvement is the best part of the program." "The center is only a half block from my house, in the middle of my neighborhood." "They're good teachers because my boy learns so much." "It frees both me and my wife to work." "She is more considerate of everyone in the family, making for a happier family."

What parents don't like:

"I feel I should be involved in the program a lot more." "I don't really know the staff very well." "I haven't been to a meeting yet; I'm too busy." "They ignore some bad behavior." "Community support could be better." "She is picking up undesirable words from other children." "She has better manners at the table but seems to be eating less." "Only a handful of parents are involved." "I spank. I don't think they punish my child."

Staff remarks:

"A good teacher must be patient, enthusiastic and understanding." "Preschoolers need a good self-image." "The families are normal but in need of social services." "I like working with children. I don't like making family contacts and administrative duties." "Sometimes when I'm reading a story, I'm interrupted because I also have to keep an eye on all the children in the room." "I evaluate a child by looking at him and listening to him." "They need love and individual help and attention." "I try to get them playing quietly and to play with each other." "At age ten I hope they will be informed enough to do well in school and to get along with other people." "Sometimes decisions are made efficiently, depends on the decision." "Sometimes I feel I do more than I'm supposed to." "We need more places like Parent Child Center for older children coming home from school." "We need another building, more staff and of course more money." "A teacher must be a listener, rather than talking to or at a child too much." "The most important thing is tender loving care." "I don't expect miracles because their culture, heredity, and environment work against them, but I expect to see our children make greater gains than those who do not attend preschool. Our program is the beginning (stressing individual needs, building self-image, social awareness). The school system needs to follow through with parent as well as child involvement." "Center building is owned by the parent group. Fathers of children are remodeling and repairing the building. Mothers will cook lunches when school is not in session. Mothers sometimes volunteer as aides. Parents are more aware of the program and the 'why' of things being done. This leads to carryover in the home. Good public relations result from this involvement." "Would not leave under any circumstances, unless relieved." "We need a nursery for children younger than two. We also need a second or third preschool, more funding, facilities, equipment and staff. There is never enough time."

Chapter 15

"They Brag on a Child to Make Him Feel Good"
Rural Child Care Project
Frankfort, Kentucky

At a Glance

19 centers
in 9 Eastern Kentucky counties

Sponsored by
Kentucky Child Welfare Research Foundation, Inc. (private, non-profit organization)

Admission criteria
Family within OEO poverty guidelines and accessible to center's transportation

Total children
639 enrolled/558 average daily attendance preschool (school year)
247 enrolled/199 average daily attendance preschool (summer months)

Total paid staff
182 (162 full-time): 6,830 hours/week

Total in-kind staff
Not available

System started
May 1965

Ethnic distribution
Children: 96% white, 4% black

Sex distribution
Children: 53% girls, 47% boys

Adult/child ratio
1 to 3.4 (not including volunteer hours)

Adult/child contact hour ratio
1 to 6.7 (not including volunteer hours)

Family status
73 % complete, 21% mother only, 1% father only, 5% surrogate

Parent employment
36% employed, 60% unemployed, 4% in school or training

Costs to parents
None

Costs to system
$2,663 per child per year; $1.37 per child per hour

Actual funding, 1969-1970
OEO	$948,200
In-kind Kentucky Research Foundation, Inc.	54,000
In-kind other	214,900
	$1,217,100

Notable elements
Social services and homemakers, parent involvement, staff development, volunteers

Contact
Director
Kentucky Child Welfare Research Foundation, Inc.
314 West Main Street
Frankfort, Kentucky
502-223-2376

Auxier Day Care Center (presented as representative of the 19 centers)
Hours
M-F, 8 A.M.-3 P.M., 42 weeks

Space (sq ft/child)
Indoor: 32.8
Outdoor: 170.7 (a gym)

Total children
29 preschool (3-5 years)

Total paid staff
6 (5 full-time): 220 hours/week

Total in-kind staff
Variable (0 full-time): 120 hours/week

Staff positions
Senior Teacher, Teacher, 2 Teacher Aides, Cook, Transportation Aide

Adult/child ratio
1 to 2 (including volunteer hours)

Adult/child contact hour ratio
1 to 3 (including volunteer hours)

Overview
The Rural Child Care Project operates 19 day-care centers scattered throughout nine counties in eastern Kentucky. Some of the counties are agricultural, and some of them used to be coal-mining areas. The houses are wood frame, the vistas are bleak, and the people are poor.

Unemployment is widespread, especially in the mining counties. While the mines were going strong, local men constituted the labor force. It was more efficient, however, for the mining companies to bring in experienced managerial talent than to train local residents, so when the mines closed and management went elsewhere, they left behind untrained, unemployed, and often physically debilitated men. Although some miners left to seek other work, many stayed behind, living in the mountain hollows in primitive conditions, with limited access to the outside world. The Rural Child Care Project serves a number of these families, some suffering from the malnutrition, anemia, and tuberculosis associated with poverty. Lack of sanitary water is one of the major problems in the area, plaguing children with intestinal parasites.

The hollows in which many of the children live are isolated, often miles from a paved road, and severe winters make them even less accessible. The rural population is very distrustful of outsiders. Proud and suspicious of change, they are not easily approached, nor do they seek outside help (which might be construed as charity) for their problems. Children in this setting, exposed to few people, often are limited in their language development and social skills.

Because families are scattered through remote areas and because funds could not be used for construction of centers, the project has had to take any space it could get. Centers are located in churches, abandoned schoolhouses, and storefronts. Community buildings used only part-time, such as Masonic Lodges and American Legion halls, made their basements available. In other areas, the project has obtained rooms in community center buildings, which were

formerly coal commissaries, hotels, and rooming houses. The
availability of outside play space differs widely from center to
center. Space is limited, but it is well used. By necessity, some
version of the open floor plan is found in most centers.

The centers deal with the simple survival needs of the children:
psychological problems common to children growing up in socially
isolated and economically deprived areas. While the project has
had to make do with whatever facilities were donated by the
various communities, parents, staff, and volunteers have put much
effort into making them workable, cheerful, and comfortable for
children. Transportation, a major problem for the centers, is
handled by school buses and private cars driven by hired
transportation aides and volunteers.

Recognizing that a child's life will not be improved simply by
taking him out of his home for a few hours daily, the project
attaches major importance to improving the lives of center
families. It does this through direct social services, including a
highly successful homemaker program, and through extensive referrals to local agencies and resources.

The Auxier Center in Floyd County is fairly typical of the
project's facilities. Once a small community store, it now fills its
two large display windows with children's artwork. Inside, the
large room is subdivided by child-size lockers and clusters of tables
and chairs. Storage shelves run along one side of the room, and an
ample supply locker dominates the opposite wall. At the back, a
kitchen area is separated from the main floor space by a counter.
Also in the rear of the building is a small bathroom with two com-
modes, two sinks, and a mirror at child level. Figure 15.1 is a typical floor plan of a project center.

From the beginning, even prior to its Head Start funding and
guidelines concerning parental involvement, the project employed
parents and community members as its center staff. In accordance
with its commitment to community development and because of a
lack of formally qualified personnel in the rural areas, all teachers
are paraprofessionals. As a result of on-the-job training, continuing
supervision, and a low turnover rate, the project has developed an
experienced and competent staff of community residents who had
little, if any, original formal training.

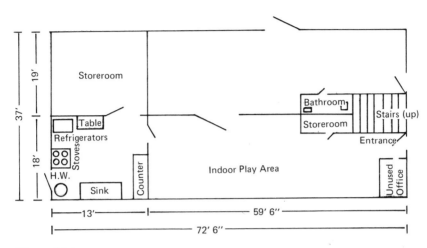

Figure 15.1
Floor plan of a typical Rural Child Care Project center

By staffing the centers with paraprofessionals from the community and providing close and supportive supervision, the project has ensured a warm, accepting atmosphere for its children. Staff and children speak each other's language. Moreover, there are usually several volunteers in attendance on any given day, increasing the adult/child ratio and the variety of adult contact. The Kentucky Rural Child Care Project is making a wholehearted effort to serve the greater community through preschool children. It has done so with a great measure of success, even though the needs of that community have, at times, appeared overwhelming.

Notable Elements
Above and beyond its basic day-care capabilities, the Rural Child Care Project does some other things particularly well. It is these elements that account for a major part of the overall project's quality and success.

Social Services and Homemakers The social services program extends the benefits the child receives in the center to the whole family. This is crucial if the project's work with children is to have any real long-term effect. While staff provide direct service or access to area services, the real role of the social service program is one of demonstration and teaching, so that families can develop the skills and management to improve their living conditions and be self-reliant. The greatest problems facing center families are defined by system personnel as poverty, lack of education, social isolation, lack of sanitation and medical resources, improper nutrition, and lack of transportation.

Each county has a social worker who makes the initial contact with prospective center families and introduces them to the project. As a relationship develops between the social worker and the family, the worker gradually offers services other than the child care provided by the project. Social workers have become leaders in the community in developing new services where there were none, coordinating existing services, and locating resources outside their immediate areas. (For instance, staff members will go beyond their duties by driving a 350-mile round trip twice a month to take children to hearing specialists.) If the social worker finds a need, he or she may offer the services of a homemaker.

The homemaker service is one of the most striking features of the project. As a liaison between the home and the center, the homemaker has the important job of visiting parents in their homes—not to check up on them or to obtain information, as is the case with welfare agency workers, but simply to be at the disposal of the mother in any way she might be useful (cooking, cleaning, helping out a sick or disabled parent, etc.). It is the homemaker who can eventually stimulate parents' interest in their children, get parents into the center and involved in community life.

Homemakers work very closely with mothers. Many of these women are withdrawn, in poor health, and overburdened with several small children. Many would be socially isolated even in an urban setting. They are not ready to reach out, look for opportunities, or even to avail themselves of opportunities presented to them unless some personal contact is maintained. They are often shy with teachers who deal with their children, feeling that they themselves are being judged.

There are three homemakers in each county, reaching up to 60 families. Homemakers may work with families for several years,

until there is no longer a need for their services. They may spend
up to half a day in one home, or less than an hour, depending on
the amount of support needed or desired. Homemakers are trained
in the basic home management skills, such as cooking, nutrition,
and sewing. They are also acquainted with the various medical and
social service agencies available in the community. As the program
has grown and confidence in these workers has been consolidated,
homemakers have been able to apply their experience to almost all
aspects of family life—family planning, budgeting, child development, home repair, job counseling, adult and consumer education,
personal hygiene, good grooming, and general home management.
When parents indicate an interest in such subjects, homemakers
arrange meetings for group discussions and demonstrations. Meetings are held at the centers, with specialists in various fields giving
parents practical instruction.

The homemaker's first responsibility is to help families learn to
help themselves. Homemakers are aware that they must not become crutches for families; rather, they must teach them to improve their own living conditions. At the same time, they must not
alienate families by imposing their own standards on them. One
mother was interested only in getting help in making new curtains
for the house. Once the curtains were completed, the homemaker
was able to motivate the mother to give the house a good cleaning,
which they did together before the new curtains went up. In
another case, a family was living on a diet of only one or two
dishes. As she gained the family's trust, the homemaker began to
introduce new kinds of foods into the home—just as center cooks
introduce new foods to the children. The homemaker can demonstrate different ways of preparing food and may take parents to a
market where better foods are available at modest prices. If there
is no money, she can help them get and budget food stamps. Problems arise frequently. Families may have no stove, no pots and
pans, no utensils to speak of. In such cases, the homemaker helps
them budget so they can begin to buy the things they need.

Many homemakers are project parents. They become good
friends to whom the families can turn, and often they are the only
outsiders the mothers see. The kind and pace of services given are
dictated by the needs and wishes of the families. The relationship

is delicate and cannot be forced. But when trust has been established, the homemaker can help families resolve many problems.
The project estimates that, through its homemaker and social
service programs, it has helped roughly one-third of its families
obtain employment.

Referrals made by homemakers are extensive. An example of
referrals made in Letcher County, shown in Table 15.1, is typical
of the other eight counties served.

At times, the project's social and homemaker services have been
hampered by a negative attitude in the community. Isolated families are very suspicious of outsiders and benefits they interpret as
charity, and the project has had to move with great caution to avoid
alienating parents over procedures considered routine elsewhere—
things like physical examinations and basic educational testing for
center children. Such suspicion has usually diminished as people
have become familiar with the project, but there are still a number
of families who are afraid to accept an outsider in their homes and
who feel threatened by this intrusion into their lives. It often takes
years for the effects of homemaker services to begin to show.

The demand for services is tremendous, and in some understaffed counties, the homemaker caseload is too large. In one

Table 15.1
Homemaker Referral Services in Letcher County

Service	Percentage of Families Referred by Homemaker
Food Stamp Program	100
Family Planning Service	100
General Health Clinic	50
Child Health Services*	40
Salvation Army*	40
Neighborhood Youth Corps	40
Emergency Food	33
Visiting Nurses	33
Employment Security Office	33

*Referrals also made at center.

county, the average number of homemaker hours per month from
July 1969 to June 1970 was 218.

Parent Involvement Parent involvement at every level in this system is high, remarkably so in an area in which a majority of residents lead moderately to severely isolated and deprived lives.
Initially, the Rural Child Care Project was dealing with people who
had little experience in community organization and cooperation—
people who were, in fact, in need of basic social contact. The
in-home service provided by social workers and homemakers was a
key to encouraging parents to participate in center affairs. These
accepting and concerned people encouraged parents first to take
an interest in their children's lives while they were in the centers,
next to help out as volunteers, and then to begin participating in
decisions about center operations and programs.

Parents are represented on all levels of the project's decision-
making apparatus on center, county, and the full project policy
advisory committees, as well as on the Board of Directors. This
participation is outlined in the "Organization" section of this
chapter, and the minutes of one center's policy advisory committee meeting are included in the appendix to this chapter.

Parent meetings, organized by homemakers, are fulfilling basic
socialization needs as well as more practical ones. Parent requests
have generated instruction in such diverse subjects as quilting,
sewing and clothing alteration, upholstering, furniture refinishing,
home repair, carpentry, plumbing, landscaping, picture framing,
automobile maintenance and repair, family planning, nutrition,
canning and food preserving, personal hygiene, health education,
child behavior, sanitation, driver education, drug abuse, first aid,
home safety, vital statistics and the census, income tax, FHA and
low-cost home loans, and food stamps. Aside from practical advice
geared to helping parents improve their standard of living by their
own efforts, these discussions can also help parents overcome fear
and embarrassment born of misinformation and inexperience with
the world; it is also hoped that such discussions will allow parents
to take advantage of community resources at their disposal. These
parent meetings are seen as a first step toward helping families

become self-supporting. A summary of homemaker-parent meetings can be found in the appendix to this chapter.

Parents, in turn, have contributed in immeasurable ways to their centers. Many parents are homemakers themselves, many staff the centers, others are transportation aides, and still others volunteer their time as they are able. Parents have raised funds to repair and improve their centers and have bought, donated, and built playground and indoor equipment for the children. The examples that follow are indicative of the care and imagination parents, staff, and volunteers have applied to a real center problem: that of low-cost play materials.

There's a tree house inside one center, accessible by ladder, with an entrance only children can get through easily. It's a quiet spot with its own small library. Made of used lumber donated by a project father, it was built by Neighborhood Youth Corps and Operation Mainstream workers assigned to the center. Another center feature is a carpenter's corner, with real log stumps for sawing. Indoor swings and a spacious sandbox allow children outdoor-type play on rainy days.

At other centers, parents have been just as imaginative. Large telephone cable spools have become trains (or whatever the children want them to be), with huge building blocks for coaches. Discarded milk crates are stepping stones, swings are made of old tires, lumber has been fashioned into small cars (with real steering wheels) and horses (with horse heads and broomstick tails). Board ladders are attached to the walls of another center, each rung a different color to help children devise their own climbing games. Hard-surfaced playgrounds are covered with sawdust to soften falls, but at one site the ground was too rocky for equipment to be anchored. So a "sliding board" was fastened to a tree trunk, and braided rope ladders dangled from its limbs. After thorough sanitation, outdoor privies have been converted to playhouses.

Parents have cut triangles, squares, rectangles, and circles in the sides of a huge old barrel so children could learn their geometric shapes as they crawled in and out. Another center has an old car and worn-out parking meters for its children. One parent donated some pipe and made handwalking bars; others built anchored

balancing ropes. Donated oil barrels, with tops and bottoms removed, were covered with dirt to make tunnels; there's a gate that
swings around a pole. Pieces from an old dinette set magically
became a horse. The chairman of one policy advisory committee
made an ingenious bouncing device out of a gaily painted pole, an
old tire, and a washing machine chassis. A parent made his center a
play motorcycle out of scrap materials and then donated a crash
helmet. Another took the panels off an old washing machine and
made a slide.

By being active in the project, parents have also been able to
make their needs known to the community and have helped other
community members find acceptable ways of meeting those needs.
For example, many children needed clothing. A seemingly simple
way of dealing with the need would be to buy or solicit clothing
and distribute it to the children. This solution was unacceptable to
parents, who objected to their children coming home in clothes
that were not their own. So when one center received some colorful fabric, parents decided that pants could be made of it—pants
easily identified as center pants, used when necessary, and then
returned to the center when no longer needed. Homemakers also
arranged for meetings where mothers could learn how to follow
patterns and sew and how to remake old clothing for their children. These meetings brought mothers together, taught them
skills, made them feel active and in control of their lives, and in the
end resulted in new clothes for the children.

Centers have had difficulty involving fathers in the program on a
daily basis. Many fathers do participate when equipment is being
rebuilt or repaired, but their interest is difficult to maintain in
between such times. Many men resent having their wives leave
home to attend meetings at the centers. Some husbands have
resented any discussion of family planning since large numbers of
children are not only traditional to the area but are often the only
available index of masculine accomplishment. The only males
present at the centers have been those from Department of Labor
manpower training programs such as Operation Mainstream and
the Nelson Program, who are assigned to the centers for maintenance work.

Staff Development From the beginning, staff training and career development were essential to the project's philosophy of working with paraprofessionals. The program's aims were to develop skills for a large number of employees, most of whom had no experience in the kinds of jobs in which they would be working, and many of whom had never been employed full-time. Staff had to be trained in a wide variety of skills, including child development, center management, cooking and nutrition, social casework and social group work, family management and consumer education, use of medical, dental, and other agency resources, clerical skills, supervision, and so on. Initially, project-wide training sessions were held using consultants from many fields. Follow-up training was done by six regional training supervisors who made weekly visits to center and county offices.

There are two unique aspects of the project's large-scale training. One is that a staff member with one specific job was frequently in on sessions devoted to other kinds of work. For instance, cooks were included in sessions on child management, unit planning, and music for preschool children. This overlapping exposure not only broadened the staff's outlook, giving them a feel for the goals of the total program, but it also provided them with skills useful across the traditional labor divisions so they could assist and fill in for other staff members.

Second, these training sessions were held outside the geographic area served by the project. For some employees, this was the first time they had been away from their home towns overnight, and their experiences in learning how to make hotel reservations, shopping in an urban area, and generally functioning in a wider environment were recognized as highly useful. In looking back at this first phase of training, some staff feel it would have been helpful to supplement this job skill approach with a similar effort to meet the basic adult education needs of the staff.

The entire Head Start Training and Technical Assistance program was cut from the 1969-1970 budget because the program was judged to have sufficiently developed its staff. Certain training positions have had to be eliminated: the position of child development training specialist was dropped, as was one regional training supervisor. Other supervisors were reassigned, and training has

been conducted on the county rather than the full-project level by
project staff, since funds no longer covered fees to outside consultants. Three additional social workers with B.A.s have been hired,
and other social workers are being encouraged to work toward
their degrees. Although training has been limited, sessions last year
covered the following: orientation to the Rural Child Care Project,
reorientation of staff, how to use volunteers effectively, child
development, consumer education, role of homemaker in the
family, group meetings, handicrafts, and indoor-outdoor play
equipment.

Even before OEO career development guidelines were issued, the
Rural Child Care Project realized it would have to move in this
direction, and staff were encouraged to enroll in high-school and
college-level courses to supplement their in-service training. For the
first time, many of the women were becoming qualified for jobs
other than domestic service or baby-sitting. The project is the only
available career opportunity for many women. As parents became
better trained and more sophisticated, they were capable of usurp-
ing some staff functions or at least making the staff feel less useful. This was particularly true of homemakers, whose roles in the
community became less vital as they passed along their skills.
Providing opportunities for all staff to take advanced education
and acquire new skills has been one way of overcoming this built-
in obsolescence.

A career development committee was organized, composed of
one representative of each kind of job in the project, elected by
his peers. The committee locates career development opportunities
for staff members and evaluates the program's own career advancement and personnel policies. At this early stage, OEO career development funds were not available, and the project allocated part of
its own budget to the committee. In this phase, it spent about
$1,700 to supplement employees working on their General Equiv-
alency Degrees or taking college courses. The project had
OEO funding for this purpose for a time but lost it along with
training funds when staff was considered to be developed. The
program was abandoned for a time, but a $3,000 grant from the
Kentucky Social Welfare Foundation has revived it.

Ten scholarships have allowed employees to participate in an

Education Professions Development Institute at Alice Lloyd College. Many staff members have taken college courses through a Head Start Supplementary Training grant at Morehead State University, Morehead, Kentucky. Nine employees have participated in Head Start Leadership Development training at the University of North Carolina. Project staff have also been consultants to other programs, and their fees have been donated to the career development fund.

Since the committee's inception in 1968, approximately twenty employees have received their General Equivalency Degrees; about thirty have taken their first college courses; and some 350 college hours have been paid for through career development activities. In all, more than 60 staff members have been promoted. Individual efforts have also been outstanding. A staff member who had been on public assistance before being hired has received her GED and acquired 17 college hours. In another instance, an employee who began as a clerical aide was promoted to case aide and subsequently to social worker, a position in which she supervises 13 other employees in administering an entire county program.

Volunteers The Rural Child Care Project uses volunteers extensively and appreciates them. In addition to the labor they perform at no cost to the system, volunteers bring new skills into the centers and can offer objective suggestions for program improvement without representing a threat to the paid staff. Each county has an unpaid, full-time parent working as volunteer coordinator, recruiting, training, and assigning volunteers to various jobs in the program. Coordinators also work in the centers and keep track of volunteer hours.

Volunteers are recruited through the news media, committees, personal contacts, the social worker's newsletter, and, perhaps most successfully, by other volunteers. Parents, skilled and unskilled community members, and paid help from Department of Labor programs, such as Neighborhood Youth Corps (2-3 days a week), Concentrated Employment Program, Operation Mainstream, and the Nelson Program, give their time. Co-op students are paid partially by their schools and partially (20 percent) by the project. Others come from church and civic organizations, local and county agencies, and the local school systems. The project would like to involve more retired and senior citizen volunteers, who, it is felt, have a great deal of experience to offer. Training is accomplished through orientation sessions, parent meetings, home visits, and on-the-job supervision by paid staff. Formal training sessions are held every six months.

In the social services area of the project, volunteers help interview prospective project families, schedule and accompany children to medical and dental appointments, and assist in clothing drives, fund raising, bake and candy sales, and clerical work in the offices. They have made burlap purses for fund raising, sheets for center cots, and dresses, pants, shirts, and paint smocks for center children.

Inside the centers, volunteers are used as teachers, aides, cooks, janitors—anywhere they can help. They pitch in for special activities, such as parties or dinners. One parent took speech lessons to help her own child and then taught speech therapy in the center. Volunteers are used on field trips and as the all-important transportation aides, driving the children to and from the center, accompanying them on school buses, and providing transportation for parents to meetings and volunteer assignments.

Some parents, originally brought in as volunteers, took advantage of General Equivalency Degree, vocational, and college courses available and have now moved on to other work. Some are aides in the summer Head Start program, some are aides with the local health department, some are employed in local businesses. Still others have been hired as project staff members. One parent who volunteered as a cook in her center is now employed as a cook for the county school system.

The project has devised a system of recognition for volunteers who donate their time and efforts. Pins and certificates are awarded at the county and the full-project level, and local news media publicize these presentations. The certificates indicate the monetary value of the time donated. It is both an expression of appreciation to the volunteer and a record of volunteer time for the project.

In addition, special help for the project has come from many groups:

The Catholic Church in Magoffin County helped with recreation, music, arts and crafts, and members volunteered for two days a week.

The Chicago, Illinois, branch of the American Medical Association bought play equipment and provides vitamins, antiseptic salves, and shampoos for Knott County.

The Methodist Church of Ann Arbor, Michigan, has adopted the Pippa Passes Center families and provides Christmas gifts and dinners; an Ann Arbor women's club sews dresses for project children.

A Pennsylvania social club has adopted the Mousie Center and gives clothing and Christmas gifts to the families.

The Mennonite Central Committee provides college students as full-time summer volunteers in the centers; families from Floyd, Knott, and Letcher counties have been referred to these workers for social and medical services.

The Brothers of Charity of the Catholic Mission in David, Kentucky, supplied paint and labor to renovate the McDowell Center in Floyd County and have given volunteer time as well.

A volunteer program such as this one is feasible for those centers willing and able to have parents and community members involved in their operations. It is also possible because most of the mothers are not employed during the hours their children are at the center. In other situations, however, it is often unrealistic to expect that a mother who is working full-time and has the additional responsibility of caring for a household and older children would have either time or energy to donate to the day-care center. Project staff feel the full-time position of volunteer coordinator is essential, as is good training and supervision. In addition, the project's volunteers are given only as much responsibility as they feel they can handle to maximize their chances of success.

Background Information

History The Kentucky Child Welfare Research Foundation has been in operation since 1962. It is a nonprofit organization for research, training, and demonstration in the field of child welfare. The Board of Directors of the foundation, after learning that federal funds were available for expanding rural child care, wrote a project proposal. The Rural Child Care Project was originally funded in March 1964 by OEO to establish child development, social work, and homemaking services in isolated rural communities. These services were to be provided by a local paraprofessional staff trained and supervised by a central office of professionals. The project was established as a single-purpose agency in order to promote flexibility of operation. In 1967-1968, it was funded as a Head Start program.

As the project began to develop, it encountered resistance both in the community and on the local government level. Community resistance has diminished as the residents of the area have become familiar with the purpose and operation of the program, but as it has gained success and acceptance in the community, the project has had difficulty with local pressure groups who, according to project staff, wish to use the centers as a power base. In a version of these circumstances, four of the original project centers (all in Harlan County) were recently transferred to the Harlan County Community Action Agency, with resultant bad feelings. The remaining 19 centers are still part of the Rural Child Care Project.[1]

Community Most of the center families get some federal assistance. Unemployment rates for 1969 in the nine counties varied from 6.4 percent to 23.9 percent. One county had a rate of 3.7 percent because of a new industry in the area. Four of the nine counties are basically agricultural, with tobacco as a major crop. The remaining counties were once mining areas rich in coal.

The ethnic composition of the nine-county area is 90 percent white and 10 percent black. The project estimates that it serves 28 percent of those in need of its services. There are an estimated 2,339 children in need of day care and 13,682 persons (counting all family members) in need of social and homemaking services.

Because of lack of employment and size of the families, the day-care service in Kentucky is primarily a service to the child and not to the mother. The project's aim is to place the children in a setting conducive to physical and psychological development and one that will prepare them for the school years ahead.

Parents Ethnic distributions of children as well as family composition statistics are included in "At a Glance" at the beginning of this chapter. Income levels of the families served by the project are low: approximately 37 percent have annual incomes under $2,000; 51 percent are between $2,000 and $4,000; only 12 percent have incomes higher than $5,000 a year. This is especially low considering that center families average seven children. Most of these families use the project's homemaker and social services programs, and project staff estimate that the various Rural Child Care services reach more than four thousand children.

The quality of education offered in the area is poor, partly because tax revenues do not stay in the region. In addition, many of the children reside in remote areas, and if transportation is not available, there is little incentive for people to stay in school. Even with schooling, there are few job prospects. Table 15.2 shows the educational level of project parents.

The scarcity of industries and the consolidation of the few that do exist severely limit employment opportunities even for those who might have the skills and education to take advantage of them. While some mothers work in the centers and others take part in training programs, 87.5 percent of them are unemployed. Only 65 percent of the fathers are employed either full- or part-time.

The project uses the OEO poverty guidelines to determine eligibility for its services. A social worker and the policy advisory

Table 15.2
Parent Educational Achievement

Education Level	Percentage of Mothers	Percentage of Fathers
6th grade or less	21	34
Grades 7 to 11	61	52
High school completion	16	11
College study	2	3

committee of the center make the final decision about which
families have the greatest need.

Basic Program

Education The Rural Child Care centers try to provide a warm,
understanding, and stimulating atmosphere in which economically
and socially deprived children can learn cognitive skills. When the
project got underway, the paraprofessional staff was not qualified
to develop and implement an educational program, but since a
good number of people have been with the program from the
start, they have, over time, acquired the necessary skills and experience. The educational program is not formal, and centers do not
use a written curriculum. Rather, emphasis is placed on individual
expression through the use of creative materials. Both free and
structured activities are included in the program, especially those
that develop decision-making abilities. Unit planning is used to
coordinate the week's group activities around a common theme.
An outline and teacher evaluation of a sample curriculum unit is
contained in the appendix to this chapter.

The 19 centers are open from September to June, and 17 centers
run a nine-week schedule during the summer. There are generally
30 preschool children in a center, divided into two groups of 15,
according to age, maturity, length of time in the program, and
need for socialization and adult contact. Each group has a teacher
(one is a senior teacher), an aide, and often several volunteers. Each
center also has a cook who works directly with the children on
nutrition education, a custodian (Operation Mainstream or other),
and one or more transportation aides.

Since all staff are paraprofessionals, each center has posted a
detailed schedule of arrival procedures, calling teachers' attention
to the importance of greeting each child as he arrives, helping him
with his coat, making a quick, informal health inspection (for
colds, sores, fevers, and so on), and expressing warmth and cheer-
fulness while performing these duties. As transportation aides
arrive with the children, they recount the morning's sights and
experiences during the often long ride to the center, and the teachers use this information to ease the child into discussion and the

day's activities. A sample daily schedule is included in the appendix to this chapter.

Free play activities are set up before the children arrive, and those who come in early are directed to these areas until everyone is present. At 9 o'clock, breakfast is served to those who need it, and snacks are set out for other children. The procedure is very informal, with children helping the center's cook serve and clean up. Staff, volunteers, and usually a male aide (from Operation Mainstream or another program) eat with the children. There is a lively flow of conversation. Structured morning activities include art, science, music, language development, and dramatic play. Weather permitting, there's a period of outdoor play before lunch.

An effort has been made to capitalize on the children's experience and environment. A science table in each center has materials that the children have gathered: lumps of coal, wasp nests, leaves and plants. These are often labeled and discussed. Native animals (opossums, woodchucks) are drawn, identified, and sometimes kept as pets. Naming of familiar objects and verbalization in play are particularly stressed to compensate for the often limited range of the children's verbal expression. The children appeared to talk freely and fluently to the staff, though they were occasionally shy with strangers.

Children have their own toothbrushes at the center (at Auxier, the maintenance man has made a long wooden wall rack for them), and after lunch the routine is toothbrushing and hand washing. Cots and blankets are set out, and children are read a story as they drop off to sleep. They sleep for at least an hour, and after the cots are put away, there's another light snack before they start getting ready to go home.

Unit plans are developed around a particular subject by each center's staff. Activities in these units aim at bettering the child's self-image, encouraging him to express himself with confidence, and improving his language skills. The latter is particularly important, since many of the children are extremely shy and withdrawn. Some highly successful activities have been a beauty-parlor day for the girls, discovery boxes, and a tradition in which a teacher makes up a story for the class featuring a child who has been sad or un-

responsive. Overall, the curriculum is quite flexible; if one activity is not going well, teachers are free to substitute something
else.

Children visit local farms, dairies, and cane mills, and some centers have organized hay rides with a mule-drawn wagon. Children
have gone to a parent's home for pony rides. Finger painting and
art activities are moved outside at one center during the summer.
Another center has an adult-size "sock-it-to-me" doll the children
can hit. Some centers have filmstrip projectors, and some have the
Peabody Language Kit. The local bookmobile service is used extensively.

Though several television sets have been donated to the centers,
the mountainous terrain makes reception so difficult that they are
virtually useless. Furthermore, the local networks have been un-
willing to carry "Sesame Street" in the mornings. The program
comes on the air after the centers are already closed. Some centers
have asked to trade in their television sets for something that would
be of more use to them.

All centers have a variety of materials such as puzzles, blocks,
dolls, lotto games, art supplies, and so on. In addition, children
use the equipment made and donated by parents and community
members for indoor and outdoor play.

The Rural Child Care Program has been concerned with the effect
of its program on the children's progress in later school grades. So
far the research on this effect has been inconclusive. One finding
indicates that the more services the family requires, the less likely
it is that the children will make good progress in school. This il-
lustrates the detrimental effect multiproblem families can have on
the cognitive development of children. The project intends to ex-
periment with more structured curriculum in the hope that this
will strengthen its compensatory developmental effort.

Food Widespread malnutrition and anemia among center children
make both compensatory and maintenance nutrition programs
necessary. Centers serve breakfast to those who need it and two
snacks and lunch to all children. At the beginning of the year, the
program is basically compensatory. The cooks attend workshops

on special foods and meal preparation. Children with special problems are given attention.

The children are fully involved in the nutrition program. It is the cook's responsibility to introduce them to new foods and different forms of food preparation. She also works with the children on serving, eating procedures, menu planning, and clean-up. The children are taken to grocery stores. Deprivation in the area is so extensive that some families do not know how to use utensils and can prepare only one very fatty or starchy meal. Educating the children in nutrition augments the work of the homemaker in introducing new and better foods to the home.

Health Care The county social worker is responsible for providing medical and dental services to the centers. When needed health care cannot be provided at the center, children are taken to local clinics and doctors. For special attention, they may have to be taken farther away. All children are given physical examinations, inoculations, and other treatment as needed. In addition to providing services, the centers encourage parents to obtain services for themselves and other family members.

The project uses as many community resources as it can, particularly Title XIX of the Social Security Amendments, which provides Medicaid for poverty-level and low-income families. Each county has a medical advisory board consisting of area doctors and dentists, one parent from each center, and a member of the public health profession. These people assess the medical needs and resources of the county and allocate funds. The participation of parents has been useful in making the members of the health professions more directly aware of the needs of the community.

When a child is ill for a period of time, the social worker or homemaker visits the home to see how he is doing and to make sure he is getting medication. The social worker also determines whether money for care is needed. Lack of medical personnel and improper sanitation are the major obstacles to keeping the children in better health.

Transportation Transportation is an enormous problem in this mountainous area, and a good portion of the project's budget is spent on this service. Centers solve this problem by using school buses, transportation aides, and, occasionally, contracted taxi service. Obtaining adequate insurance coverage has also been a problem.

A few children can walk to their centers, but most are picked up and returned home by aides who use their own cars and are paid hourly salaries, mileage, and insurance. Some aides must start their routes by 7:00 A.M. to have the children at the center by 9:00 A.M. Many children have to walk a few miles before they reach a road where they can be picked up. One child has to be rowed across a creek every morning by his father before he can get to the school bus. Another four-year-old gets himself dressed and scrambles up a high bank to get to a spot where a transportation aide can meet him. A presently insurmountable problem is that severe winters close down some of the area roads, denying service to many families until spring. Families that cannot be reached by a serviceable road—either because they are too isolated or the child is too young to walk to the road—must also be excluded from the program. Centers also provide transportation for families taking advantage of social service referrals and for parent meetings at the centers as well.

Transportation aides are more than chauffeurs. They are a communication channel between home and center. They meet the parents, see the homes, and learn something about the child's environment and his relationship with his parents in the course of picking up and delivering. They communicate all this to the teacher to help her better understand the child. Most work four hours a day, and many elect to spend time helping out in the centers, thus easing the child's transition to and from his home.

Organization
Figure 15.2 is an organization chart of the entire Rural Child Care Project. Figure 15.3 shows the organization of Auxier Day Care Center, which is typical of the other 18 centers in the project.

Policy Making The Board of Directors of the Kentucky Child Welfare Research Foundation is the governing board of the Rural Child Care Project. Membership on the board varies between five and

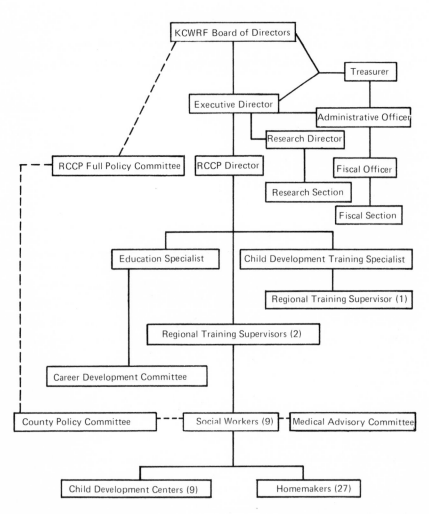

Figure 15.2
Organization chart of Rural Child Care Project

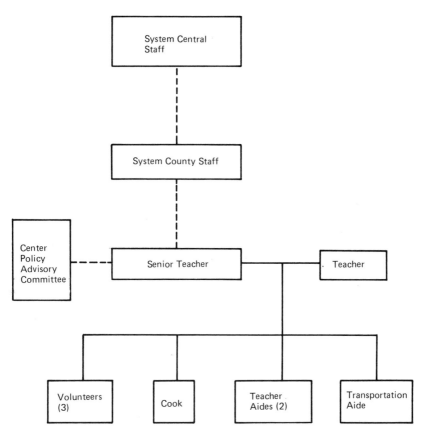

Figure 15.3
Organization chart of Auxier Day Care Center

twelve people and currently includes four social workers, two educators, and one businessman. The possibility of adding two parents from the Rural Child Care Project is now under consideration. The board has policy authority for the program and sets all personnel and fiscal policies.

The board responds to three kinds of advisory committees: (1) The Center Policy Advisory Committees (PACs) consist of four parents and two community members. Their responsibilities revolve around community and parent interest in center operations. They meet monthly to discuss issues and center business. (2) The County Policy Advisory Committees coordinate the PACs (usually two per county). These committees are regarded as the core decision-making groups. Composed of eight parents and eight community members, they discuss resource development within the county. They form personnel selection committees and medical advisory boards, which set some policies and make recommendations to the Full Project Policy Advisory Committee. (3) The Full Project Policy Advisory Committee is composed of one parent and one community resident from each of the nine counties. At this level, the problems of the nine counties are compared, ideas and solutions are shared, and issues such as program, budget, and legislation are addressed. This committee recommends directly to the project director and the Board of Directors. Total membership of the three kinds of policy advisory committees is 172.

The project director is involved in almost all program functions. Figures 15.4 and 15.5 break down the project director's duties and the techniques and time involved in performing them. The project director and an education specialist are responsible for setting overall curriculum. The education specialist also controls planning. Staff members and teachers assist in both areas. The overall project budget is developed jointly by the project director, the Board of Directors, and the Full Project Policy Advisory Committee. Joint control is exercised over the total nine-county area, which is considered a single administrative unit. For example, funds may be transferred from one county to another if necessary. The project director makes the final decisions regarding hiring and firing of staff on the advice of the policy advisory personnel committee (county level), which interviews candidates. Program content is the same for all

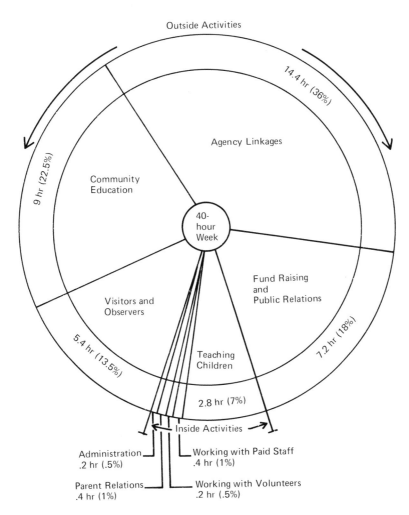

Figure 15.4
Breakdown of administrative duties of Rural Child Care Project director

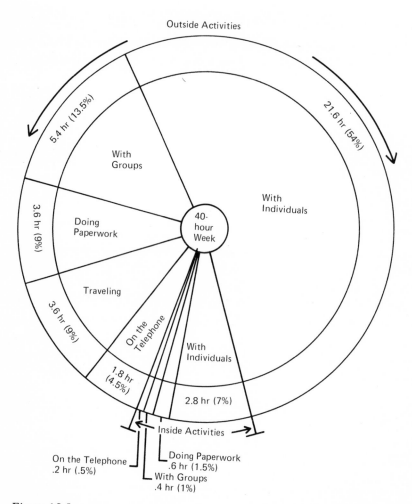

Figure 15.5
How the Rural Child Care Project director spends his time in the performance of his administrative duties

centers, subject to modification by and for local needs. The education specialist and the project director have responsibility for daily
program activities, but other staff and parents may make decisions.

Because of the hierarchy of policy advisory committees and the
other administrative channels, decision making has often been a
lengthy and frustrating business, with up to a 90-day gap between
proposal and implementation. Despite the obvious drawbacks of
this hierarchy, however, the central administration believes in
having as much group process as possible. They feel that the more
parents and staff are involved in the decision making, the more
accurately their needs and views will be reflected, the more likely
program implementations are to succeed, and the sooner parents
will be able to take full control of the centers' operations.

Staff Organization There is joint administration, supervision, and
training among the nine county operations. Each center is auton-
omous, however, in its specific program, and the centers are linked
through the County and Full Project Policy Advisory Committees.

The social worker is the focus of county coordination. A recent
budget cut has placed greater responsibilities at the county level.
Social workers with some assistance from the regional training
supervisors are directly responsible to the project director for each
county's operation—this usually includes two centers (each with 30
children), three homemakers, and clerical aides. Social workers are
also charged with community organization and the medical and
policy advisory committees involved, as well as direct casework
with families. They work closely with the homemakers.

Table 15.3 lists the staff roster of the entire system with average
work weeks in hours; Tables 15.4 and 15.5 give similar information,
as well as a paid staff profile, for a single center in the project,
Auxier Day Care Center.

Staff Meetings and Records Each center holds a weekly meeting
for paid staff and interested volunteers. All children are regularly
discussed at this session, and informal meetings often develop for
a particular child's problems. A short report on the progress of
each child is filed monthly with the county social worker. Sample
child progress reports are included in the appendix to this chapter.

Table 15.3
Average Work Week of Rural Child Care Project Staff by Position

Staff Position	Hours/Week	Child Contact Hours/Week
Director's office (10 full-time)	400	N.A.
Project director	40+	
Child development training specialist	40	
Education specialist	40	
Regional training supervisors (3)	120 (40)	
Clerical aides (4)	160 (40)	
Fiscal staff (8: 7.3 full-time equiv.)	290	N.A.
Fiscal officer	30	
Administrative officer	30	
Clerical aides (5)	200 (40)	
Clerical aide (1)	30	
Research staff (12 full-time)	480	N.A.
Research director	40	
Research associate	40	
Research assistants (4)	160 (40)	
Research clerks (2)	80 (40)	
Clerical aides (4)	160 (40)	
County staff (45 full-time)	1,800	N.A.
Social workers (9)	360 (40)	
Homemakers (27)	1,080 (40)	
Clerical aides (9)	360 (40)	
Local center staff (105: 96.5 full-time equiv.)	3,860	3,226
Senior teachers (19)	760 (40)	684 (36)
Classroom teachers (19)	760 (40)	684 (36)
Classroom aides (37)	1,480 (40)	1,332 (36)
Cooks (13)	520 (40)	260 (20)
Transportation aides (17)	340 (20)	306 (18)
In-kind staff	N.A.	
Total paid staff (182: 171 full-time equiv.)	6,830	3,326

Table 15.4
Average Work Week of Auxier Day Care Center Staff by Position

Staff Position	Hours/Week	Child Contact Hours/Week
Paid staff (6: 5.5 full-time equiv.)	220	185
Senior teacher	40+	40+
Teacher	40	40
Teacher aides (2)	80 (40)	80 (40)
Cook	40	5
Transportation aide	20	20
In-kind staff (3 full-time equiv.)		
Volunteers (equivalent of 3 full-time)	120(40)	108 (36)
Total staff (8.5 full-time equiv.)	560	478

Table 15.5
Auxier Overall Paid Staff Profile

Education	
College experience	3
High school	2
Working on GED	1
Sex	
Male	0
Female	6
Ethnicity	
White	6
Parents of project children	0

The social worker periodically evaluates the centers he or she is responsible for.

How Resources Are Used
Tables 15.6 and 15.7 present the functional breakdown, in summary and in detail, of the way 1969-1970 income (shown in "At A Glance") was used.

Conclusion
This study has not attempted to deal in depth with the issues and problems facing the Rural Child Care Project. There are problems, of course, especially in a system of this size. The problems and concerns have been summarized by Edward E. Ellis, the director of the Rural Child Care Project:

Problems of the Rural Child Care Project Centers have been many. The most persistent one has been finding facilities that could be adequately renovated and maintained at a minimum cost over a period of time. In order not to compromise any of the Kentucky statutes regarding day-care services, all Project Centers meet all requirements for fire, sanitation, health, and space necessary to obtain a license to operate.
Transportation is another major problem faced by the Project Centers. This is due to the extreme isolation so common to Appalachian Kentucky. The centers have had considerable problems in bringing in the most isolated children to the area where the cen-

Table 15.6
Summary of Rural Child Care Project Estimated Dollar and In-Kind Expenditures 1969-1970*

	Percentage of Total	Total Cost	Cost/Child/ Year	Cost/Child/ Hour
Standard core	52	$ 621,900	$1,361	$ .70
Varying core	7	87,100	190	.10
Occupancy	10	125,100	274	.14
Supplemental services	31	383,000	838	.43
Totals	100	$1,217,100	$2,663	$1.37

*Costs rounded to nearest $100; percentages to nearest 1%.

Table 15.7
Detail of Rural Child Care Project Estimated Dollar and In-Kind Expenditures 1969-1970*

	Percentage of Total	Total	Dollar Cost	In-Kind Dollar Value
Basic Care				
Standard core costs				
Child care and teaching	26	$ 309,600	$209,600	$100,000
Administration	16	$ 192,600	$192,600	—
Feeding	10	$ 119,700	$119,700	—
Varying core costs				
Health	1	13,900	13,900	—
Transportation	6	73,200	73,200	—
Occupancy costs	10	125,100	38,200	86,900
Supplemental service costs				
Social services and homemakers	22	263,000	235,000	28,000
Staff development	5	66,000	66,000	—
Research	4	54,000	—	54,000
Overall personnel costs	72	876,300	701,700 (74%)	182,900 (68%)
Totals	100	$1,217,100	$948,200 (80%)	$268,900 (20%)

*Costs rounded to nearest $100; percentages to nearest 1%.

ters are located. The hard winters of Eastern Kentucky with their floods and snows only add to the problem of transportation, which is bad enough when the weather is good.

Unsanitary water is another problem the Project has to deal with. It has been necessary at some centers to dig and maintain deep wells with electric pumps, tile fields, and septic tanks so we could put in complete bathroom facilities. It has also been necessary to install heating devices and to rewire most centers for major electric appliances, such as hot water heaters and electric stoves.

We have overcome many of the above problems in the nine counties of operation, but only by constant repair and maintenance. At the same time, we have learned to utilize all possible resources in accomplishing these objects and have involved a maximum participation on the part of the communities helping us overcome these deficits.

Despite the fact that we have been able to use school buses, transportation employees, contractual arrangements with individual carriers, plus volunteers in getting the children from isolated hollows to the Centers, there is yet another problem created by the topography of the area. This relates to the necessity of transporting the children in different groups, which means doubling back after delivering one group and picking up another group who live in a different direction. This creates problems of time scheduling in the centers as well as in meeting curriculum standards of hours and subject materials. This, coupled with the use of nonprofessional Child Development staff, has been a major concern.

With the consistent cutback in funding during the last three and a half years we have fewer academically trained staff giving support, supervision, and ongoing training than we would like. With the increased burden of meeting these gaps in services in the Social Service, Homemaking, and Child Development programs, we have had to redefine practically all employee roles and responsibilities as they relate to these components to accomplish more. One of the conditions of this year's funding grant has caused us considerable concern due to our instructions to serve even more children in the centers and to give participation and involvement to the parents in the target areas. This is to be carried out despite the 8-10 percent budget cut of which we were just recently informed after five months of operation this fiscal year.

In order to meet the conditions of the grant, it has been necessary to cut back the social services so vital in coordinating county and community services in this rural area. We have at the same time been asked to upgrade our center program, to hire more parents, to recruit more volunteers, even though program staff and support staff have been cut to the bone in these same vital areas of training and supervision.

Much time on the part of the Social Services staff has been devoted to parent involvement both on the Policy Advisory Committee and on community organizations where they might benefit from all services available. As transportation is involved in getting parents to such meetings, these cuts in the travel budget really curtail these activities, as staff is usually involved.

Greater effort will still have to be devoted to parent participation, and new techniques of involving them will of necessity have to be developed.

Staff recruitment has been less of a problem the last two years because we have been able to maintain a center core of trained paraprofessionals who are indigenous to the areas they serve. When resignations or attrition take place, the training and supervision of new employees has had to be considerably curtailed due to financial cutbacks. This is now carried out on a one-to-one basis or in small group training sessions, using those consultants and facilities available for the least cost.

The Project has never been adequately financed, and there has never seemed to be enough money to do all that needs to be done. Additional seed money would make it possible to attract other monies for resources for those areas where they do not now exist.

Changes in the type of program have had to be made as OEO and HEW have changed their responsibilities and guidelines considerably. This has made it extremely difficult for us to develop many of the long-range policies that should be developed.

In the opinion of the study team, the Rural Child Care Project is providing children with their basic needs and parents with a wide variety of essential services, despite geographical drawbacks and underfunding. Among these services are:

For children:
opportunities for basic socialization and peer cooperation; language development and self-expression; medical attention; compensatory and maintenance nutrition; special needs (for example, clothing)

For staff:
advancement through training and education opportunities; adequate pay; community involvement; training in a variety of skills

For parents:
employment; medical and social service referrals; direct help through
homemaking; skills for improvement of family life; involvement in
decision making; educational benefits; basic socialization; awareness of adequate care for children

For community:
significant volunteer opportunities; coordination of community
services and development of new services; realistic identification
of needs and ways to meet them; training of community people
to become new resources.

  Most aspects of the Kentucky Rural Child Care Project are not
innovations. They can be found in various programs around the
country. What is exceptional here, above all else, is the engage-
ment and activity the project has generated despite economic and
topographic problems and a heretofore passive and isolated rural
population.

Note

1. By the summer of 1972 the project was setting up two more centers in new
counties and had plans for infant and preschool programs in three additional
counties. Total children served in these new programs would be 220, and plans
call for smaller classes and higher staff/child ratios.

Minutes of Policy Advisory Committee Meeting
Summary of Homemaker-Parent Meetings
Curriculum Unit Outline and Evaluation of Activities
Sample Daily Schedule
Child Recording Forms
Parent and Staff Comments

Minutes of Policy Advisory Committee Meeting
McDowell Child Development Center
April 21, 1970
Tuesday, 7:00 P.M.

The meeting was called to order at 7:15 P.M. by Mr. S., Chairman.
He opened the meeting with the Lord's Prayer. Mr. S. introduced
Mr. L. for the benefit of the ones who were not present at our last
meeting.

Old Business

Mr. L., social worker, brought up the subject of an old bill from
the Culligan Water Service. The bill was for $198. Mr. D. made the
motion that $25 be paid on the bill now. Mr. S. seconded the
motion.

New Business

Mr. S. then expressed his sincere thanks to the volunteer fathers
who put the new floor covering down. The floor covering was
purchased from Sandy Valley Hardware. Cost was $97. Mr. S. also
expressed thanks to Mr. A. who is from the mission at Martin,
Kentucky. He donated paint, also helped do the work. Mr. S.
informed everyone that C. S. has donated a large refrigerator for
the center. This refrigerator needs a part, which will cost $16.

Mr. S. asked for ideas on raising money for the center. Everyone
decided on having a chicken-n-dumpling dinner. Mr. M. made a
motion to vote on buying a lawn mower. A. M. seconded this
motion. The mower will be raffled off at $1.00 per ticket. The
dinner will cost $1.00 per ticket. The dinner will be held May 24
at the McDowell Child Development Center. Dinner will be served
from 11:00 A.M. to 3:00 P.M. B. D. and A. M. and E. T. volunteered to plan the dinner.

E. S., Treasurer, came in after the meeting started. The minutes
were read to her by M. H., Secretary.

E. S., Treasurer, stated that there is a balance of $103.04 in the
treasury now.

D. F. from the mission at Martin volunteered to be in charge of
advertising for the dinner and raffle, also for the printing of the

tickets. The PAC decided to purchase 15 live hens for the dinner. Mr. S. volunteered to keep the hens and care for them until they are to be used. Mr. M. made a motion that the meeting be adjourned. This motion was seconded by J. M.

M. H., Secretary

Summary of Homemaker-Parent Meetings
Floyd County
April 1970

Auxier Homemaker-Parent Meeting
April 3, 1970, Floyd County Office

Since our office furniture needed painting, we discussed antiquing.
Most of the mothers had never done any antiquing so they suggested we do the office furniture so they could help and learn how
themselves. The furniture turned out real nice, and the parents are
going to antique something of their own at our next meeting. We
discussed the Home Nursing Training that we have just finished.
All the mothers seem very interested and are looking forward to
our teaching them what we have learned. Refreshments were
served.

McDowell Homemaker-Parent Meeting
April 10, 1970, Mr. & Mrs. M. Home

The McDowell Homemaker-Parent Meeting was held at the home
of D. M. on April 10, 1970. It was the biggest turnout we have
ever had. The ladies cut out dress patterns for their little girls. All
the ladies discussed birth control and getting together and having
what they called an old-fashioned working and helping each other
do their spring housecleaning. They all enjoyed the meeting and
socializing so much some of them decided to go green picking.
Mrs. M. made coffee and served to all the ladies.

Curriculum Unit Outline and Evaluation of Activities
Schedule: May 4 through 8
Theme: Colors and Shapes

Science
1. Pop bottles filled with colored water.
2. Rainbow—teacher makes an arc of colors and the children follow her. Children have choice of colors.
3. Field trip to discuss colors and shapes of our surroundings.
Alternate:
4. Kool-Aid popsicles—colors and shapes.

Objective: Test the children's knowledge of colors.
Evaluation: All the children enjoyed the bottles with colored water, especially the younger ones. Children most enjoyed field trip and discussion afterwards.

Art
1. 12 X 18″ newsprint—draw teddy bear (head, arms, legs). Let child choose his own colors in painting circles.
Alternate:
2. Clown—circles and triangles for body.
3. Totem pole using shapes and colors.
4. Mural—colored construction paper flowers.

Objective: Teach the small children their basic colors; large children, reinforce color concepts
Evaluation: Patterns used in excess. Found when patterns weren't used, children enjoyed making bears more.

Supervised Free Play Activities
1. Block corner—encourage the use of different sizes and shapes.
2. Housekeeping—different shapes and colors of packaged food.
3. Reading and listening—nature book.
4. Manipulative table—peg boards, puzzles, bead stringing.

Music
Early morning activity with all groups.

"Little Red Caboose"
"Little Green Frog"

Game: Go Back

Objective: Teach the children to share; prepare them for first-grade play.
Evaluation: Children always enjoy singing but need to learn to express themselves more openly.

Speech
1. Discovery box—objects that have different shapes and colors.
Alternate activity:
2. Flannel board—use construction paper shapes and colors on flannel board and have child tell what they are.
3. Developing number experiences kit.

Objective: Concentrate on shy children and develop self-image.
Evaluation: GREAT!! But had to be changed for older ones. Numbers were added.

As a whole, children did learn new colors, but shapes were more difficult. Used only squares and circles. Suggest using shapes as a unit alone.

Sample Daily Schedule

7:30 A.M.	Early arrival of Aide
8:00 A.M.	Arrival of other Aides
8:00 - 9:00 A.M.	Supervised free indoor play and subgroup activities—Aides II and I
9:00 - 9:30 A.M.	Aides supervise morning wash-up and snack
9:30 - 10:00 A.M.	Younger group has organized activities. Older group has indoor or outdoor activities
10:00 - 10:45 A.M.	Older group has organized activities. Younger group has indoor or outdoor activities
10:45 - 11:00 A.M.	All children have table games and quiet activities
11:00 - 11:45 A.M.	One Aide supervises lunch wash-up. One Aide supervises lunch table preparation with children Lunch—all Aides eat with children
11:45 - 12 noon	All Aides supervise after lunch wash-up, get children settled for nap
12:45 - 1:45 P.M.	Nap for children—Aides alternate nap supervision, record keeping, preparation for next day's activities
1:45 - 2:00 P.M.	Aides supervise toileting and after nap wash-up
2:00 - 2:15 P.M.	Afternoon snack
2:15 - 3:00 P.M.	Free indoor or outdoor play. At proper time, Aides supervise safe departure of children.

CHILD RECORDING

CHILD: I., Billy

PARENTS: S., Katherine

MC DOWELL CENTER # 2

FLOYD COUNTY

SR. TEACHER: A. W.

June 1970

Billy was off the whole week in June with sore throat and in-
fected ears. However, he came to the graduation and did quite well.
His family were real proud and rather surprised that he could do so
well.

CHILD RECORDING

CHILD: I. , Billy

PARENTS: S. , Katherine

HEIGHT: 46"

WEIGHT: 41 lbs.

MC DOWELL CENTER # 2

FLOYD COUNTY

SR. TEACHER: A. W.

October 1970

Billy seems somewhat subdued from his former boisterous self in the spring. He asks often about his best friend, Roger, who is in first grade this year. Billy seems somewhat overwhelmed by so many new faces. So he reacts somewhat hesitantly. However, the summer at home has definitely hurt him in his associations with others. He had become rather possessive and selfish as before. He had made some very slow progress in his consideration of others before the June closing of the center.

CHILD RECORDING

CHILD: H., Brad

PARENTS: H., Earl and Mabel

MC DOWELL CENTER # 2

FLOYD COUNTY

SR. TEACHER: A. W.

June 1970

Brad has remained very controversial. He continues to strike out at anyone or anything that crosses him. His mother was taken to a hospital in Lexington, but his attitude has only continued and is not of a new nature.

Brad is happy at the center and seemed delighted that he was not graduating. He says that he is not going to the big school but is going to stay here. So even if he does make life rough for the rest of us, he is happy about it all.

CHILD RECORDING

CHILD: H., Brad

PARENTS: H., Earl and Mabel

HEIGHT: 42"

WEIGHT: 37 lbs.

MC DOWELL CENTER # 2

FLOYD COUNTY

SR. TEACHER: A. W.

October 1970

I'm sorry to say that Brad continues along his provocative way. But he has more fun than anyone. It is rather hard to keep a step ahead of him. We must be firm in our restrictions for him and try to keep him busy. His attention span has lengthened somewhat, but he has been at the center so long that it is especially hard to find something that interests him. He is so sweet and mischievous at the same time that it is difficult for us to be firm with him without a smile, and he is smart enough to know it.

Comments

What parents like for their children:

"Children learn to be around other children and adults." "Children talk about how they love the teachers and want to go home with them. Also, teachers learn the child something different every day." "The teacher sends work home for children to do and enjoy." "When their teeth give them trouble they are taken care of at the center." "I like the progress of the children, the manners they have been taught, the things the center can give that they cannot get at home." "Now they help their mother in the kitchen. They have learned to associate with other children and overcome shyness. They have better manners and say a prayer at meal time." "The teachers are good to them. They learn the children things they should know. They learn table manners, good discipline, and they give thanks before meals." "The neighbor's children had learned a lot in this program—I thought he could learn to talk to people." "Children learn togetherness and good manners. They get hot meals." "Children will now talk more with people. It's made our family life better. He's now able to get along with his brothers. Also, he's not fussy about foods anymore—he eats all foods." "My child can build with blocks and play with other children. He learns to use books and other play toys and goes on walks and gathers things such as rocks, wood, leaves, and insects." "The teachers are real good to the children. They pat the child when he does something good or nice. They brag on a child to make him feel good. They try to learn the children right." "I like the table manners that the child learns away from home, and the brushing of teeth after meals. Also the learning to share and getting along with other children." "The children mind at home a lot better. They never forget to say the blessing at the table at home now." "Our child is well fed and given good care and can play with other children." "Children learn their manners and parents or people in the community feel welcomed by the teachers. The teachers understand the children." "He is able to get along with older brothers and sisters—there's less fighting." "They treat the children nicely when I'm there—other people say they treat them nicely when parents aren't around. The children learned to say prayers and have better manners." "The program buys them clothes, gives them a place to play and plenty to eat." "He draws better now."

What parents like for themselves:

"We've gotten medical help, clothing, and other things since he's been at the center. There's more time for me to take care of the family." "I can attend meetings on food and nutrition. I feel better and am less nervous. The children get good care." "I have time to work part-time. It helps to know they're well taken care of, that they are getting naps. I don't worry about them. I can go to meetings and some classes." "I have more time to take care of the house and a younger child." "I'm on both policy advisory committees." "I have time to get food stamps and take care of my sick mother. I volunteered to take a sick patient to the doctor." "Our family life is better. I'm able to work in the center as a volunteer and learn about child activities. I've been chairman of the policy advisory committee." "I'm on the parent committee. I help hire or dismiss staff for the center. I can do what needs to be done at home while the child's in the center."

What staff has to say:

"I like the involvement with children and being able to work with the total family. I get satisfaction from providing the children with good food." "I have freedom to be creative with the children." "Teachers are allowed to try any ideas that might work, after those ideas have been discussed with the center staff." "There are no bad children or bad behavior—only children with special needs, who need more help." "I like the health and nutritional care. The conditions of the families served are so inadequate that it is difficult to raise the standard of living."

Appendix   **Basic Data on Centers and
                              Systems**

Four tables are provided for the reader, with brief interpretations, which present basic data on the 20 child care centers studied. The full names and locations of the 20 programs are listed in the Introduction.

Table A1—General Information
Table A1 presents a quick summary description of the centers studied. Sponsorship includes all segments of the economy. Most of the centers serve poverty populations. This fact is somewhat surprising, for although OEO funded the study, the centers were not in general explicitly selected because they served poverty populations.

Centers offering programs for all age ranges are included, though the bulk of the services offered are for preschoolers. Center hours seem rather short in some cases. If we consider that the parent will need time after delivering the child to the center to get to work, and time to get to the center to pick up the child, it appears that the center hours are such that a parent would have difficulty working full-time.

Table A2—Notable Elements
Table A2 details the exemplary features of the centers studied. The failure to cite a center as having a notable element does not necessarily mean that the center was of low quality in that respect, but rather that considering other programs *and other aspects* of that center, it was more informative to feature something else. Similar elements have been combined under general headings. We note that parent or community participation was broadly represented as exemplary, as was staff and career development. This finding is in accord with the fact that so many centers serve poverty populations and that OEO guidelines emphasize community development.

Table A3—Distributions
Table A3 presents capsule statistics describing each center. The number of children is given in terms of average daily attendance (ADA) rather than enrollment. The number of staff is given in terms of full-time equivalent staff (FTE) including volunteers.

Forty hours of staff effort counts as one FTE. Thus, one FTE could represent one person working 40 hours, two persons working 20 hours each, etc. We note that centers tended to be moderate in size, although some very large systems were represented. Adult/child ratios and contact hour ratios tended to be quite favorable (few children per staff). Contrary to expectation, child care is not offered primarily to children in single-parent households. A substantial number of complete families are represented.

Centers served a variety of ethnic groups, although considering center size, the largest number of children were black. Blacks are, however, seriously underrepresented on center staffs. Like other institutions in society, child-care centers appear to be somewhat slow to hire minority group members.

Table A4—Estimated Funding and Expenditures

Table A4 summarizes center budgets. It shows expenditures, income, and functional allocation of funds for each center or system. Unweighted center and system averages are also presented. One should exercise care, however, in interpreting these averages. Because our centers were not scientifically chosen and are not representative of any particular population, they cannot be interpreted to reflect the national population.

We note considerable variation in costs per child, but in most cases they were somewhat higher than those usually cited in discussing child care. In part, this is due to the fact that a substantial portion of center costs are defrayed by using donated time and equipment. These donations were counted as expenditures for two reasons: (1) Experience with other programs indicates that as the supply of child care expands, volunteers, donated space, etc., will become scarce. (2) These donations do constitute a cost to society and are real even though it is not common to consider them in cash terms.

Table A1
General Information—Centers

	Total	Amalgamated	American (Woodmont Ctr.)	Avco	Casper	Central City	5th City	Georgetown	Greeley	Haight-Ashbury	Holland	Syracuse	Ute	West 80th
Sponsorship														
Private nonprofit	10	X		X	X		X	X	X	X	X	X		X
Private profit	1		X											
Public	2					X							X	
Head Start affiliate	4					X			X		X		X	
Admission criteria														
Poverty	11	X		X	X	X	X		X	X	X	X	X	X
Nonpoverty	8	X	X	X	X		X	X		X				X
Programs														
Infants	3			X			X					X		
Toddlers	6			X	X		X			X		X		X
Preschool	12	X	X	X	X	X	X	X	X	X	X		X	X
School-age	2						X						X	

Hours

A.M.		6	7	7:30	7:30	7:30	7:30	7	7:30	7:30	7:30	8
P.M.		6	6	6	5:30	4	4:30	6	4:30	4:30	5	6
Days open (average 247)		250	250	247	250	225	250	250	255	244	250	246
Full day	13	X	X	X	X	X	X	X	X	X	X	X
Half day	3		X		X	X				X	X	
Summer program	1			X								

Table A1 (continued)
General Information—Systems

	Total	Berkeley	Family Day Care	Rural Child Care	Mecklenburg County	Neighborhood Centers	Northwest Rural Opportunities	Springfield
Sponsorship								
Private nonprofit	4			X		X	X	X
Private profit	0							
Public	3	X	X		X			
Head Start affiliate	2			X			X	
Admission criteria								
Poverty	7	X	X	X	X	X	X	X
Nonpoverty	2	X						X
Programs								
Infants	3		X			X	X	
Toddlers	4		X		X	X	X	
Preschool	7	X	X	X	X	X	X	X
School-age	5	X	X		X	X		X

Hours

A.M.

P.M.   Center hours vary within systems.

		247	254	238	254	253	248	250
Days open (average 249)								
Full day	7	X	X	X		X	X	X
Half day	4	X	X		X	X	X	X
Summer program	2			X			X	—

Table A2
Notable Elements—Centers

	Amalgamated	American (Woodmont Ctr.)	Avco	Casper	Central City	5th City	Georgetown	Greeley	Haight-Ashbury	Holland	Syracuse	Ute	West 80th
General													
Sponsorship	X		X				X						
Parent and/or community					X	X		X	X		X	X	X
Volunteers				X									
Home care													
Standard core													
Educational program:													
Curriculum	X	X				X		X	X		X		X
Bilingual/bicultural					X							X	
Staff (training, quality, career development)			X		X	X			X				
Administration (planning, positions, stability)		X											
Other (financial management, making do, nutrition)	X												

Varying core

Health and remedial care	X		X	X	X
Transportation					
Occupancy					
Plant and facilities		X			X
Supplemental services			X		

Table A2 (continued)
Notable Elements—Systems

	Berkeley	Family Day Care	Rural Child Care	Mecklenburg County	Neighborhood Centers	Northwest Rural Opportunities	Springfield
General							
Sponsorship							
Parent and/or community			X				
Volunteers			X				
Home care		X		X	X		
Standard core							
Educational program:							
Curriculum						X	
Bilingual/bicultural							X
Staff (training, quality, career development)	X	X			X	X	
Administration (planning, positions, stability)		X		X	X		
Other (financial management, making do, nutrition)		X		X			

Varying core		
Health and remedial care		X
Transportation	X	
Occupancy		
Plant and facilities		X
Supplemental services	X	X

Table A3
Distributions—Centers

	Amalgamated	American (Woodmont Ctr.)	Avco	Casper	Central City	5th City	Georgetown	Greeley	Haight-Ashbury	Holland	Syracuse	Ute	West 80th
Overall													
Total children (ADA)	54	118	27	77	55	197	10.5	38	54	66	92	22	38
Total staff (FTE)	12	17	7.6	18.4	14.3	33.6	3.1	8	27.6	17	43	9.2	15
Total volunteers (FTE)	0.5	1	1.3	9.1	0.9	13	1.1	4	7	1	0	1.3	2
Adult/child ratio	1/4.5	1/6.5	1/3.9	1/4.3	1/3.5	1/5.6	1/3.6	1/3.3	1/2.2	1/3.4	1/2.3	1/2.7	1/2.8
Adult/child contact hour ratio	1/4.9	1/9.4	1/5.5	1/5.9	1/5.6	1/7	1/4.2	1/5.5	1/4.1	1/5	1/4.2	1/3.6	1/4.5
Sex (in percentages)													
Children:													
Male	52	56	50	57	47	57	64	51	52	60	49	53	45
Female	48	44	50	43	53	43	36	49	48	40	51	47	55
Staff:													
Male	33	11	33	0	21	21	0	17	30	11	18	11	25
Female	67	89	67	100	79	79	100	83	70	89	82	89	75
Family status (in percentages)													
Complete	85	81	58	11	15	49	64	51	17	43	23	80	60
Mother only	15	18	42	85	77	45	36	49	77	55	77	14	20
Father only	—	—	—	—	—	3	—	—	4	—	—	—	5
Surrogate	—	1	—	4	8	3	—	—	2	2	—	6	15

Parent employment (in percentages)

Employed	100	81	90	75	58	58	100	36[1]	67	39	44	[2]	71
Unemployed	–	15	5	3	13	33	–	25	17	10	6		3
In school or training	–	4	5	18	29	6	–	9	14	2	19		26
Not seeking work	–	–	–	4	–	3	–	30	2	49	31		–

Ethnicity–children (in percentages)

Anglo	29	91	12	88	23	22	50	4	30	40	35	13	15
Black	42	7	88	3	32	78	43	–	54	8	65	–	35
Chicano	19	–	–	3	39	–	–	96	6	49	–	–	28[3]
Indian	–	1	–	5	5	–	–	–	–	–	–	87	–
Oriental	–	1	–	–	1	–	7	–	8	–	–	–	–
Puerto Rican	4	–	–	–	–	–	–	–	–	3	–	–	–
Other	9[3]	–	–	1	–	–	–	–	2	–	–	–	22

Ethnicity–staff (in percentages)

Anglo	53	80	17	89	43	75	100	23	37	39	57	33	12
Black	27	20	83	–	21	25	–	–	63	5.5	43	–	69
Chicano	13	–	–	11	36	–	–	67	–	50	–	–	–
Indian	–	–	–	–	–	–	–	–	–	–	–	67	–
Oriental	–	–	–	–	–	–	–	–	–	–	–	–	–
Puerto Rican	7	–	–	–	–	–	–	–	–	–	–	–	–
Other	–	–	–	–	–	–	–	–	–	5.5	–	–	19

(1) Mothers only
(2) 100% employed, in school, or in training
(3) Spanish-speaking

Table A3 (continued)
Distributions—Systems

	Berkeley	Family Day Care	Rural Child Care	Mecklenburg County	Neighborhood Centers	Northwest Rural Opportunities	Springfield
Overall							
Total children (ADA)	269	3,570	787	239	1,072	425	106
Total staff (FTE)	93	1,568	171	59	269	154	31
Total volunteers (FTE)	10	0	(1)	14.25	0	38	8
Adult/child ratio	1/2.8	1/2.1	1/3.4[2]	1/5	1/3.5	1/3.2	1/3.4
Adult/child contact hour ratio	1/5	1/2.6	1/6.7[2]	1/6	1/4.3	1/4.6	1/5.7
Sex (in percentages)							
Children:							
Male	47	50	47	55	49	52	42[3]
Female	53	50	53	45	51	48	58
Staff:							
Male	12	3	(1)	0	2	0	20
Female	88	97		100	98	100	80

Family status (in percentages)

Complete	32	99	15	15	73	25	25
Mother only	62	.5	75	81	21	75	65
Father only	—	.5	—	2	1	—	5
Surrogate	6	—	10	2	5	—	5

Parent employment (in percentages)

Employed	39	95(5)	66	60	36	(4)	(1)
Unemployed	8	4	9	21	60		
In school or training	20	1	25	19	4		
Not seeking work	33	—	—	—	—		

Ethnicity—children (in percentages)

Anglo	28	6	17	24	96	4	42
Black	13	1	77	76	4	63	56
Chicano	—	90	6	—	—	31(6)	1
Indian	—	3	—	—	—	—	—
Oriental	—	—	—	—	—	—	—
Puerto Rican	56	—	—	—	—	—	—
Other	3(6)	—	—	—	2	2	1

Table A3 (continued)
Distributions—Systems

Ethnicity—staff (in percentages)

		(7)	(1)				
Anglo	56	–	–	50	20	10	20
Black	38	–	–	50	76	–	30
Chicano	–	–	–	–	4	90	–
Indian	–	–	–	–	–	–	–
Oriental	–	–	–	–	–	–	–
Puerto Rican	–	–	–	–	–	–	30
Other	6	–	–	–	–	–	20(6)

(1) Insufficient data
(2) Does not include volunteer hours. Auxier Center ratios are 1/2 and 1/3 (contact hours) including 120 volunteer hours per week.
(3) Remaining data for Brightwood Center only
(4) 100% employed, in school, or in training
(5) In season
(6) Spanish-speaking
(7) Principally black, Spanish-speaking

Table A4
1970-1971 Estimated Funding and Expenditures—Centers

	Amalgamated	American	Avco	Casper	Central City	5th City	Georgetown	Greeley	Haight-Ashbury	Holland	Syracuse	Ute	West 80th	Average
Summary data														
Cost/child/hour (in dollars)	1.42	.59	1.08	.62	1.18	.75	1.38	.89	1.71	1.37	2.06	1.59	1.90	1.27
Cost/child/year (in dollars)	2,925	1,295	2,453	1,438	2,442	1,301	2,933	1,445	3,895	2,590	3,517	3,604	4,147	2,614
Percentage of budget for personnel	81	65	62	81	79	78	75	81	81	70	77	78	73	75.5
Sources of revenue (in percentages)														
Federal					55				54	14	88	67		21
State and local		100	21	5	20			44	14	62			70	18
Parent fees			30	27			22	5					5	14
Other	98		15	15		36	53	5	8	3	10			18
In-kind	2		49	53	25	64	25	51	24	21	2	33	25	29
Total budget (in thousands of dollars)	158	133.4	65	110.7	134.3	256.2	30.8	54.9	208.4	170.9	323.6[1]	78.5	168[2]	139
Expenditures (in percentages)														
Teaching and child care	56	48	52	48	43	69	70	35	46	47	37	39	54	50
Administration	14	23	15	24	18	11	9	27	16	8	17	19	11	16
Feeding	10	11	9	13	6	9	10	11	12	15	6	19	7	11

Health	4	0	2	1	8	1	0	9	7	4	3	14	3	4
Occupancy	16	18	22	14	11	10	11	12	12	14	9	9	12	13
Other (transportation, social services, etc.)	0	0	0	0	14	0	0	6	7	12	28	0	13	6

(1) 429 including research
(2) 155.5 excluding growth costs

Table A-4 (continued)
1970-1971 Estimated Funding and Expenditures—Systems

	Berkeley	Family Day Care	Rural Child Care	Mecklenburg County	Neighborhood Centers	Northwest Rural Opportunities	Springfield	Average
Summary data								
Cost/child/hour (in dollars)	1.93	.92	1.37	.83	.57	.58	1.12	1.05
Cost/child/year (in dollars)	3,055	2,287	2,663	2,036	1,170	1,509	2,197	2,131
Percentage of budget for personnel	83	75	72	77	71	80	75	76
Sources of revenue (in percentages)								
Federal	6			58	68	80		32
State and local	85	80	80	20		8	5	38
Parent fees	6			1	10		48	9
Other	2				19		35	8
In-kind	1	20	20	21	3	12	12	13
Total budget (in thousands of dollars)	821.9	8,163	1,217	486	1,088	641.2	232.3	1,807
Expenditures (in percentages)								
Teaching and child care	52	39	26	48	40	44	44	42
Administration	28	27	16	23	22	18	20	22

Feeding	7	23	10	14	14	15	11	13
Health	1	3	1	1	2	6	1	2
Occupancy	9	3	10	12	19	12	19	12
Other (transportation, social services, etc.)	3	5	37	2	3	5	5	9

Index